# Qualitative Methodology

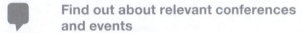

# Qualitative Methodology
# A Practical Guide

## Jane Mills and Melanie Birks

Los Angeles | London | New Delhi
Singapore | Washington DC

Los Angeles | London | New Delhi
Singapore | Washington DC

SAGE Publications Ltd
1 Oliver's Yard
55 City Road
London EC1Y 1SP

SAGE Publications Inc.
2455 Teller Road
Thousand Oaks, California 91320

SAGE Publications India Pvt Ltd
B 1/I 1 Mohan Cooperative Industrial Area
Mathura Road
New Delhi 110 044

SAGE Publications Asia-Pacific Pte Ltd
3 Church Street
#10-04 Samsung Hub
Singapore 049483

Editor: Jai Seaman
Production editor: Ian Antcliff
Copyeditor: Jen Hinchliffe
Proofreader: Lynda Watson
Indexer: Silvia Benvenuto
Marketing manager: Ben Griffin-sherwood
Cover design: Naomi Robinson
Typeset by: C&M Digitals (P) Ltd, Chennai, India
Printed and bound in Great Britain by Ashford
Colour Press Ltd, Gosport, Hants

MIX
Paper from
responsible sources
FSC
www.fsc.org    FSC® C011748

**Library of Congress Control Number: 2013939198**

**British Library Cataloguing in Publication data**

A catalogue record for this book is available from the British Library

ISBN 978-1-4462-4897-3
ISBN 978-1-4462-4898-0 (pbk)

# Table of Contents

# Notes on editors and contributors

**Robin Adeney** completed her doctorate at the University of Regina in Saskatchewan in 2011 using a narrative inquiry methodology for her research design on children's play. She has worked as a singer/songwriter, storyteller, pre-school, kindergarten and grade one teacher and museum educator. Her varied interests include children's play, histories of childhood, the arts as ways of knowing, folklore and games, inclusive education, and understanding children's culture. Recently, Robin's attention shifted to include post-secondary education and she is currently employed with the provincial government in the colleges and private vocational schools area.

**Melanie Birks** is recognised internationally for her work in grounded theory methodology. In addition to the text co-authored with Jane Mills, Melanie has published numerous journal articles that address methodological processes in qualitative research, in particular in grounded theory. She has a number of other publications in the form of books, book chapters and peer reviewed articles. Melanie has worked and researched extensively in the area of nursing education and is passionate about instilling a culture of evidence based practice in health care professionals both in Australia and overseas. Melanie is a recipient of the Australian Defence Medal for her work in educating Royal Australian Air Force personnel. She has spent time teaching and researching in the international environment, particularly in East Malaysia, which was the setting for her PhD research.

**Simon Burgess** received his PhD in moral and political philosophy from Monash University in 2006. Since then he has worked in policy development, project management, and academia. He is currently the head of Central Queensland University's Master of Indigenous Studies program. He has published in philosophy, curriculum evaluation and workplace management but his principal research interests are in philosophy, particularly as it relates to moral evaluation and the wider social world.

**Ysanne Chapman** is an independent scholar and consultant in education. She currently holds adjunct appointments with James Cook University, Charles Sturt University and Monash University in Australia. Professor Chapman has an extensive history in academia including experience in working in the international environment. Professor Chapman has produced numerous books, book chapters and journal articles, and has been commissioned to co-author further books, including a textbook on communication.

**Bob Dick** is an independent scholar, an occasional academic, a consultant and facilitator in the fields of participative community and organizational change and evaluation, and a concerned citizen. For the past 40 years he has helped people (and himself) improve their own performance and satisfaction, and that of their organisations and communities. As educator, consultant and facilitator, Bob has used action research, action learning and participative methods in communities, organisations and university classrooms. He has published in the areas of facilitation, action research, and change. Much of his current work has involved the use of action research and action learning to bring about change, leadership development, and the enhancement of organizational and community resilience.

**Urmitapa Dutta** is an Assistant Professor of Psychology and a member of the graduate committee of Peace and Conflict Studies at the University of Massachusetts Lowell. Informed by a critical social justice agenda, her research tries to understand and address marginality where it is intimately connected to violence. Urmitapa's doctoral dissertation was a critical ethnographic investigation of the struggles over cultural representations and their relationship to varied expressions of ethnic violence in Northeast India. As part of this project, Urmitapa has worked with youth to develop innovative, community-based approaches to address everyday violence and to promote 'everyday peace'. While continuing her critical ethnographic research in Northeast India, Urmitapa's current research also focuses on developing participatory action research projects with people from marginalized contexts in the greater Boston area. She was recently awarded the 2012 Exemplary Diversity Scholar Citation from the National Center for Institutional Diversity, University of Michigan Ann Arbor.

**Karen Hoare** is a Nurse Practitioner for Children and Young People and partners with five general practitioners in a clinic in South Auckland. Additionally she has a joint appointment as a Senior Lecturer across the School of Nursing and the Department of General Practice and Primary Health Care within the University of Auckland. Karen is developing her research expertise as a constructivist grounded theorist. Originally trained as primarily a children's nurse at Great Ormond Street hospital, London, her experiences working with children and young people span the globe, emigrating to New Zealand from the UK in 2003. She has lived in South and West Africa and also worked in Peru. In 2000 she set up the charity and company 'Development Direct Global Partnerships' (see www.developmentdirect.org.uk), the aim of this organization is to alleviate global poverty and improve the health of children.

**Janice Huber** is an Associate Professor in Preservice and graduate teacher in education at the University of Regina. Growing from doctoral and postdoctoral study, her relational narrative inquiries and coauthored publications, including *Composing Diverse Identities: Narrative Inquiries into the Interwoven Lives of Children and Teachers* (Routledge, 2006) and *Places of Curriculum Making: Children's Lives in Motion* (Emerald, 2011), continue to explore narrative understandings of identity in relation with the curriculum-, identity-, and assessment-making experiences of children, families, and teachers. She is a co-author of *Warrior Women: Remaking Postsecondary Education Through Relational Narrative Inquiry*, which explores the experiences of diverse Aboriginal teachers in Canada as they navigate postsecondary, public and First Nation school contexts (Emerald, 2012). In 2006 she was awarded the Early Career Award of the American Educational Research Association Narrative Research Special Interest Group.

**Debra Jackson** has been an academic nurse for over 15 years. An outstanding scholar and researcher, Professor Jackson has a strong international profile and her experience and expertise includes leading two impressive research programs in women's and family health and workforce development and adversity.  Much of her research has been funded by national competitive grants. She is an experienced supervisor of research higher degrees. She has examined numerous theses for national and international universities, and has supervised more than 20 research students to completion. In 2007 Professor Jackson won the Vice Chancellors Award for Outstanding Research Higher Degree Supervision (UWS). Professor Jackson has been published in over 250 publications including journal articles, books and book chapters. She has co-edited three widely used textbooks, two of which are into their 3rd editions. Professor Jackson is an experienced writing mentor and coach.  She is an active Editor and Editorial Board member and peer reviewer for Australian and international journals and funding bodies.

**Marianne LeGreco** is Associate Professor in the Department of Communication Studies at the University of North Carolina at Greensboro. She focuses her scholarly work on organizational and health communication, discourse tracing, and community-based research methods. Her interests in practical approaches to qualitative research coincide with her work on discourse tracing. This methodology calls attention to discursive practices, social change, and multi-level analysis. Dr. LeGreco applies her theoretical and methodological work primarily in food-related contexts including community-based food programs, food policy, and the construction of healthy eating practices. Her curiosity around food stems from her family, many of who have worked as farmers, chefs, catering directors, and nutritionists.

**Patrick J. Lewis** is a storyteller-teacher-researcher working with children, undergraduate and graduate students in Early Childhood and Elementary in the Faculty of Education at the University of Regina.

**Seán L'Estrange** is a Lecturer in Sociology at University College Dublin whose main research areas include the study of nationalism, religion and science. He is currently researching a book on classical political sociology.

**Jane Mills** is an internationally recognized grounded theorist with a background in community nursing practice. Jane has authored over 100 peer reviewed publications including journal articles, book chapters and books, many of which have focused on qualitative research methodologies. Her recent publication *Grounded Theory: A Practical Guide*, co-authored with Melanie Birks has been particularly well received. Since 2009, Jane has been employed at James Cook University in the tropical region of far north Queensland, Australia. As the Director, Centre for Nursing and Midwifery Research Jane's research focuses on teaching and learning in the tertiary setting, public health issues including tropical disease prevention, primary health care and rural health workforce. As well, Jane is an experienced higher degree supervisor and has examined higher degree theses for both Australian and international universities. Jane is the recipient of a number of awards including an Australian Government Office of Teaching and Learning Citation for Outstanding Contributions to Student Learning in 2012, and a National Health and Medical Research Council Primary Health Care Post-doctoral Fellowship (2007–2009).

**Eamonn Molloy** is an accomplished scholar, who is currently engaged in teaching and research at Pembroke College, University of Oxford. Eamonn has held academic posts at the Universities of Warwick, Bath and Lancaster. He has worked on collaborative research projects with numerous Government bodies including the National Health Service, Department for Education and Skills, Department for International Development, Natural Environment Research Council and the Economic and Social Research Council. He has also worked closely with private sector organizations including Cadbury Schweppes, Unilever, United Utilities, BNFL and major mining, oil and gas companies in South Africa and Mozambique.

**Gayatri Moorthi** is an interdisciplinary health researcher, who is the Project Supervisor and Ethnographer for the IDU Peer Recruitment Dynamics and Network Structure in Respondent Driven Sampling project. The project is working with high risk injecting drug users in Hartford, CT. Her research interests include harm reduction, drug use, HIV risk, health policy, qualitative research methods, critical medical anthropology and public health. She recently concluded her dissertation research, a multi-sited ethnography, which examined the harm reduction policy and interventions in New Delhi, India. The research evaluated the efficacy and impact of these measures on injecting drug users as well as the dynamics of a peer driven model of intervention. She has worked on projects involving vulnerable families and communities, at risk foster children, and schools, both in India and the US. She aims to continue working in the area of public health, to fuel practical solutions for community concerns.

**Martin Müller** has been Assistant Professor for Cultures, Institutions and Markets at Universität St. Gallen in Switzerland since 2009. He read for his MPhil in Development Studies at the University of Cambridge and received a PhD in Human Geography at Goethe-Universität Frankfurt am Main. His work engages with post-structuralist theories, particularly discourse theory and actor–network theory, often through an ethnographic lens. His current research examines the governance of the Olympic Games and the perception and management of natural disturbances such as wildfires or insect pests in protected areas. His regional focus is on the post-Soviet space, Russia in particular, and he has more than 12 months of fieldwork experience in Russia. Past research has appeared in journals such as *Organization, Environment and Planning A, Political Geography* and *Global Environmental Change*. For further information see www.martin-muller.net.

**Russell Ó Ríagáin** is currently a Benefactors Scholar of St John's College, Cambridge. He is working on a PhD that deals with the processes, both political and cultural, associated with colonialism by examining the changes in the control over ideological, military, economic and political resources as evinced in settlement form and patterning in the landscape in Scotland and Ireland in the Iron Age and medieval period, c.500 BC to c.1500 AD, taking an approach marrying archaeological, historical, geographical and sociological methods. Recent publications include the editing of a thematic issue of the Archaeological Review from Cambridge on the relationship between archaeology and the (de)construction of national and supranational political configurations, a co-authored article in the same issue dealing with the relationship between archaeology and nationalism in Ireland and Romania, the relationship between literary texts and social history, and various articles on Neolithic and medieval secular and ritual buildings.

**Michelle Redman-MacLaren** has experience in hospital and community health social work, community development, health promotion, NGO management (including refugee settlement) and more recently public health research. Michelle has had the privilege of living and working in rural and remote Australia (including Torres Strait Islands), rural New Zealand, Kosovo, Solomon Islands and Papua New Guinea (PNG). Michelle is passionate about working in the Pacific, especially with women. Michelle is currently undertaking her PhD using a grounded theory methodology. In partnership with colleagues in PNG, Michelle is exploring the impact of male circumcision practices for women in PNG, including women's risk of HIV transmission. Michelle is also working with colleagues in PNG and Solomon Islands to explore church-based responses to HIV (PNG), research capacity strengthening utilising decolonising methodologies (PNG and Solomon Islands) and action research/action learning.

**Sonali Shah's** research adopts different qualitative methodologies to examine the impact of public policy on the private lives of disabled people over historical time and in a national and international context. She is the Principal Investigator on a collaborative ESRC funded project, with Prof Mick Wallis (School of Performing Arts and Cultural Industries) to transmit oral history texts of disabled people, generated through social scientific disability research, to 21st-Century secondary school audiences via different performance methods (theatre and installation). This work is based on material from her Nuffield Fellowship and recently published co-authored book *Disability and Social Change: Private Lives and Public Policies* (2011, Policy Press) which combines biographical narratives and historical policy analysis to explore social changes in the lives of disabled people from the Second World War to the present day. Sonali is the sole author of *Career Success of Disabled High-Flyers*

(2005, Jessica Kingsley Publishers), and *Young Disabled People: Choices, Aspirations and Constraints* (2008, Ashgate). She is also a tutor on the Distance Learning Masters in Disability Studies and teaching on different programmes across education, medicine, social policy, psychology and disability studies. Her teaching interests focus on disability and social policy, particularly in relation to childhood and family, education and employment.

**Allison Stewart** is an Associate Fellow at the Saïd Business School, University of Oxford, and a doctoral graduate of the Institute for Science, Innovation and Society, and the BT Centre for Major Programme Management at the School. Her research focuses on sharing knowledge and ignorance between major programmes, with an empirical focus on the Olympic and Commonwealth Games. Allison held a lectureship in Management at Christ Church, Oxford from 2009–2012. She completed her MSc in Management Research at the Saïd Business School and earned her Bachelor of Commerce degree with a major in organisational psychology from McGill University in Canada. Allison is now a Capital Projects Manager at BG Group, and has previously worked at a number of global consulting organisations including Deloitte and Accenture, where she focused on organisation design and change management for private and public sector clients.

**Karen Tracy** is a discourse analyst who studies and teaches about institutional talk, particularly in justice, academic, and governance sites. She is the author of three books. Her first, *Colloquium: Dilemmas of Academic Discourse* (1997), was the recipient of the Outstanding Book Award given by the Language and Social Interaction Division of NCA. The second, *Everyday Talk, Building and Reflecting Identities* (2002), is a text used in college classes that explores how discourse, cultures and identities link. A second edition is underway. Her most recent book is *Challenges of Ordinary Democracy* (2010, Penn State University Press), a 35-month case study of the meetings of a school board and its community. Her current project involves analysing discourse about same-sex marriage in state supreme courts doing oral argument and public hearings of legislative bodies.

**Kim Usher** is Professor of Nursing and Head of School of Health at the University of New England. Kim's research areas of interest include psychopharmacology and the health of people with mental illness, chronic illness, the psychosocial impact of emergencies and disasters, adolescent substance use and the impact on the family unit, alcohol related injuries, family centred care and family carers, consumer experiences in health services, and workforce issues. During her time as an academic, Kim has developed an interest in research methodologies, including the use of innovative methodologies. Kim has published extensively in the nursing and health related literature and has co-authored numerous book chapters. In addition, Kim has supervised 20 PhD students to completion and has many current students.

**Yoland Wadsworth** has been a pioneer practitioner, facilitator and theorist in the development of transformative research and evaluation methodologies, including participatory, dialogic and 'whole systems' action research in health, community and human services for 38 years. She has authored Australia's best-selling texts *Do It Yourself Social Research* and *Everyday Evaluation on the Run* and the most recent work in this methodology trilogy: *Building in Research and Evaluation: Human Inquiry for Living Systems* (all 2011). She is an Adjunct Professor with the Centre for Applied Social Research, RMIT University; Hon Principal Fellow with the University of Melbourne's McCaughey VicHealth Centre, and Distinguished Fellow of the Action Research Center, University of Cincinnati. She has received the Australasian Evaluation Society's ET&S Award for an 'outstanding contribution to evaluation in Australia' and in 2007 was made a Fellow. She is a past president and life member of the international Action Learning, Action Research Association.

**Karen Yates** is a registered nurse and registered midwife, with a strong interest and background in midwifery clinical care, education and maternity service provision. Karen completed initial nursing and midwifery education in the hospital setting and has since been awarded a post-registration Bachelor of Nursing, Master of Nursing, Graduate Certificate of Education (Tertiary Teaching) and Doctor of Philosophy. Karen has worked in both private and public settings and in both regional and rural facilities. Her roles in these facilities included clinical and advanced clinical practice roles, education, senior management and project administration. Karen has worked for James Cook University on a sessional basis for over ten years and commenced a permanent position as Lecturer in 2012, coordinating subjects at both undergraduate and postgraduate levels. Karen completed her PhD in 2010 using a phenomenological approach to research the experience of midwives who work in a dual role as midwife and nurse in rural far north Queensland. Her research interests are in rural and remote nursing and midwifery workforce, models of maternity care and midwifery practice. Karen is a member of the Australian College of Midwives and the Australian College of Nursing.

**Mary Isabelle Young** is *Anishinabe Kwe* from Bloodvein First Nation. She received her early education, Grades 1–8, in Bloodvein, Manitoba. She attended residential school for three years and graduated from Kelvin High School in Winnipeg. She obtained her Bachelor of Arts from the University of Winnipeg, Post-Baccalaureate in Education and Masters of Education from the University of Manitoba. She completed her PhD in First Nations Education from the University of Alberta. Notwithstanding these degrees, Mary consistently honours the ways her parents taught and educated her. She believes they were truly her first teachers. Her parents were the ones who encouraged her and insisted she speaks *Anishinabemowin*. In 1984 Mary began as a Native Student Advisor and became the first Director of the Aboriginal Student Services Centre at the University of Winnipeg. She is currently an Assistant Professor in the Faculty of Education at the University of Winnipeg. Mary is the author of *Pimatisiwin: Walking in a Good Way: A Narrative Inquiry into Language as Identity* (Pemmican, 2005). She is a coauthor of *Warrior Women: Remaking Postsecondary Places Through Relational Narrative Inquiry* (Emerald, 2012).

**SAGE**

# QUALITATIVE  METHODOLOGY

Book Home | Instructor Resources | Student Resources

Authors: Melanie Burks and Jane Mills

Pub Date: January 2014

Pages: 280

Learn more about this book

## Book Home

Welcome to the companion website for *Qualitative Methodology: A Practical Guide* by Jane Mills and Melanie Birks.

## About the Book

Fresh, insightful and clear, this exciting textbook provides an engaging introduction to the application of qualitative methodology in the real world.

Expert researchers then trace the history and philosophical underpinnings of different methodologies, explore the specific demands each places upon the researcher and robustly set out relevant issues surrounding quality and rigor. Featured methodologies include action research, discourse analysis, ethnography, grounded theory, case studies and narrative inquiry.

This practical book provides a helpful guide to the research process - it introduces the relevant methods of generating, collecting and analysing data for each discrete methodology and then looks at best practice for presenting findings. This enables new researchers to compare qualitative methods and to confidently select the approach most appropriate for their own research projects.

Key features include:

- Summary table for each chapter - allowing quick checks to test knowledge
- 'Window into' sections - real world examples showing each methodology in action
- Student activities
- Learning objectives
- Full glossary
- Annotated suggestions for further reading
- Links to downloadable SAGE articles
- Links to relevant websites and organizations

This is an invaluable resource for students and researchers across the social sciences and a must-have guide for those embarking on a research project.

## Instructor Resources

This site is password protected 🔒

*Please read the information to your right. To access the site, click on the sign in button on the right hand side below.*

The section of the companion website contains resources which are available free of charge to lecturers who adopt *Qualitative Methodology: A Practical Guide.*

The following material is available for lecturers:

- PowerPoint slides
- Testbank of Multiple Choice Questions

## First-time Users

Many of the materials on the instructor site, are only available to Faculty and Administrative Staff at Higher Education Institutions who have been approved to request Review Copies by SAGE.

To create an account,  please click here. In order to be approved, you must provide your institution and the course that you are or will be teaching. Once you have created an account and you have been validated as a faculty member, you will be able to access the instructor site.

*Please note: Validation usually takes approximately 24-48 hours to be completed.*

If you have any questions, please contact SAGE Customer Service at +44 (0) 20 7 324 8500 from 8:30 am to 5:00 pm.

## Returning Users

If you already have an account with SAGE, log in using the email address and password created when registering with SAGE.

**Sign In ▶**

# Preface

## Jane Mills and Melanie Birks

The aim of this book is to provide a practical guide to the very early stages of designing a qualitative research study, with readers introduced to concepts that are the building blocks of this process. Qualitative methodologies as opposed to qualitative methods are the main focus of this book although we do briefly address common methods used in each to provide context. Elsewhere (Birks and Mills, 2011), we define the difference between methodology and methods as follows:

> Stemming from a congruent philosophy, a methodology is a set of principles and ideas that inform the design of a research study. Methods, on the other hand, are practical procedures used to generate and analyse data. (p. 4)

A research design therefore includes three components: philosophy, methodology and methods. There are many excellent research methods books (Flick, 2009; Nagy Hesse-Biber and Leavy, 2011; Silverman, 2009, 2011) providing guidance on the 'nuts and bolts' of conducting a qualitative study, however before heading out into the field, there is a lot of important 'thinking' work that needs to be accomplished to make sure the mechanics of a research study successfully generate quality data that meet the aim of the study. Methodology is all about thinking, reflecting and positioning yourself as a researcher so that you are both informed and confident in implementing the subsequent research design to achieve a quality outcome. As Denzin and Lincoln (2011) state 'the question of methods begins with the design of the qualitative research project. This always begins with a socially situated researcher who moves from a research question, to a paradigm or perspective, to the empirical world' (p. xi). In this book we will challenge and support you to locate yourself philosophically and methodologically in relation to your qualitative research question prior to entering the field.

Part I addresses the foundations of qualitative research. We introduce the development of qualitative research over time, and address the concept of a generic qualitative research process. The first building block of a qualitative research study is writing a research question that works, followed by an exploration of the idea of practical philosophy as a place to begin positioning yourself methodologically. The differences between methodology and methods, and the impact that choosing a particular philosophical stance and methodology can have on how methods are used and the resultant outcome generated, will be illustrated through the use of a number of examples in the final chapter in this section.

Part II scaffolds the reader's learning by examining eight qualitative methodologies: action research, discourse analysis, ethnography, grounded theory, historical research, case study, narrative inquiry and phenomenology. Choosing methodologies for inclusion in this text was an arbitrary process guided by our experiences of teaching, listening to international conference presentations and reading both journal articles and books. A recent analysis of articles published in *Qualitative Health Research* between the years of 1999–2007 supports the majority of our choices, ranking the most popular research designs in the following order: grounded theory, phenomenology, ethnography and narrative analysis (Shin et al., 2009). Case study and historical research we consider important as they offer researchers the methods necessary to capture, and most importantly contextualize, the experience of individuals and communities during a particular point in time, while action research creates a space where researchers can work with participants to develop both understanding and incremental change. An examination of discourse analysis, with its roots in post-structural and postmodern thinking, provides the reader with an opportunity to consider the relevance of qualitative enquiry denoting the 'humanist individual' (Adams St Pierre, 2011) possessive of agency and usually the subject of many of the other seven methodologies discussed in Part II. We are the first to acknowledge however, that qualitative research studies are never as clear-cut as this list makes out. Kincheloe (2001), famously extends the discussion first posited by Denzin and Lincoln (2000) that the work of a qualitative researcher is that of a bricoleur or a 'handyman or handywoman who makes use of the tools available to complete a task' (Kincheloe, 2001: 680). Often, qualitative researchers will draw upon a range of research traditions in order to best answer the question they pose, however it is the congruence of the philosophical underpinnings with the methodology and methods adopted that makes for a rigorous design, an argument we will extend in Chapters 3, 13 and 14.

Each chapter in Part II is written using an identical format to enable easy comparison between different aspects of each qualitative methodology and includes:

- History of the methodology
- Philosophical underpinnings
- Positioning the researcher
- Aligning philosophy and methodology with purpose
- Data generation and collection
- Analysis of data
- Quality and rigour
- Presentation and dissemination of findings

When reading Part II, a solid qualitative research question formulated as an outcome of Part I can be used as the basis for a cross methodological examination. What would it mean if phenomenology as opposed to ethnography is used to answer the question posed? How does grounded theory compare to action research from the perspective of positioning the researcher? Clearly, this book will not provide all the answers to these types of questions relating to each of the qualitative methodologies included, however it's a starting point, with some signposts about where to go next. Being a new qualitative researcher can be difficult and sometimes a simple explanation provides enough direction to start the proverbial 'journey' to acquire knowledge and skills on the right path, rather than getting lost and taking a lot of time consuming wrong turns before even getting going.

Part III examines planning a qualitative study in detail. Concrete strategies for writing a full, qualitative research proposal, including an ethics application, are provided. Processes for appraising the quality of your own and others' qualitative research findings are addressed, while the final chapter discusses current debates in qualitative research using the theory of generational difference as a framework for discussion. The politics of evidence, causality and impact, and the challenges faced by Generation Y are explored in the context of qualitative research.

Throughout the book there are a number of recurring features to support the reader's knowledge and skill development in qualitative research. Case studies titled 'windows into' illustrate particular points made in the text. Contributors to the 'windows into' series, speak from their own experience about the pragmatics of conducting a qualitative research study. Activities are provided to prompt reader activity and help connect their own potential study to theory. Key points from each chapter are summarized to give a 'snapshot' of each methodology for the purpose of succinct comparison.

We wish to thank our families, Hew, Emma and Alec Mills and Benjamin Birks for their continued, patient support of our investment in scholarly discourse. We also wish to acknowledge our mentors, Karen Francis and Ysanne Chapman, along with our colleagues and students who inspire us to continue to make a practical contribution to the qualitative methodological literature. We also thank the contributors to this book and our supportive and efficient team at SAGE, Patrick Brindle, Jai Seaman and Anna Horvai who have been instrumental in bringing this project to fruition. To those who find value in our contribution, we extend our appreciation and commitment to continue to make a difference in this field.

## References

Adams St Pierre, E. (2011) 'Refusing human being in humanist qualitative inquiry', in N. Denzin and M. Giardina (eds), *Qualitative Inquiry and Global Crises*. Walnut Creek, CA: Left Coast Press, pp. 40–55.

Birks, M. and Mills, J. (2011) *Grounded Theory: A Practical Guide*. London: SAGE Publications.

Denzin, N. and Lincoln, Y. (2000) *The Handbook of Qualitative Research*. Thousand Oaks, CA: SAGE Publications.

Denzin, N. and Lincoln, Y. (2011) 'Preface', In N. Denzin and Y. Lincoln (eds), *The SAGE Handbook of Qualitative Research*. 4th edn. Thousand Oaks: SAGE Publications, p. 766.

Flick, U. (2009) *An Introduction to Qualitative Research*. London: SAGE Publications.

Kincheloe, J. (2001) 'Describing the bricolage: conceptualizing a new rigor in qualitative research', *Qualitative Inquiry*, 7: 679–692.

Nagy Hesse-Biber, S. and Leavy, P. (2011) *The Practice of Qualitative Research*. Thousand Oaks: SAGE Publications.

Shin, K.R., Kim, M.Y. and Chung, S.E. (2009) 'Methods and strategies utilized in published qualitative research', *Qualitative Health Research*, 19: 850–858.

Silverman, D. (2009) *Doing Qualitative Research*. London: SAGE.

Silverman, D. (2011) *Interpreting Qualitative Data*. London: SAGE Publications, Ltd.

# PART I

# 1
# Introducing Qualitative Research

Jane Mills and Melanie Birks

## Learning objectives

After reading this chapter, you should be able to:

- Identify key milestones in the evolution of qualitative research
- Discuss the definition of qualitative research
- Explore the concept of a generic form of qualitative research
- Discuss the purpose and structure of qualitative research questions
- Construct a qualitative research question

## Introduction

Ambition

Desire

Curiosity

Trepidation

Frustration

Excitement

Fear

Confusion … and then we begin.

For beginning researchers, planning to undertake a qualitative study is motivated by a range of factors. For some it is a requirement of their employment that they achieve a PhD, the highest degree that a university awards. For others, engaging in this type of work results from a long-held desire to exercise their intellect; while curiosity is a characteristic that all potential researchers display. Once the decision is made to commence, most people experience trepidation at the prospect, quickly followed by frustration with university processes, culminating in excitement when they receive their ethics approval letter. For students of research, after their first initial supervisory meetings working through potential research questions and designs before being sent off to read, and read, and read; feelings of tension and confusion often begin to fill them with doubt.

Feelings of tension and confusion are more intense for qualitative researchers at the beginning of their career because of the complex lineage of many research designs. You may find you relate to the words of the doctoral candidate and supervisor in Box 1.1. In qualitative research the mandate that the design must match the question, and not the other way around, makes the situation even more complicated. Beginning researchers approach their higher degree studies with a research question of sorts, or at least a substantive area of enquiry that they wish to investigate. To be accepted into a program of study, a research proposal is written that includes a research design, however, there is often limited understanding of what this means in reality. As a result, it is normal for higher degree qualitative research students to spend the first 6–12 months of their candidature exploring not only their original methodological ideas, but also others that might provide a better fit with their research question – which is at the same time being refined.

---

**BOX 1.1**

### Window into qualitative research

A poem by Michelle Redman-MacLaren (Doctoral candidate)

*Tension*
As I begin, Tension begins with me
How am I contributing today?
By sitting at my desk, growing my brain
How is this healing the world?
Tension snickers 'your ego is back'
Her soft, knowing chuckle
Reminding me of my familiar foe
The need to produce, to work, to do
A gentle counterpoint required.

A sabbatical, a journey, a spiritual quest
A quieting of doing
A louding of being
My challenge now and throughout
My PhD

A poem by Ysanne Chapman (Supervisor)

*In Waiting*
The expectant student
always looking for that first word
that springboards into fluency –

---

Spilling forth a thousand words
And a thousand more
grabbing at the pages
before the brain silences the fingers.

This chapter will explore the evolution of qualitative research and how a changing society has contributed to the field of enquiry as it stands today. The purpose and outcomes of a qualitative study will be discussed, and generic concepts relevant to this approach to research will be outlined. To conclude the chapter, we will explain what makes a research question work well and provide you with some strategies to build a strong foundation for your own study.

| Activity 1.1 | You and qualitative research |
|---|---|

Take a minute to jot down a few words that describe your understanding of qualitative research. How do you feel about the prospect of undertaking a study using a qualitative methodology?

## The evolution of qualitative research

Tracing the evolution of qualitative research is traditionally linked to periods of time, beginning with early ethnographies (Vidich and Lyman, 2000) conducted between the fifteenth and nineteenth centuries as a part of explorers' voyages to the 'New World' and the colonialization of both vast tracts of land and the traditional owners of that land. Ethnography during this time, and on into the late nineteenth and early twentieth centuries was founded on the premise that the researcher was a detached observer of cultures other than their own, falling in line with scientific thought at that time, which perceived the world as an entity for which there were general, uniform laws to explain both the physical world and the causal relationships that supported its being (Erickson, 2011). It was not until the late nineteenth century that the philosopher Wilhelm Dilthey wrote of a form of social inquiry that aimed to understand human experience, as opposed to garnering proof for the purpose of prediction and ultimately generalization. Dilthey's 'science of the spirit' (Erickson, 2011: 44) informed the work of early phenomenologist's and anthropologists. At the beginning of the twentieth century the genre of realist ethnography, positioning researchers as objectively able to capture the totality of community life through careful observation and interview, dominated qualitative research. In the United States (US), a tradition of community ethnographic studies was established in the Chicago School of Sociology that continued to be anchored in a realist, or positivist ontology. Scholars at this institution later developed the perspective of symbolic interactionism (Blumer, 1969), based on the work of Mead (1934), which moved qualitative research into a sphere of relativism that was 'proudly anti-positivistic' (Fine, 1993: 64). Strauss was a student of Mead and Blumer, who together with Glaser (Glaser and Strauss, 1967) began to question the appropriateness of a scientific method of verification, developing the alternative methodology of grounded theory while generating a sociological theory of dying (Glaser and Strauss, 1965).

Denzin and Lincoln (2000, 1994, 2011, 2005) have iteratively argued a conceptualization of the history of the field of qualitative research in eight moments (Box 1.2), of which the first two, traditional (1900–1950) and modernist or 'golden age' (1950–1970) include our discussion to this point, with a number of qualitative researchers during this time gravitating from the foundationalism of positivistic thought to a position more akin to constructivism (Mills, Bonner and Francis, 2006). Atkinson, Coffey and Delamont (2003) struggle with the use of Denzin and Lincoln's heuristic, arguing that the development of qualitative research is far from linear after what they term the 'ruptures of 1968' (p. 6), even though linearity is not the original authors' intent believing instead that each of the eight moments 'overlap and coexist in the present' (Denzin, 2011: xv). Juxtaposing a clearly delineated timeline against this broad overarching statement of coexistence can result in a state of confusion, unless one considers these moments not as phases, but as the point of origin for particular schools of thought, many of which will be explored in Part II in relation to contemporary qualitative methodologies.

---

**BOX 1.2**

**Denzin and Lincoln's Moments of Qualitative Inquiry**

| Years | Moment |
|---|---|
| 1900–1950 | Traditional |
| 1950–1970 | Modernist or 'Golden Age' |
| 1970–1986 | Blurred Genres |
| 1986–1990 | Crisis of Representation |
| 1990–1995 | Postmodernism |
| 1995–2000 | Post-experimental Inquiry |
| 2000–2004 | The Methodologically-Contested Present |
| 2005–Present | Fractured Future |

---

So what happened in 1968? A number of momentous events made it an amazing year to be alive (if you were old enough to understand what was happening). US engagement in the Vietnam War sparks a series of often-violent protests across the world. Dr Martin Luther King was assassinated on the 4th of April, with a subsequent wave of race riots lasting days in a number of major American cities. Ironically, President Lyndon B. Johnson signed the US Civil Rights Act seven days later and James Anderson, Jr., the first black US Marine, was posthumously awarded the Medal of Honor. In the United Kingdom, the anti-immigration speech *Rivers of Blood* was delivered in response to the passing of an act of parliament (the *Race Relations Act 1968*) generating immense social controversy in this country. France was led to the brink of a communist revolution with a million students and workers marching through Paris in response to Charles de Gaulle's government. Again in the US, militant student protests occurred at the University of Wisconsin-Madison, North Carolina at Chapel Hill, Howard University, and Columbia University in New York City. Nuclear weapons testing proliferated in the US, and France exploded its first hydrogen bomb. The US presidential candidate Robert F. Kennedy was assassinated in connection to the Arab Israeli conflict in the Middle East. Saddam Hussein came into power in Iraq as the result of a coup d'état, while Pope Paul VI published the encyclical *Humanae Vitae* condemning birth control. The women's liberation movement gained traction with a large demonstration against the Miss America pageant. CNN launched the investigative journalism television show, *60 Minutes*, Richard Nixon was elected the President of the United States and *Apollo 8* orbited the moon (Dunnigan and Hartman-Strom, unknown).

The social and political ruptures of 1968 impacted profoundly on the way qualitative researchers perceived themselves during this time, including: their role, their place in the world and the relationship they sustain with participants throughout the research process, including the presentation of findings. In 1967, Howard Becker, an eminent scholar and member of the second wave Chicago School, presages many of the methodological dilemmas that dominate the literature to come. In his presidential address to the Society for the Study of Social Problems, entitled *Whose Side Are We On?* (Becker, 1967), he disabuses the notion

**Figure 1.1**

that sociological researchers can be value free. The extensive critique and resultant development of Becker's original thesis (Atkinson et al., 2003), that there is no such thing as value free research, is representative of much that has been written about qualitative research in the past four plus decades. Many of the standards that contemporary qualitative researchers account for in the design and implementation of their studies stem from these methodological discussions and debates. Erickson (2011), in his historical account of qualitative inquiry in social and educational research, likens the fifteen years from 1967 onwards to a 'firestorm of criticism of realist general ethnography' (p. 49) resulting in part from the growing influence of Native American, African American and feminist researchers concerned with power, oppression, the researcher's position in a study, and the importance of reflexivity. In particular, qualitative researchers, committed to action research, identify 1970 as a turning point when many broke away from universities as centres of research that they considered unsympathetic to understanding the world in a way outside of 'conceptions of Cartesian rationality, dualism and "normal science"' (Fals Borda, 2006: 27). At this time, the publication of Freire's (1972) *Pedagogy of the Oppressed* provided the impetus for many qualitative researchers to reposition themselves in relation to 'how and why' they engaged in the process of inquiry. Freire's battle cry to work '*with*, not *for*, the oppressed [so as to] make oppression and its causes objects of reflection by the oppressed, and from that reflection will come their necessary engagement in the struggle for their liberation' (Freire, 1972: 25) resonated with many, providing a platform for both participatory action research and critical ethnographic research. Shortly after this, Feyerabend published the seminal text *Against Method* (1975) where he argued that 'science knows no "bare facts" at all but that the "facts" that enter our knowledge are already viewed in a certain way and are, therefore, essentially ideational' (p. 19), adding more fuel to the firestorm raging through the modernist landscape of research.

In the late 1970s and early 1980s the conceptualization of paradigms of inquiry gained currency, with particular paradigms delimited through answering questions of ontology, epistemology and methodology (Guba, 1990; Lincoln, Lynham and Guba, 2011). In the history of qualitative research this time was dominated by the 'paradigm wars' (Denzin, 2010), with postpositivists, constructivists and critical theorists all 'pushing back' against the dominant positivistic research culture, while at the same time competing with each other for legitimacy and recognition. In 1989 a landmark event, the *Alternative Paradigms Conference*, was held in San Francisco with the aim of clarifying and exploring issues of concern for scholars identifying with each of these three paradigms of thought (Guba, 1990). Reflecting back, Denzin (2010) identifies this process of respectful dialogue as signalling the end of the paradigm wars of the 1980s, while positing there were two more conflicts to come; in the field of mixed-methods research where the incompatibility thesis of postpositivist and 'other' paradigms was debated in the 1990s/00s, and the current politicized conflict with regard to what constitutes valid evidence as an outcome of research (Hammersley, 2008; Denzin, 2009).

# Qualitative research

Teaching undergraduate research students for many years, out of necessity we have both addressed the idea of a 'common or garden variety' version of qualitative research. Breaking down the concept of qualitative research to simple component parts results in the lecturer rapidly moving to generic explanations of the research process as opposed to initially situating a design methodologically which requires the student to have a basic understanding of philosophical and often sociological thought, absent in the many practice-based professions in which qualitative research proliferates. A traditional, dichotomously situated, definition of qualitative research is that:

> … if researchers choose to gather experiential data more than measurements, they call their research 'qualitative' – but they still may emphasize either the particular or the general. If findings are drawn primarily from the aggregate of many individual observations, we call the study 'quantitative,' but the researcher still may emphasize either the particular or the general (Stake, 2010: 19).

This simple division of research into either qualitative or quantitative is largely rejected by qualitative methodologists as inadequate in describing the nuances and multiplicity of research designs (Flick, 2007) – however we would argue that in the current 'crisis' of evidence, Stake's definition resonates with many from outside qualitative research such as policymakers and funders (Birks and Mills, 2011). As an alternative to defining qualitative research by what it is not – quantitative – Atkinson, Coffey and Delamont (2001) consider qualitative research an umbrella term dimensionalized by discipline; methods; topic and substance; voices and text. The importance of the researcher's discipline in shaping the mores of qualitative methodologies shouldn't be underestimated, particularly in relation to the choice of topic and substance, and the place of voices and text. Method, however, is the one dimension that incorporates elements common to the majority of qualitative research studies – leading to the idea of generic planning and implementation processes. It's not unusual to read reports of research labelled 'qualitative', usually accompanied by a caveat term such as descriptive or exploratory. Naïve or methodologically free studies such as these are framed in terms of methods that often include: purposive sampling, the generation or collection of textual data as a result of observation and interviews, thematic analysis of the data and a reliance on measures of trustworthiness (Guba and Lincoln, 1989) to ensure rigour.

So what's wrong with conducting a generic 'qualitative research study'? While overall, the purpose of a qualitative research study is to examine phenomena that impact on the lived reality of individuals or groups in a particular cultural and social context, studies firmly anchored in a methodological school of thought are finely textured and nuanced – producing a much higher quality outcome. It is the question asked by the researcher that determines the methodology used and it is this choice of methodology that guides the researcher, already ensconced in their discipline, to consider dimensions of topic and substance, voice and text.

# Writing a qualitative research question

Knowing how to write a research question that is clear and unambiguous, while allowing sufficient scope for the unexpected directions that a qualitative research study can take, is an important skill for the research student to develop. As you review texts discussing research design you will no doubt see reference to a wide variety of terminology. Research questions? Hypotheses? Aims? Objectives? The differences between each of these terms are often not clear and cause confusion in the novice researcher. An understanding of these differences in language and the purpose of using particular terminology is important in clarifying the researcher's thinking about their particular study.

Different researchers will define concepts relating to research using different language. Table 1.1 provides a summary of our definitions of terms used to describe a researcher's intention in relation to their proposed research and their use in practice.

In qualitative research, a well-constructed research question will guide the selection of an appropriate methodology and development of the research design. Underestimating the importance of ensuring clarity in the meaning, structure and intention of research questions can negatively impact on the ability of the researcher to find the answer to these questions (Bragge, 2010). Quality research questions potentiate quality research outcomes. Agee (2009) suggests that while a good research question does not automatically lead to good research, poorly-constructed questions will almost certainly impact on the quality of a study.

It should be expected that the research question, its aims and objectives may be modified as a research study progresses (more so in some qualitative designs than others) but this does not detract from the importance that the initial research question brings to the project as a whole. Koro-Ljungberg and Hayes (2010)

**Table 1.1**  Defining key research terms

| Term | Definition | Usage |
|------|-----------|-------|
| Topic | The research focus | Provides generic statement of the focus of the study |
| Research statement | A brief paragraph outlining the purpose and significance of the proposed research study | Summarizes the intent of the researcher |
| Hypothesis | A suggested or proposed explanation for a phenomenon | Common in quantitative research<br>Used in qualitative research to hypothesize relationships |
| Research question | An interrogative statement of the research intent | Asserts the research intent<br>Directs the study design |
| Aim | A statement of intent or anticipated outcome | Guides action towards the research goal |
| Objective | Aim or goal that includes reference to specific object or phenomenon to be achieved | Acts as a tangible subset of the stated research question or aims to support the research |

propose that the research question promotes methodological congruence and furthermore provides direction for the use of research methods and strategies within a methodological framework. These authors refer to the 'permeable boundaries' that research questions permit within a 'helpful and informative methodological space' (p. 117).

Many readers will come to this text with an idea or topic area for research but have yet to formulate it into a researchable question. Some will have formulated a question yet are struggling to align it with an appropriate methodology. Others may come to a study with an unfocused or unmanageable topic area or in some cases, a hope that the topic will somehow simply show itself (Silverman, 2009). Koro-Ljungberg and Hayes (2010) warn that questions that are vague, broad or absent can potentially impede thorough, detailed and rigorous analysis.

One of the frustrations experienced by graduate students in the early stages of a study is their inability to establish a clear focus for their research. It is important here to point out that a lack of focus in the early stages of research is common and to be expected as a normal part of the process. A student's desire to know more about a topic through research is a result of a lack of knowledge about the subject matter and this deficit is evident in their inability to narrow the focus of the research. It is indeed the acquisition of a growing familiarity with the phenomenon of study that provides the impetus for continually refining the research question (Creswell and Tashakkori, 2007). As Agee (2009) points out, research question refinement is an iterative process.

Nevertheless, in the early stages of a study an 'answerable' question must be formulated in order for the research to progress (Bragge, 2010). What makes a qualitative research question 'answerable' or 'good'? Agee (2009) suggests that the individual(s) who is/are the focus of the research and the situational context should be evident in the question. Koro-Ljungberg and Hayes (2010) also identify the study-context and setting as guiding parameters for the construction of research questions, along with instrumentalization (which we interpret as meaning the use of a research question as a tool to guide the conduct of the study) and epistemology, which once again refers to the constructive alignment that exists between the question posed and the overarching methodology. Agee (2009) adds that research questions should have a reflexive and ethical dimension and must be feasible for study in terms of the resources of the researcher.

What then does a 'good' research question look like? We need to draw on Koro-Ljungberg and Hayes' (2010) element of 'instrumentation' to answer this question. The intent of the outcome of the study will determine the interrogative that heralds the question's content. Closed questions are of no use in qualitative research as they have no scope. For example, the question 'Do farmers experience depression following prolonged drought' calls for a yes or no answer and does not give the necessary direction to the study. Interrogatives such as 'how' or 'what' generally provide a broad opening for a research question. If the researcher proposes to explicate the process, then 'how' questions should be used, e.g., 'How do female engineers in the Middle East achieve professional development in the work place?'

Studies that attempt to examine an individual's experience of a phenomenon will usually be phrased from a 'what' or 'how' perspective, e.g., 'What is the experience of Sudanese refugees attempting to resettle in urban American environments?' or 'How do children of military service personnel experience transition to new schools following relocation?' The desire to explore and describe may be formed as a 'why' statement, such as 'Why does post-natal depression occur more often following the birth of a second child?'

This last example brings us to an important point. Neither your research question nor the study that follows can be founded on any pre-existing assumptions. Agee (2009) warns against such pre-suppositions as these stifle the discovery of meaning that characterizes qualitative research. Be clear about how your study sits in the context of existing disciplinary knowledge otherwise you risk building your study on a faulty foundation.

Drawing from this discussion and our own experience, we propose the following principles for the development of an effective research question. The researcher needs to ask whether the research question:

- Is answerable in terms of the researcher's expertise and available resources
- Is free from assumptions that are not based in valid evidence
- Contains only one question rather than a number of questions strung together
- Is phrased as an open-ended question
- Makes reference to the context of the phenomena of interest
- Includes reference to participant individuals or groups
- Uses language that indicates the philosophical position of the researcher
- Is concise, stating the question briefly and with clarity

Depending on the nature and stage of the study, few or all of these principles may be addressed. The intent of these principles is to give you some guidance in the construction of your own research question without being regarded as hard-and-fast rules.

---

**Activity 1.2** — **Effective research questions**

Review a research question you are currently working with or select one from a published piece of work to which you have access. Using the above principles as a guide, evaluate the research question and identify any ways in which the research question could be improved. Attempt to rephrase the question in your own words to ensure it is more appropriate for its purpose.

---

It is important to note that a research study may contain more than one research question as Koro-Ljungberg and Hayes (2010) found. We concur with Agee (2009), however, that a single overarching research question is necessary to guide the study, with sub-questions being used as and if necessary. You may find, however, that your inclusion of distinct aims and objectives may be sufficient to support your research question, particularly in the early stages of your study.

# Conclusion

Qualitative research has evolved over recent decades to achieve credibility for its ability to explore the human condition and its many truths. Undertaking a study using a qualitative methodology requires an understanding of the philosophy that underpins the proposed research design. The development of a research question that reflects the intent of the research and directs its conduct is pivotal to success in qualitative research. This chapter has explored concepts relevant to qualitative inquiry and has outlined generic processes in the planning and implementation of a study based on a well-constructed research question. As you progress through this text, you will no doubt return to this chapter to revise and reground your understanding of qualitative research.

## KEY POINTS

- Embarking on a qualitative research study can be a daunting process accompanied by mixed emotions
- The evolution of qualitative research can be linked to specific periods of time, beginning with the ethnographic movement that commenced in the early fifteenth century
- While generic qualitative research exists as a concept, such an approach removes the philosophical anchor of a situational methodology
- A well-constructed research question directs the selection of methodology and provides guidance for conducting of a qualitative study

## CRITICAL THINKING QUESTIONS

- How have historical milestones influenced the evolution of research in the qualitative paradigm and its position in contemporary social enquiry?
- What are your thoughts on the concept of generic qualitative research? Does the absence of a methodological anchor diminish the value of a qualitative study?
- How important is the research question in the conceptualization and implementation of a research study? How much scope should be given for the evolution of a qualitative research question as a study progresses?

# Suggested further reading

Silverman, D. (2013) *A Very Short, Fairly Interesting and Reasonably Cheap Book About Qualitative Research*. London: SAGE Publications.

'David Silverman's second edition of this book provides a refreshing introduction to doing and debating qualitative research. An antidote to the standard textbook, this new edition shows how research can be methodologically inventive, empirically rigorous, theoretically-alive and practically relevant. Using materials ranging from photographs to novels and newspaper stories, the book demonstrates that getting to grips with qualitative methods means asking ourselves fundamental questions about how we are influenced by contemporary culture. By drawing on examples from websites and social media in the new edition, Silverman's text acknowledges how our social worlds are changing and explores new arenas for data collection. A new Glossary of Received Ideas aims to challenge conventional understandings of terms central to qualitative research and will inform, amuse and stimulate readers' (SAGE Publications, 2013).

## References

Agee, J. (2009) 'Developing qualitative research questions: a reflective process', *International Journal of Qualitative Studies in Education*, 22: 431–447.

Atkinson, P., Coffey, A. and Delamont, S. (2001) 'A debate about our canon', *Qualitative Research*, 1: 5–21.

Atkinson, P., Coffey, A. and Delamont, S. (2003) *Key Themes in Qualitative Research: Continuities and Change*. Walnut Creek, CA: AltaMira Press.

Becker, H.S. (1967) 'Whose Side Are We On?', *Social Problems*, 14: 239–247.

Birks, M. and Mills, J. (2011) *Grounded Theory: A Practical Guide*. London: SAGE Publications.

Blumer, H. (1969) *Symbolic Interactionism: Perspective and Method*. Berkeley: University of California Press.

Bragge, P. (2010) 'Asking good clinical research questions and choosing the right study design', *Injury*, 41, Supplement 1: S3–S6.

Creswell, J. and Tashakkori, A. (2007) 'Editorial: differing perspectives on mixed methods research', *Journal of Mixed Methods*, 1: 303–308.

Denzin, N. (2009) *Qualitative Inquiry Under Fire: Toward a New Paradigm Dialogue*. Walnut Creek, California: Left Coast Press.

Denzin, N. (2010) *The Qualitative Manifesto*. Walnut Creek, CA.: Left Coast Press.

Denzin, N. and Lincoln, Y. (2011) *SAGE Handbook of Qualitative Research*, 4th edn. Thousand Oaks: SAGE Publications.

Dunnigan, K. and Hartman-Strom, S. (unknown) *The Whole World Was Watching: An Oral History of 1968*. Available at: http://www.stg.brown.edu/projects/1968/reference/timeline.html.

Erickson, F. (2011) 'A history of qualitative inquiry in social and educational research', in N. Denzin and Y. Lincoln (eds), *The SAGE Handbook of Qualitative Research*, 4th edn. Thousand Oaks: SAGE Publications, pp. 43–59.

Fals Borda, O. (2006) 'Participatory (action) research in social theory: origins and challenges', in P. Reason and H. Bradbury (eds), *Handbook of Action Research: Concise Paperback Edition*, 2nd edn. London: SAGE Publications, pp. 27–37.

Feyerabend, P. (1975) *Against Method: Outline of an Anarchistic Theory of Knowledge*. London: New Left Books.

Fine, G. (1993) 'The sad demise, mysterious disappearance, and glorious triumph of symbolic interactionism', *Annual Review of Sociology*, 19: 61–87.

Flick, U. (2007) *Designing Qualitative Research*. London: SAGE Publications.

Freire, P. (1972) *Pedagogy of the Oppressed*. London: Penguin Books.

Glaser, B.G. and Strauss, A.L. (1965) *Awareness of Dying*. New York: Aldine.

Glaser, B.G. and Strauss, A.L. (1967) *The Discovery of Grounded Theory: Strategies for Qualitative Research*. New York: Aldine.

Guba, E.G. (1990) *The Paradigm Dialog*. Newbury Park: SAGE.

Guba, E.G. and Lincoln, Y.S. (1989) *Fourth Generation Evaluation*. Newbury Park: SAGE.

Hammersley, M. (2008) *Questioning Qualitative Inquiry: Critical Essays*. Los Angeles; London: SAGE.

Koro-Ljungberg, M. and Hayes, S. (2010) 'Proposing an argument for research questions that could create permeable boundaries within qualitative research', *Journal of Ethnographic & Qualitative Research*, 4: 114–124.

Lincoln, Y., Lynham, S. and Guba, E. (2011) 'Paradigmatic controversies, contradictions, and emerging confluences, revisited', in N. Denzin and Y. Lincoln (eds), *SAGE Handbook of Qualitative Research*, 4th edn. Thousand Oaks: SAGE Publications, pp. 97–128.

Mead, G. (1934) *Self, and Society*. The University of Chicago Press.

Mills, J., Bonner, A. and Francis, K. (2006) 'The development of constructivist grounded theory', *International Journal of Qualitative Methods*, 5: Article 3.

Silverman, D. (2009) *Doing Qualitative Research*. London: SAGE.

Silverman, D. (2013) *A Very Short, Fairly Interesting and Reasonably Cheap Book About Qualitative Research*. London: SAGE Publications. Available at: http://www.uk.sagepub.com/books/Book238751?siteId=sage-uk&prodTypes=any&q=silverman&fs=1.

Stake, R. (2010) *Qualitative Research: Studying How Things Work*. New York: The Guilford Press.

Vidich, A. and Lyman, S. (2000) 'Qualitative methods: their history in sociology and anthropology', in N. Denzin and Y. Lincoln (eds), *Handbook of Qualitative Research*, 2nd edn. Thousand Oaks: SAGE Publications, pp. 37–84.

# 2
# Practical Philosophy

## Melanie Birks

| Learning outcomes |
|---|

After reading this chapter, you should be able to:

- Discuss basic philosophical concepts
- Outline the history of philosophical thought
- Reflect on the relationship between philosophy and qualitative research
- Articulate your personal philosophical position

## Introduction

Philosophy is recognized as a specific area of study, yet it permeates our everyday existence. Philosophical concepts can be complex and many students struggle to understand their relevance to research and their applicability within the qualitative paradigm. In this chapter, we examine philosophy and its relationship to qualitative research. The chapter commences with a definition of philosophy and a brief exploration of the history of philosophy, followed by an examination of philosophical concepts relevant to qualitative research. The chapter concludes with a discussion of the significance of the researcher's personal philosophical position in promoting congruence between research question, methodology and the conduct of a qualitative research study.

## What is philosophy?

Philosophy can be defined in many ways. It can be seen as the consideration of higher order problems and how we attempt to solve them, such as *what is the meaning of life? Is there a god?* (Wilson, 2002). The questions that attract philosophical thinking are usually broad and abstract (Teichman and Evans, 1995) and the inherent complexity of such concepts tends to lead many of us to shy away from engaging in philosophical thought as the prospect can be daunting. We need not think of philosophy as an estranged and ethereal concept, however. Each and every day we make decisions based on how we view the world. The lens through which we view the world is our personal philosophy. Philosophy can be seen as 'an attempt to provide for oneself an outlook on life based on the discovery of broad, fundamental principles' (Stewart, Blocker and Petrik, 2010: 1). We draw from contemporary thinking on philosophy to define it as *a view of the world encompassing the questions and mechanisms for finding answers that inform that view.*

The approach we take in solving everyday problems in our personal lives is founded on our individual philosophy. The process of reflecting on the events of our lives, how we frame them and what we learn from them occurs in the context of our personal philosophy.

# History of philosophy

An exploration of historical developments in philosophy provides a foundation for understanding how different stages of philosophical thought have influenced the evolution of major research paradigms. Paradigms are variously defined as models, patterns or exemplars. In respect of research, they are frameworks that represent a shared way of thinking in respect of how we view the world and we generate knowledge from that perspective. In Box 2.1, Simon Burgess provides an overview of major philosophical developments in history and their contribution to the research traditions that have evolved in concert with these developments.

---

**BOX 2.1**

### Window into qualitative research

#### Simon Burgess on major philosophical developments

The ancient Greek philosopher Socrates (469–399 B.C.E.) was eccentric, challenging and sometimes maddening. He was always questioning people about their assumptions concerning justice, courage, temperance and wisdom, and he invariably showed that their initial statements were actually rather difficult to defend. Socrates knew that his habit of questioning everything could seem impious and even dangerous to many people. In fact, he ultimately paid the supreme price for it; the people of Athens convicted and killed him for being irreverent towards the gods and corrupting the youth. But of course Socrates has certainly not been forgotten. His dialectical approach to the clarification and refutation of assumptions and ideas is often loosely referred to as the 'Socratic method', and he is rightly regarded as being central to the Western philosophical tradition.

The branch of philosophy concerned with the study of knowledge is known as epistemology, and it has featured various schools of thought since ancient times. Roughly speaking there are the rationalists who argue that at least some forms of knowledge can be gained simply through reasoning; and then there are the empiricists who argue that all knowledge is really dependent on observations, experiments, and other forms of sensory

*(Continued)*

---

*(Continued)*

experience. Rationalists point out that many truths of logic, mathematics and geometry, for example, appear to be provable through pure reasoning. The great French philosopher René Descartes (1596–1650) argued that each of us can also know about our own existence through a process of pure reasoning; 'I think, therefore I am', he declared. Yet empiricism has remained popular down the ages. By emphasizing the role of observation and experience, empiricism helped provide the philosophical underpinnings of the scientific revolution, and for many it gained further credibility in the process.

The burgeoning success and prestige of science in the 18th and 19th centuries prompted many to think that the empirical methods of science should be applied to our understanding of society. Positivists such as Auguste Comte (1798–1857) were particularly enthused by this line of thought. Yet there have always been sceptics about the idea that moral, social and political questions can be solved by science alone. According to the great Scottish philosopher David Hume (1711–1776), an essentially scientific line of inquiry can help us to understand the way the world is; working out how the world ought to be, however, requires something more. In his view, our decisions about social policy, for example, require us to draw upon our moral and political values, and there is no purely scientific way of saying what these should be.

Not all philosophers particularly care for a sharp distinction between the purely descriptive and scientific questions of what is, on the one hand, and evaluative questions of what ought to be, on the other. Nonetheless, something that roughly corresponds to this contrast is the methodological division between naturalism on the one hand, and interpretivism (sometimes known as constructivism) on the other. Methodological naturalism can be thought of as essentially scientific, and it is often of great assistance in gaining a better understanding of particular aspects of human life and human society. For example, in many cases it can be used to quite conclusively demonstrate the effects of certain specific social policies, therapeutic remedies and dietary choices that may be available. In and of itself, however, methodological naturalism will not determine which of these responses is the most ethically sound, wise or desirable.

Interpretivism draws upon a tradition in philosophy that owes much to thinkers such as Immanuel Kant (1724–1804), Wilhelm Dilthey (1833–1911), Edmund Husserl (1859–1938) and Max Weber (1864–1920). It plainly recognizes that human beings are not simply thoughtless and helpless; our actions are the product of our judgements, reasons and intentions. So, unlike ordinary billiard balls, for example, human concerns and human behaviour cannot be explained simply as the result of various external causes. With such considerations in mind, interpretivism is a methodology that is much narrower in scope than naturalism. It deals with human beings, human society, our stories and cultural artifacts and a host of human problems, but it does not pretend to provide any insights into physics, chemistry or biology. Most importantly, interpretivism allows its descriptions and explanations of human beings and their concerns to be subtly and thoughtfully imbued with human values. Many historians, psychologists and social commentators are quite happy to be regarded as adherents of methodological interpretivism. The fact that their work is imbued with complex human judgements and values may mean that their explanations and conclusions are forever open to reinterpretation and social critique. In the context of their discipline and the tasks that they have set for themselves, however, many accept that this is entirely as it should be.

In Box 2.1, Simon Burgess makes reference to some basic philosophical approaches that lead to research paradigms and refers to the inability of positivist philosophy to find answers to questions of relevance to social science researchers. Thus, we see the evolution of approaches borne from both postpositivist and interpretivist, paradigms. In addition to the research paradigms that have evolved concurrently with historical developments in philosophy referred to in Box 2.1, social justice movements since the middle of the last century have seen critical approaches develop as a philosophical framework to guide research. Critical approaches seek to understand concepts of justice in the context of society (Onwuegbuzie, Johnson and Collins, 2009).

Table 2.1 summarizes major research paradigms that influence qualitative methodologies. As will be gleaned from the following discussion, qualitative researchers are often drawn to methodologies founded on research paradigms other than positivism because they permit assumptions about perceptions of reality and knowledge that align with the researcher's area of inquiry. Of these paradigms, postpositivism, postmodernism, critical theory and constructivism have largely been the frameworks of choice for qualitative researchers. There are, however, examples of philosophical positions and research paradigms stretching beyond these usual boundaries (Alvesson and Skoldberg, 2009). Critical approaches, for example, share commonalities with both constructivism and postpostivism that sits them on a continuum between the reductionist perspective of postpositivism and the subjectivity of social context that drives constructivism (Onwuegbuzie et al., 2009). Critical realism, in particular, is a philosophical variant that requires special consideration because of its uniqueness in this regard (Kilduff, Mehra and Dunn, 2011). Reed (2009) in fact suggests that critical realists 'want things both ways' (p. 52). Critical realism takes the middle road through positivism and constructivism in asserting the existence of fixed structures within which society functions, while acknowledging that we have the capacity to exert influence through the constructions that result from social interaction (Reed, 2009).

The relationship between philosophical moments and research paradigms is therefore not fixed in nature and the alignment may be considered more 'elastic' than quantitative and qualitative fundamentalist would tend to acknowledge (Fig 2.1).

**Table 2.1**  Research paradigms

| Paradigm | Characteristics |
| --- | --- |
| Positivism | Asserts the existence of a single reality that is there to be discovered. |
| Postpositivism | Rejects the concept of a measurable reality that exists in isolation of the observer. |
| Postmodernism | Posits that the reality of a phenomenon is subjectively relative to those who experience it. |
| Critical theory | Seeks to redress perceived societal injustices through research. |
| Constructivism | Recognizes that reality is constructed by those who experience it and thus research is a process of reconstructing that reality. |

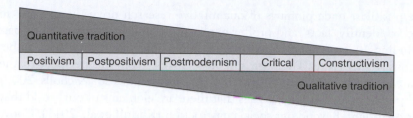

**Figure 2.1** Philosophical moments and research paradigms

# Philosophical concepts

Philosophy consists of a number of branches of study. Broadly these can be categorized as *metaphysics, ethics, politics, science, logic, mathematics, language, law* and *art* (Teichman and Evans, 1995). The extent to which individuals will apply themselves to a specific area of study will vary depending on the purpose and priorities of the philosopher. Those who concern themselves with human values, for example, will explore concepts relevant to ethics, while those concerned with social justice will place greater emphasis on political philosophy (Stewart et al., 2010). The exploration of all branches of philosophy is beyond the intent and scope of this chapter and thus we will focus on metaphysical philosophical concepts relevant to the conduct of qualitative research – *ontology* and *epistemology*.

## Ontology

Ontology is the study of being. The potential practical application of philosophical concepts is evident in one of the most simplified explanations of the term originating from the world of information technology (IT). From this perspective, Gruber (1993) provides a definition of ontology that views knowledge as an abstract representation of the world conceptualized either implicitly or explicitly. With such conceptualization, a shared understanding of a particular subject is secured through a common world view (Gruninger and Lee, 2002). Research in the qualitative domain requires an understanding of the ontological concepts of *existence* and *reality*.

Greek ontology as espoused by Plato identifies things in nature to be as distinguishable as existence or essence (Feenberg, 2003). Simply put, existence refers to the 'that' and 'how' a thing is in the world while the essence of something is 'what' it is (Garsdal, 2012). These concepts as defined may seem obvious, but in the context of research they are significant. In the research traditions of quantitative and qualitative inquiry, the distinction between them is palpable. Quantitative researchers are more concerned with proof 'that' a natural phenomenon exists, whereas qualitative researchers concern themselves more with 'how' and 'why' situations occur in the social world. The distinction is particularly evident when we explore perspectives of truth and reality.

The positivist underpinnings of quantitative research drive the use of scientific method to identify 'facts' and proffer explanations and make predictions based on these findings. A fact is considered to be a single objective reality that can be measured consistently (Petty, Thomson and Stew, 2012). From this perspective, the reality of a concept is linked to its existence in a physical sense (Nicholls, 2009). The 'realist' perspective, therefore, argues that there are elements of our world that exist in their own right, beyond our social construction (Kilduff et al., 2011). Conversely, philosophical movements that subsequently saw a turn away from positivist concepts provide the foundations upon which many qualitative research methodologies have evolved. These paradigmatic moments reject the concept of a single objective reality and propose the existence of multiple realities that acknowledge the significance of subjective interpretation. From such a 'relativist' perspective, truth is not a black and white entity, but is subject to various interpretations as a social construct.

## Epistemology

As stated in Box 2.1, epistemology is the branch of philosophy concerned with knowledge. While ontology explores the concept of reality, epistemology examines 'the ways in which it is possible to gain knowledge of this reality' (Petty et al., 2012: 270). We *know* something when what we believe coincides with our reality (Stewart et al., 2010). We can believe many things, true or false, but only belief that is true can be considered knowledge (Teichman and Evans, 1995). For example, historically, people believed that the world was flat. This was not a truth and thus they could not assert that they *knew* this to be the case.

**Figure 2.2**

Often when we consider knowledge we think of logic. Logic is 'the study of correct thinking' (Stewart et al., 2010: 2). Logic employs a systematic approach to thinking to ensure arrival at knowledge that we know to be truth. Logic enables us to establish the truth of knowledge in that it provides proof of that knowledge. In lay terms, we consider this proof to be some form of evidence, while empirical scientists will seek to establish the truth of knowledge through deductive processes (Teichman and Evans, 1995). The ability to prove knowledge through deduction is fundamental to the positivist paradigm, wherein truth and facts are the products of inquiry. As discussed in Box 2.1, the complexity of humanity and society falls within the realm of research paradigms in which qualitative enquiry is imbedded. Just as the reality of individuals and groups in society are relativist, so too are concepts of knowledge and proof. The alignment of beliefs with reality in qualitative research, therefore, is achieved through different means than that which occurs in quantitative research.

This distinction can be clarified through consideration of the concept of *theory*. A theory is 'an explanatory scheme comprising a set of concepts related to each other through logical patterns of connectivity' (Birks and Mills, 2011: 112–113). Through induction, qualitative research methodologies can generate theory. Conversely, through deduction, quantitative research aims to test theory. Thus, qualitative approaches generate knowledge that is seen to reflect the reality of individuals and groups while quantitative research seeks to validate that knowledge and its potential global application through empirical testing.

---

| **Activity 2.1** | **Philosophical concepts in qualitative research** |

Reflect on the preceding discussion. What relevance do you think that concepts of existence, reality and logic have in respect of qualitative research? What is the role of theory in relationship to these concepts? Draw a concept map to illustrate your understanding.

---

## Philosophy and research

Philosophy is derived from the Greek and translates as 'the love of wisdom' (Stewart et al., 2010: 1). Research is an attempt to generate knowledge and as such requires a foundation to guide the conduct of research or the interpretation of findings or both. Russell (2009) argues that philosophy involves identifying the defects in knowledge in order to ensure that it is comprehensive, consistent and indefinite. Research is the tool that assists us to fill the gaps in what is known in our world.

Qualitative methodologies are often distinguishable from each other, and indeed from quantitative research, on the basis of the major philosophical foundations that underpin them. You will see through your exploration of Part II of this text that each chapter provides a discussion of the philosophical foundations upon which each methodology is built. Such is the importance of philosophy in qualitative research. You may struggle with understanding the concepts that underpin philosophical thinking, but the take home message from your reading of this chapter should be that philosophy cannot be extricated from qualitative research without removing substance. Philosophy is what makes a set of methods a methodology.

## Positioning yourself as a researcher

In this chapter we are exploring philosophical concepts and their relationship to research. Qualitative research, by its very nature, requires an investment of the self. In qualitative research, methodology is not simply selected by the researcher, it is chosen on the basis of its suitability to answer the research question. Furthermore, the most successful research studies in the qualitative paradigm are those that see alignment between the methodology and the philosophical position of the researcher.

As one person's conceptualization of existence and their perception of reality differs from the next, it is important when embarking on a study for the researcher to examine how they view existence and reality. Each chapter in Part II of this text includes a discussion of the position of the research in recognition of the importance of the alignment of personal and methodological philosophy. In previous work (Birks and Mills, 2011) we have examined the significance of the position of the researcher, and processes that can be employed to promote and enhance effective positioning. The following discussion is based on and further expands our earlier work.

Ontology and epistemology are intrinsically linked. Your philosophical beliefs about reality guide your thoughts about how legitimate knowledge can be acquired. Interrogating your own philosophical position requires thinking through what you believe to be true about the nature of reality. Once you have made a decision about where you are ontologically, you need to examine your beliefs about how researchers can legitimately gain knowledge about the world.

---

**Activity 2.2** — **Perspectives of existence and reality**

Consider your perspective of existence and reality. Write down your responses to the following questions:

How do you define your self?
What is the nature of reality?
How do you know the world, or gain knowledge of it?
What can be the relationship between researcher and participant?

---

The questions posed in the previous activity are intended to help you identify some of your underlying assumptions about the world. Some people get very uncomfortable thinking about what they consider to be 'fluffy' questions such as these. We strongly encourage researchers to employ techniques such as memoing or journaling (Birks, Mills, Francis and Chapman, 2009) to assist in articulating assumptions such as these that can tell you something of your philosophical position, which in turn informs your methodological preference. The ability to answer questions regarding your philosophical position will guide how you position yourself as a researcher and, in turn, how you work with participants, the approach you take to data generation/collection and analysis, and the way you present your findings.

When considering the question of how you define your self, think about the various roles that you engage in on a daily basis. You might consider yourself an expert in your chosen professional field, but a novice researcher. In addition, you may have other 'selves' where you are a member of a religious congregation, a minority cultural group, play a team sport, parent young or older children, be a spouse, a daughter, a son. All of us have multiple selves that we live out, and all of these roles impact on how we think about the world. When we begin a research study we do not only think about this work as a novice researcher – rather we draw upon the totality of our life experience in deciding how to proceed. The multiple selves that we live out, or the many 'hats' that we wear, influence the questions we ask, the methodological approach we choose and in turn how we go about our research. For example, if you are an experienced architect who relies upon exact, reliable measurements to carry out your work, your methodological preference may well be for a methodology couched in the postpositivist paradigm. This is because your experience tells you there is a fundamental truth about the concept of measurement that you use in your everyday life. Surely this same principle applies to discovering a fundamental process that individuals draw upon to manage their lives. A world governed by fundamental truth is for you a possibility, which therefore influences how you approach your qualitative research study.

What relevance does all this have for you as a qualitative researcher? Figuring out where you are methodologically will 'overtly reshape the interactive relationship between researcher and participants in the research process' (Mills et al., 2006: 9). Ultimately, it is about the relationship between the researcher and the data, how it is collected or generated, what the data consists of and how it is analysed. In order to be methodologically congruent in your research design you need to be conscious of your philosophical position. You must also remain responsive to how this position impacts on the conduct of your research through the process of reflexivity.

## Reflexivity

Regardless of your methodological position, there is an imperative for qualitative researchers to be reflexive. We define reflexivity as an active process of systematically developing insight into your work as a researcher to guide your future actions. Qualitative research requires an investment of the self in the research. The potential for this investment to influence the research and the extent to which such influence is valued depends to a great extent on the methodology employed. Maintaining a reflexive approach ensures a critical review of the involvement of the researcher in the research and how this impacts on the processes and outcomes of the research (Newton, Rothlingova, Gutteridge, LeMarchand and Raphael, 2012).

In spite of the obvious importance of the researcher being reflexive in the conduct of their research, the question of what constitutes reflexivity, the value of reflexive practices in ensuring the quality of research processes and the contribution that reflexivity can make to the generation and analysis of data are the topics of an ongoing debate in qualitative enquiry literature (Birks and Mills, 2011). Newton et al. (2012) in their study of published qualitative research found that most researchers fail to present an account of how reflexivity is achieved and maintained. While inattention to the reporting of reflexive processes does not necessarily point to a failure of the researcher to engage in reflexivity, it does call in to question the importance placed on reflexivity by those in the qualitative research community.

So practically, how do you 'do' reflexivity? We included the word 'systematically' in our definition of reflexivity as a reference to assuring the quality of your work as a qualitative research. Maintenance of a reflective journal and writing of memos can provide a written record of reflexivity, if, as you write about your actions and feelings and the influences on your thinking, you incorporate an analysis of impact and outcome. Taylor (2011) reports on the use of digital video recording as a means of promoting reflexivity in doctoral research students. Regardless of how you choose to do it, consciously creating a record of how you feel during the research process will allow you reflexively to analyse much more than just an audit trail of decisions made in relation to operational or analytical processes.

Peshkin (1988) investigated his own subjectivity by recording how he felt during particular moments of the fieldwork phase of one of his research studies on community school relationships in different contexts. Using 5″ × 8″ cards, Peshkin wrote about specific situations that aroused his feelings, be they positive or negative, happy or sad, and importantly when he felt motivated to move beyond the role of a researcher into being a participant advocate. Even though Peshkin did not use the word 'reflexivity' to describe this aspect of his work as a researcher, his action of analysing the written records of his subjectivity to identify what he called 'subjective I's' (p. 18) resulted in developing insight into how his underlying assumptions about the world influenced both data analysis and presentation of the findings. As he says, 'I have looked for myself where, knowingly or not, I think we all are – and unavoidably belong: in the subjective underbrush of our own research experience' (Peshkin, 1988: 20).

Incorporating a reflexive agenda that seeks to find subjective 'I's', multiple perspectives of self or the vantage points of influence on your qualitative research is important work for those who consider themselves not to be positivistic researchers, as the idea of maintaining objective separation without a mechanism for monitoring behaviour, feelings and thought is impossible. After all, it is only through the analysis of your subjectivity through the judicious process of reflexivity that you can guide your own actions in a more insightful way.

---

**Activity 2.3** | **Identifying multiple selves**

This is an activity for those of you who have had some experience or involvement with qualitative research. Choose a journal entry or memo that is about your thoughts and feelings in relation to the research process. Can you identify any moments where you spoke from one of your multiple 'selves'? Can you name that persona? What might that mean for your overall analysis of the data?

---

# Conclusion

This chapter has presented an overview of philosophy and associated concepts as a means for understanding how philosophical thought has influenced the development of the qualitative research tradition. As you will see when you read through the chapters in Part II of this text, each qualitative methodology is founded on a particular philosophy of thought that influences the type of methods used and how they are applied in the conduct of a research study. The position of the researcher is the bridge between philosophy, methodology and the application of these methods. Thus, the alignment between the research question, chosen methodology and personal philosophy, and ability of the researcher to be reflexive in relation to the research is critical to ensure congruence in the study that will be manifested in the products of the research.

---

**KEY POINTS**

- Philosophy is the study of higher order problems and our attempts to address them
- The history of philosophical thinking aligns with the development of research paradigms including positivism, postpositivism, postmodernism, critical theory and constructivism
- Areas of philosophical study relevant to qualitative research are ontology, in particular the concepts of existence and reality, and epistemology, including the concept of logic
- Qualitative research aims to make a contribution to what is known and thus relies on philosophical thought as a foundation to frame the generation of knowledge
- The selection of qualitative methodology is driven by the research question but cannot be separated from the personal philosophy of the researcher
- In qualitative research, the researcher's philosophical position should be identified at the outset to ensure congruence with the methodological approach

---

- Reflect on the basic philosophical concepts discussed in this chapter. How might these concepts manifest covertly in everyday life? How do they relate to research methodologies with which you are familiar?
- Consider the history of philosophical thought presented in Box 2.1. Draw a diagram aligning the philosophical moments with paradigms of research, as you understand them.
- Think about your perception of philosophy and how it relates to qualitative research. Has it changed after reading this chapter?
- Examine your personal philosophy in relation to your research interests. How cognisant have you been about your philosophical position and its alignment with those interests and your preferred methodologies?

## Suggested further reading

Gaarder, J. (1994) *Sophie's World*. New York: Farra, Straus and Giroux.

'A page-turning novel that is also an exploration of the great philosophical concepts of Western thought. One day fourteen-year-old Sophie Amundsen comes home from school to find in her mailbox two notes, with one question on each: 'Who are you?' and 'Where does the world come from?' From that irresistible beginning, Sophie becomes obsessed with questions that take her far beyond what she knows of her Norwegian village. Through those letters, she enrols in a kind of correspondence course, covering Socrates to Sartre, with a mysterious philosopher, while receiving letters addressed to another girl. Who is Hilde? And why does her mail keep turning up? To unravel this riddle, Sophie must use the philosophy she is learning – but the truth turns out to be far more complicated than she could have imagined.' (Macmillan, 2013)

## References

Alvesson, M. and Skoldberg, K. (2009) *Reflexive Methodology: New Vistas for Qualitative Research*. London: SAGE Publications.

Birks, M. and Mills, J. (2011) *Grounded Theory: A Practical Guide*. London: SAGE Publications.

Birks, M., Mills, J., Francis, K. and Chapman, Y. (2009) 'A thousand words paint a picture: the use of storyline in grounded theory research', *Journal of Research in Nursing*, 14: 405–417.

Feenberg, A. (2003) 'What is philosophy of technology', *Retrieved from* http://www.sfu.ca/~andrewf/books/What_is_Philosophy_of_Technology.pdf.

Gaarder, J. (1994) *Sophie's World*. New York: Farra, Straus and Giroux.

Garsdal, J. (2012) 'Some reflections on existence and imagination in relation to interreligious dialogue and intercultural philosophy of religion', *Islam and Christian-Muslim Relations*, 23: 257–266.

Gruber, T.R. (1993) 'A translation approach to portable ontology specifications', *Knowledge Acquisition*, 5: 199–220.

Gruninger, M. and Lee, J. (2002) 'Ontology', *Communications of the ACM*, 45: 39.

Kilduff, M., Mehra, A. and Dunn, M.B. (2011) 'From blue sky research to problem solving: a philosophy of science theory of new knowledge production', *Academy of Management Review*, 36: 297–317.

Mills, J., Bonner, A. and Francis, K. (2006) 'Adopting a constructivist approach to grounded theory: implications for research design', *International Journal of Nursing Practice*, 12: 8–13.

Newton, B.J., Rothlingova, Z., Gutteridge, R., Le Marchand, K., Raphael, J.H. (2012) 'No room for reflexivity? Critical reflections following a systematic review of qualitative research', *Journal of Health Psychology*, 17: 866–885.

Nicholls, D. (2009) 'Qualitative research: part one-philosophies', *International Journal of Therapy and Rehabilitation*, 16: 526–533.

Onwuegbuzie, A.J., Johnson, R.B. and Collins, K.M.T. (2009) 'Call for mixed analysis: a philosophical framework for combining qualitative and quantitative approaches', *International Journal of Multiple Research Approaches*, 3: 114–139.

Peshkin, A. (1988) 'In Search of Subjectivity – One's Own', *Educational Researcher*, 17: 17–21.

Petty, N.J., Thomson, O.P. and Stew, G. (2012) 'Ready for a paradigm shift? Part 1: Introducing the philosophy of qualitative research', *Manual Therapy*, 17: 267–274.

Reed, M. (2009) 'Critical realism: philosophy, method, or philosophy in search of a method', *The Sage Handbook of Organizational Research Methods*. London: SAGE, 430–448.

Russell, B. (2009) *An Outline of Philosophy*. [electronic resource] Hoboken: Taylor & Francis.

Stewart, D., Blocker, H.G. and Petrik, J. (2010) *Fundamentals of Philosophy*. Boston: Prentice Hall.

Taylor, C.A. (2011) 'More than meets the eye: the use of videonarratives to facilitate doctoral students' reflexivity on their doctoral journeys', *Studies in Higher Education*, 36: 441–458.

Teichman, J. and Evans, K. (1995) *Philosophy: A Beginner's Guide*. Oxford: Blackwell.

Wilson, B. (2002) *Simply Philosophy*. Edinburgh: Edinburgh University Press.

# 3
# Methodology and Methods

Jane Mills

---
**Learning objectives**

After reading this chapter, you should be able to:

- Differentiate between research methodology and methods
- Identify the links between philosophy, methodology and methods that result in a research design
- Discuss common critiques of the use of qualitative methodologies
- Describe methods commonly used in qualitative research designs

---

## Introduction

As scholars, and often as teachers, we all have our favourite texts, a gem that shines as a clear explanation of a difficult concept. Lincoln and Guba's paradigm mapping published in successive editions of the *Handbook of Qualitative Research* is one such text that can assist new researchers, or even old ones with an appetite to learn, to locate various paradigms in relation to each other and in relation to what to consider when designing and implementing a study (Lincoln et al., 2011). The latest iteration of this publication includes a new table titled *Themes of Knowledge: Inquiry Aims, Ideals, Design, Procedures and Methods* that examines 21 factors in relation to five themes of knowledge: positivism, postpositivism, critical (+feminism + race), constructivism (or interpretivist) and participatory (+postmodern). Included in this set of factors is methodology, accompanied by a number of methods that are influenced by the theme of knowledge selected by the researcher.

Themes of knowledge inform our thinking as qualitative researchers. The more we read about each of these themes the easier it is for us to decide where we want to locate ourselves ontologically, epistemologically and most importantly for this chapter, methodologically. In saying this however, the cross-fertilization of thought is everywhere in qualitative research designs and leads to the oft referred to 'messiness' associated with this type of enquiry. Learning to live with the complexity of qualitative research is easier for some than for others. As a new researcher, it is best to be open to the possibilities offered by assuming the role of 'bricoleur' (Kincheloe, 2001) even though a nice set of solid rules would be more comforting. At the end of the day though, one can hold on to the thought that 'qualitative research is just a different way of seeing and using new forms of language. It illuminates different corners of research areas' (Holloway and Biley, 2011: 973) and therein lies its value.

## Differentiating methodology from methods

Schwandt describes methodology as 'a particular social scientific discourse (a way of acting, thinking, and speaking) that occupies a middle ground between discussions of method (procedures, techniques) and discussions of issues in the philosophy of social science' (2007: 193). Methodology determines how the researcher thinks about a study, how they make decisions about a study, and how they position themselves to engage firstly with participants and then with the data generated/collected. Writing a research question comes before choosing a methodology (see Chapter 1). Methodology is the lens a researcher looks through when deciding on the type of methods they will use to answer this research question, and how they will use these methods for best effect. Broadly speaking, methods include: choice and recruitment of participants or sampling, data generation or collection, fieldwork, data recording, data analysis and the reporting of a study. While each of these seems fairly self-explanatory, there are many permutations available to you that can only be decided upon in relation to the methodology chosen. Therefore, as a researcher, you are also a methodologist, 'someone who sits outside methods and describes, explains, justifies, evaluates, and helps us understand them' (Carter and Little, 2007: 1318).

Choosing a methodology is strongly linked to the desired outcome of the study. What do you want to achieve by answering a particular research question in a certain way? In order to illustrate the influence methodological choice can have on the use of methods in a study and its eventual outcome, let's examine two examples of qualitative research from the worlds of business and health, both of which investigate women's experiences of a substantive area of enquiry.

Favero and Heath (2012) report a study investigating generational perspectives of women in the workplace and how these can be used to explain conflict. These researchers posed two questions: 'What are the broader discourses that constitute intergenerational conflict around work/life balance for professional women?' and 'What are the interpretive frames that professional women use to understand these discourses consistent with their generational experience?' (p. 338). In the first instance, these researchers position themselves using a feminist standpoint and outline the method of interpretive focus groups, underpinned by feminist participatory theory, used to both generate and analyse data with participants. Participants are recruited through the researchers' own networks, and then using a snowball sampling technique whereby each participant brings a friend along to the interpretive focus groups. The intellectual capital of the groups is tapped into, and participants become co-researchers through the shared analysis of two existing data sets investigating the substantive area of inquiry, leading then to the generation of new data concerning their own lived experience. Together the groups determined 'the flow of the conversation, at times reading other excerpts from the data sets to support their interpretive claims' (p. 342). The aim of the final report is to identify how different generations of women interpret the discourses of 'paying your dues and face-time' in such a way that explains 'conflict and open[s up] a hopeful space for productive dialogue' (Favero and Heath, 2012: 333). Tracing the place of methodology in the design, implementation and reporting of this study is very easy, mainly because in the text of their report, the researchers return to feminist and participatory methodology as a way to ground their actions. How the researchers position themselves alongside the participants, describe the methods of data generation incorporating strategies to minimize power differences, share the analysis and adjust the analysis to account for generational difference, include participants' words in the report as evidence to support their argument, and finally frame the research outcomes in terms of making a difference or creating change can all be justified against the methodology chosen to guide the study.

The second example of how the researchers' choice of methodology shapes their qualitative study is that of Munir, Kalawsky, Lawrence, Yarker, Haslam and Ahmed (2011). Researchers in this study examine the need for interventions related to cognitive function in women undergoing chemotherapy. This study is reported as qualitative mixed methods, however the design, implementation and reporting of the study clearly indicate it uses a postpositivistic methodology (Lincoln et al., 2011). The research question is '[are] cognitive interventions … required to help patients manage return to work and maintain satisfactory cognitive function at work?' (p. 386). Participants, living with breast cancer, are recruited as part of a larger longitudinal study of 50 women, with the sample size of this sub-study dictated by data saturation being reached after 31 interviews are conducted. As well, five oncology health professionals are interviewed about the feasibility of possible interventions generated from the analysis of patient interviews. A semi-structured interview guide is used for both sets of interviews, and patient participants are also asked to complete three questionnaires. Each interview is audio-recorded and transcribed. Data is analysed using frequency counts of participants' statements concerning three pre-determined categories. A small number of interview transcripts are then open coded to create a coding scheme. Each transcript is then coded against the scheme by two different researchers to 'ensure the reliability' (p. 388) of the analysis. Frequencies and percentages are calculated using the counts of the different codes, and relevant comments highlighted in text to provide evidence for the subsequent categorical analysis. Findings from the study identify four potential interventions and recommend further research to test the efficacy of these. The methodological grounding of this study is less obvious to the uninformed reader as the researchers fail to overtly position themselves in this way, unlike the previous example. Using a semi-structured interview guide to ensure consistency, a reliance on statistics to analyse participants' texts, measures to ensure the reliability of analysis such as comparing coding between researchers, the presentation of findings in tables and the formatting of findings into evidence for further research that will test the interventions identified, all indicate the research team conceived this study using a postpositivistic methodology or lens.

By considering each of these examples, it becomes clear that the methodology used is tied to the outcome desired by the researcher. In the first study, the researchers wanted to make a difference to professional women's lives in the workplace by explaining a generational impact on how people work and how they prioritize their work. By providing more information to professional women and their employers, they hope to make a difference through improving communication and understanding. In the second study, the researchers want to find out what women living with breast cancer and their carers think would be useful interventions to improve their cognitive functioning both at home and at work. By finding out 'grassroots' information, they can later test the efficacy of interventions they know to be acceptable. Each of these teams of researchers desire different outcomes and so choose their research question, methodology and methods to be fit-for-purpose. The question of what drives researchers' desires, and inspires them to ask questions they are interested in finding the answers to, can often be answered by how they position themselves philosophically (see Chapter 2).

---

**Activity 3.1** — **Articulating motivations and outcomes**

Think about a study that you are involved in or are planning. Jot down your motivations and anticipated or desired outcomes. Consider the discussion of the position of the researcher in the previous chapter. How does your position in respect of this research align with the motivations and outcomes you have identified?

---

If we consider the eight methodologies addressed in Part II of this book, we can see how they map across to a number of different themes of knowledge (Figure 3.1) each with different prospective outcomes. Having read Chapter 2, you would realize that philosophically, things are never particularly straightforward, and this translates to methodology. For example, grounded theory is a methodology that can be aligned with a number of different themes of knowledge. Traditional grounded theorists would see themselves as postpositivist researchers, seeking an approximation of truth through a research process that allows theory to emerge from the data. Constructivist grounded theorists position themselves quite differently in relation to the participants and consider data to be a co-constructed entity that they then analyse (Birks and Mills, 2011). Therefore, a caveat is attached to the following map: qualitative research is a creative enterprise that aims to answer questions using rigorous, flexible, best-fit approaches. It is this best-fit approach that results in methodological linking to different themes of knowledge.

| Theme of Knowledge | Qualitative Methodology | Outcome |
|---|---|---|
| Positivism | X | X |
| Postpositivism | Grounded theory | Knowledge of Process & Outcome |
| Critical +Feminism +Race | Discourse analysis | Knowledge of Discourse, Illumination & Change |
| | Ethnography | Knowledge, Illumination & Change |
| | Narrative inquiry | Knowledge, Illumination & Change |
| Constructivism or Interpretivism | Ethnography | Knowledge of Culture |
| | Grounded theory | Knowledge of Process & Outcome |
| | Historical research | Knowledge of History |
| | Case study | Situated Knowledge |
| | Phenomenology | Knowledge of Lived Experience |
| | Action research | Knowledge of Process, Outcome & Change |
| Participatory +Postmodern | Action research | Knowledge, Participatory Process, Outcome & Change |
| | Discourse analysis | Knowledge of Discourse |
| | Case study | Situated Knowledge & Change |
| | Grounded theory | Knowledge of Process, Outcome & Change |

**Figure 3.1**  Map of methodologies discussed in Part II

## Common critiques of qualitative methodologies

There are a number of critiques of qualitative methodologies which are important to consider when planning your research design. Hammersley (2008) provides an extensive argument about concerns voiced with respect to qualitative research, particularly in the present day funding environment engaged with functional research findings to underpin evidence-based practice and policymaking (Nelson, 2008). In summary, Hammersley (2008) lists the following three quantitative criticisms of qualitative research designs and posits that we have failed to address these criticisms in the areas of measurement, causal analysis and generalization:

1. Failing to rigorously operationalize concepts and thereby to document measurable differences
2. Not ruling out rival explanations through physical or statistical control
3. Failing to produce generalizable findings

The idea of a standard set of criteria to appraise the quality of qualitative research is also subject to extensive debate, much of which links to the so-called failure to answer positivist challenges to legitimacy (see Chapter 13). While there are some qualitative researchers who think 'we should be letting a thousand flowers bloom' (Seale, 2003: 169) resulting in a form of methodological anarchy that rejects any criteria of rigour (Silverman, 1998), there are many others who believe methodological slurring (Baker, Wuest and Stern, 1992), or failing to identify and explicate in the research process based on traditional forms of research, erodes the quality of the final product.

Morse's (2011) pithy commentary on key issues with qualitative research reports raises more questions than it provides answers, however, the aspects she identifies are very worthy of consideration during the process of designing a study. Where a balance needs to be sought between traditional formulaic approaches to qualitative methodologies with the flexibility required to answer particular research questions, the researcher should address the pros and cons of formulated versus free research design. Morse joins the ranks of those cautious of mixing qualitative methodologies, identifying the risk of creating 'methodological stone soup' (p. 1019). A challenge is raised about who has the prerogative to modify methods and strategies used in different qualitative methodologies, with words of warning to new researchers about collecting data sets with insufficient depth that should be heeded. Finally, the criticism that qualitative enquiry is insignificant is considered by Morse, with a realistic assessment of the potential impact of small studies, as compared to larger programs of research that mobilize a series of studies over a longer period of time, in order to address a substantive area of enquiry. For new researchers, opportunities to contribute to a larger program of research within their discipline, or across like disciplines should be sought. Seeking a role in an established program of research is a useful strategy for career development that can result in building a track record of research, increasing opportunities for research grant income, and establishing a reputation for conducting research with discernible impact (Cleary, Mackey, Hunt, Jackson, Thomspon and Walter, 2012).

Considering critiques can be disheartening, especially for the more free-spirited among us. Flexibility in the use of qualitative methodologies is essential to create a best-fit with the research question, and to optimize the desired outcome. The take home lesson from considering these critiques is to invest time in thinking through decisions made when designing a qualitative research study. As Seale (2003) advises 'reading and discussing … methodological ideas … is a sort of intellectual muscle-building exercise, time out in the brain gymnasium, before returning to the task at hand, hopefully a little stronger and more alert' (p. 181).

# Research methods

Part II of this text includes eight chapters, each addressing a different qualitative methodology using the same format to allow for easy comparison. Authors discuss methods including: data generation and collection, the analysis of data, quality and rigour and the presentation and dissemination of findings in relation to their particular methodology. As a preface to this more specific work, data generation, collection and analysis in the context of contemporary thinking and debates is discussed in the second half of this chapter. A wider perspective on quality and rigour and the presentation and dissemination of findings is provided in Chapters 13 and 14.

## Data generation and collection

A generally accepted tenant of qualitative research is that the researcher is an instrument (Creswell, 2013; Janesick, 2004; Merriam, 2009; Stake, 2010) who can both collect and generate data, depending on how they position themselves. The process of data collection is used when the researcher has 'limited influence on the data source, as occurs when data is extracted from static materials such as documents and the literature' (Birks and Mills, 2011: 174). This contrasts with data generation when the researcher 'directly engages with a data source to produce materials for analysis, such as occurs during in-depth interviewing' (Birks and Mills, 2011: 174). If we think back to the illustration of the influence of various qualitative methodologies on the research process used earlier in this chapter, both groups engaged in data generation, one through the process of interpretive focus groups (Favero and Heath, 2012), both used semi-structured interviews, while the other group also collected data by using three different questionnaires (Munir et al., 2011).

Methods of data generation and collection generally include capturing records of interviews, audio-visual materials and physical objects, documents including surveys, and observations (Sandelowski, 2002; Creswell, 2003; Birks and Mills, 2011). Primarily, qualitative researchers use participant interviews and transcribe these to create tangible data sets. Interviews can be unstructured, using a 'grand-tour' question to begin; semi-structured where the researcher has a guide or aide-memoir to prompt the course of questioning; or structured which is when the researcher asks a series of identical questions of each participant. Silverman (1998) argues there is an over-reliance on interviewing as a method of data generation in qualitative research stating that 'the fashionable identification of qualitative method with an analysis of how people "see things" ignores the importance of how people "do things"' (p. 105). In a more recent publication Silverman (2007) goes on to ask 'why assume that qualitative research involves only researchers asking questions of respondents?' (p. 40), a question founded in the assertion that interview data can only recount participants' experiences, which in effect manufactures data, as opposed to data identified through processes of observation and reading. The following window into qualitative research (Box 3.1) by Sonali Shah, illustrates how multiple methods of data generation can be used in qualitative research, creating sufficient depth in the data set to dimensionalize a phenomenon in a way that analysing interview data alone would be unable to achieve. Shah (2006) investigates how young disabled people aged between 13 and 25 years perceive the influence of their school environment on aspirations for the future, subject selection and career decisions. Rather than relying solely on interviews, Shah conducts a three stage process of data generation that includes observation, forum theatre workshops and semi-structured interviews to elicit participants' life stories while at the same time situating this story in 'the various religious, social, psychological and economic currents present in their world' (p. 217).

---

**BOX 3.1**

## Window into qualitative research

### Using multiple methods with disabled teenagers

This window reports on three methods of qualitative data generation (observation, forum theatre, and life story interviews) and how they were employed to capture the voices of young people with physical impairments in full-time education (special and mainstream) and looking to their futures. It explains how I, a disabled researcher, adopted these methods to uncover the social realities of young disabled people, providing a platform for this rich data to become known and used by policymakers.

As a disabled researcher, I shared some experiences with the researched, specifically in terms of disablement, challenging oppression and educational experiences. My ontological position coupled with the multiple strategies of data generation (described below) encouraged the vocalization of a historically marginalized group who are often subjects of research but rarely perceived as social actors able to make decisions about their occupational futures. Young disabled people are frequently ignored, not consulted about major questions that affect them, and are likely to have decisions made for them by non-disabled adults – parents, teachers or service providers (Shah, 2006). By using accessible and creative strategies of data generation I was able to tap into young disabled people's choices and aspirations with the aim of informing future research and the policy agenda.

### Observation

Classroom observation, the first method, provided a means to examine the ways in which young disabled people interact within their school environments, with their peers and adults in different contexts, and the meanings which they bring to such interactions. During each observation (within the seven different educational settings) I, the researcher/observer, positioned myself so I could clearly observe the teacher and students without being intrusive. One reason for using observation prior to interviews was to ensure the questions reflected the respondents' concerns and assumptions, not those of the researcher. It also indicated the communication styles of the potential respondents and what modifications may be needed to the interview guide. Observation also allowed me to become familiar with the environment and also make myself known to potential respondents.

*(Continued)*

(Continued)

## Forum Theatre

The Brazilian activist Augusto Boal's method of Forum Theatre inspired the second method of data generation. The intention was to generate dialogue and creative activity between young disabled people about their experiences of oppression when making transitions to adulthood, the choices available to work in a disabling society and the barriers encountered when striving to meet their career aspirations after school. Forum theatre was a flexible and democratic tool which encouraged everyone to participate, explore their own creativity, and be activated and inspired by the process.

I collaborated with a drama facilitator (also a disabled woman) to develop and plan a theatre workshop to explore issues relating to disability, aspirations and barriers. Each workshop included two brief introduction and warm-up games, followed by a 20 minute scene acted out by myself and the drama facilitator. I played the role of a 15-year-old disabled student named Angela who had just started at her local mainstream school, having previously been at a residential special school for three years, and who was thinking about her occupational future. The scene took place between Angela and her mother (played by the drama facilitator) and explored the issues surrounding Angela's experiences at school and home, and the barriers she encountered when trying to make her own career-related choices. The students watching the performance, are invited to suggest how the character (i.e. Angela) could have behaved and acted differently. Although they were not allowed to advise the actors on what to say or do, the students could cross the performing area, adopt a role and show the group exactly what they believed the characters could do differently. The sessions were video recorded which enabled retrospective analysis.

The phase of fieldwork allowed young disabled people to voice their own thoughts and feelings, and challenge assumptions and stereotypes. It also brought a positive experience to the young disabled people and created a rapport between the young participants and myself. It was this rapport that helped generate rich data during the final phase of fieldwork.

## Life story interviews

The final phase of fieldwork employed a third qualitative method of data generation through life story interviewing with each of the young disabled people who participated in the theatre workshops. The technique of life story interviewing enabled me to under-stand the young persons' history and the influence of structure and agency at critical points in their lives. I interviewed each of the young people using a semi-structured topic guide and prompts. Each of the young people told their stories about their original aspira-tions including who/what shaped them and how these aspirations had changed over time. The influence of different relationships, policies, institutions and environments that have the potential to facilitate or constrain individual choices were also explored.

Interviews typically lasted between 20 and 40 minutes. With the permission of the young people and, where they were under the age of 18, their parents, the interviews were recorded and fully transcribed. I assured the young people that their identity would be

(Continued)

*(Continued)*

protected, with them choosing their own pseudonyms. Although I carried out the interviews, a non-disabled support worker was present to facilitate my own access requirements. Her presence prevented me from becoming too immersed in the young people's stories and participating in an intersubjective exchange, and thus encouraged me to take stock in a more detached way and retain contact with an observer position. The support worker also had strategies to avoid being drawn into the interview exchange, positioning herself out of the young person's visual range.

Employing these three methods of data generation not only provided young disabled people with a way to have their own voices heard, but also an opportunity to be empowered by sharing their experiences and concerns with an empathetic other.

The argument against reifying interviews as the 'gold standard' of data collection in qualitative research is revisited by Sandelowski (2002) who states 'researchers must recognize what they are doing when they do it, and what it means to take data at face value. In short, qualitative researchers need to explicitly address the status they give to interview data' (p. 107). Audio-visual materials and physical objects, sometimes referred to as artifacts, are identified by this author as a particularly rich source of data, rarely accessed to its full potential in qualitative studies. In a theoretical paper, ironically titled *Interviewing Objects: Including Educational Technologies as Qualitative Research Participants*, Adams and Thompson (2011) proffer a useful discussion of various heuristics that can be used to work with objects or artifacts as a source of data. These authors argue that to 'interview an educational "artifact" is to catch insightful glimpses of the artifact in action, as it performs and mediates the gestures and understandings of its employer, involves others, and associates with other objects in the pedagogical environment' (p. 734). One striking example they provide of an artifact as a data source, is the use of *PowerPoint* by teachers. Interactions between teachers and this mainstream piece of software are analysed to identify the influence of the artifact, which plays out through the template design of common slides, and the invitation this provides to the shaping of knowledge and the embodied relationships between teachers, students and *Powerpoint* in the classroom. Describing *Powerpoint* as sponsoring a 'prescribed (default) framework for staging knowledge' (p. 746), findings from this study point to the need for teachers to reflect on their interactions with technology and to live more critically in relation to how these interactions influence what they say and do.

Document analysis in qualitative research can include both peer-reviewed literature and what is referred to as the 'grey' literature, simply defined as that which is not peer reviewed. Government reports, websites, minutes of meetings, patient records, policies and procedures, diaries and logbooks, newspapers and magazines are all examples of grey literature that can provide data for qualitative studies. There are various analytical frameworks for analysis that can be used to both collect and analyse documents as data, with an example of one being 'discursive frame analysis'. Brulle and Benford (2012) conducted a discursive frame analysis of documents pertaining to 'game protection', a concept which morphed to 'wildlife management' as a result of a social movement that occurred in the US between 1930 and 1940. Four sources of data were drawn upon for analysis: historical sources, texts held by the US Library of Congress, descriptions of organizations classified as environmental movement organizations in the *Conversation Directory*, and a count of the number of articles in the popular press related to the substantive area of enquiry, listed in the *Readers Guide to Periodic Literature* under the sub-headings of wildlife management and game protection. Findings from this study identify how cultural production and movement growth took place sequentially over a ten-year timeframe with the final outcome of changing legislation and policy regarding the substantive area of enquiry.

Other important documents that constitute generated data are memos and fieldnotes. Memos can be defined as 'records of thoughts, feeling, insights and ideas in relation to a research project' (Birks and Mills, 2011: 40). As such, they constitute another documentary source of data for analysis. Writing memos throughout the research process serves a number of important purposes including:

- Mapping research activities
- Extracting meaning from the data
- Maintaining momentum, and
- Opening communication. (Birks, Chapman and Francis, 2008)

Fieldnotes differ from memos in that they are written by the researcher during actual fieldwork, or shortly thereafter. 'Proximity means that fieldnotes are written more or less *contemporaneously* with the events, experiences and interactions they describe and recount' (Emerson, Fretz and Shaw, 2001: 353). Incrementally, a researcher accumulates a corpus of fieldnotes and memos for analysis, although these authors state that such a corpus is a 'loose collection of possibly usable materials, much of which will never be incorporated into a finished text' (p. 353) with many differing views among ethnographers about the form fieldnotes can take.

Like fieldnotes, observation as a method of data generation/collection is a largely ethnographic endeavour, with both of these forms of data collection less fashionable in other contemporary qualitative research designs. However, if we are open to reconsidering the dominant position of interviewing as the pre-eminent method of choice, a period of immersion in the field, generating data through field notes is a likely adjunct. There has been an expansion of the purpose of observation from the traditional province of culture to include process and outcomes of interventions. The researcher as instrument has also been supplemented by video-recordings of activity over periods of time as a method of data collection (Paterson, Bottorff and Hewat, 2003). Creswell (2013) lists four options for data generation using observation:

1. Complete participant – researcher's role is not known, full participation
2. Observer participant – researcher's role is known, participation secondary to observation
3. Participant observer – researcher's role is known, observation secondary to participation
4. Complete observer – researcher's role is known, no participation

Levels of participation in observation as a method of data generation vary depending on the context and the position of the researcher being either emic or etic, otherwise referred to as insider or outsider status. Hoare, Buetow, Mills and Francis (2012) argue that the dichotomous separation between emic (insider) and etic (outsider), which in some way corresponds to subjective or objective, is false, as all qualitative research is embodied and as such the level of researcher engagement and insight exists on a continuum between these two concepts. The researcher's insight into a particular situation, garnered by previously acquired knowledge and skills and their level of participation when using observation as a method of data generation is intertwined with a 'body of assumptions and expectations, only some of which are accessible to reflection or able to be verbalized' (Borbasi, Jackson and Wilkes, 2005: 498). Thus, the outcomes of data generation will always be influenced by the qualitative researcher's tacit knowledge – an example of which is provided in the previous window where the researcher firstly positions themselves as a 'disabled researcher', albeit one who set out to observe as opposed to overtly co-constructing data with participants who were also disabled.

---

**Activity 3.2** — **Sources of qualitative data**

Review a selection of published qualitative research studies you may have at your disposal. What sources of data were prominent in these studies? To what extent is interview data relied upon? Are there examples of where these studies may have benefited from other sources of data?

---

## Analysis of data

Only the researcher through a process of designation can answer the question of what constitutes the products of data generation or collecting. As Wolcott (1994) states, 'nothing *becomes* data without the intervention of a researcher' (emphasis in original, p. 3). Following on from this, Sandelowski (2011) challenges researcher's sometimes unacknowledged 'take' on data, arguing that the study's aim combined with the position of the researcher will shape analytical outcomes as 'data analysis always entails a process by which data are tamed or made docile to those purposes' (p. 347).

Once a new qualitative researcher 'comes to grips' with the high level of influence they have on their study, strategies to promote and ensure rigour, reflexivity and transparency in the research process become more significant. How decisions are made regarding the implementation of a research design directly corresponds to the quality of the final product. Stake (2010) asks us

> ... to consider the evidence by which you, we, all of us, make our decisions – both large and small. However disguised, they are often fortuitous, personal, and situational. This is not a claim that we make our decisions capriciously. No, we factor in matters of great importance, but the weights we assign to

different matters are subject to change, as we are burdened by new responsibility and enticed by new opportunity. (p. 122)

Data analysis is based on the researcher's decision-making processes about evidence identified in the data set. Creswell (2013) purports that three interlinked data analysis strategies form the basis for all qualitative research designs. These strategies include preparing and organizing the data, coding, and representing the data in text, tables or figures. The first two strategies for analysis often include the use of qualitative data analysis software. Data preparation involves transforming the experience of data generation and collection using interviews and periods of observation into text. Documents and artifacts may also need to be recaptured into a format more appropriate for storage and analysis. Once the data is prepared it is filed and organized using a system that allows the researcher easy access and retrieval.

Coding is the labelling of a data segment using a term that captures the researcher's interpretation of its essential meaning. Saldaña (2009, 2013) divides coding into two cycles that operate at different conceptual levels. First, cycle coding is an iterative process that involves comparing data segments with each other, codes with new data segments, and codes with codes. There are a number of different types of codes, which orientate the researcher to different aspects of the data, with Saldaña suggesting coding for attributes, structure, description and values. As well, in vivo codes, or codes that adopt participant's words are identified. Grouping like with like results in the development of categories which are higher level conceptual labels representing a group of codes (Birks and Mills, 2011). Qualitative researchers often speak of 'collapsing codes', and even categories and their sub-categories, as the process of data analysis progresses towards second cycle coding. First cycle coding can be repetitive, with researchers needing to return to the original data to recode as their thinking progresses. In second cycle, or advanced coding, the researcher focuses on conceptual development and sometimes the integration of categories to describe a theory, however this is dependent on the methodology adopted. Second cycle coding can be likened to the 'assembly process' (Saldaña, 2009: 150) of qualitative research findings. A useful technique in second cycle coding is the development of definitional statements for each category that define the parameters of this group of data, thus providing a tool for conducting comparative analysis (Birks, Chapman and Francis, 2007).

The separation of data analysis and the presentation of findings has long been viewed as an artificial construct, with Richardson's (1994) seminal essay on writing as a method of enquiry arguing that 'writing is also a way of "knowing" – a method of discovery and analysis. By writing in different ways, we discover new aspects of our topic and our relationship to it. Form and content are inseparable' (p. 516). Writing, while organizing findings into a tabular form or a model, becomes an active strategy for analysis as the researcher brings together the results of second cycle coding to describe or represent a particular phenomenon. Constructing a theoretical argument through writing will often result in the identification of gaps in the logic and questions still requiring answers. Questioning the data through writing is an effective technique to advance the conceptual depth required in a qualitative research study, with various designs using different methods to achieve this aim (see Part II). Sandelowski and Barroso (2002) provide a final thought on the step beyond writing as a method of analysis, identifying the importance of clearly differentiating the findings of your study as separate from the process of analysis. Understanding that data are different from findings, and that the process of analysis that led you to these findings is different again, is fundamental to ensuring research studies impact on policy, practice, education, and future research directions (see Chapter 14).

## Conclusion

Understanding the difference between methodology and methods will assist in developing a rigorous qualitative research design. Investing time in thinking through as many of the implications of particular methodologies as is possible will reap rewards during the data collection/generation and analysis phase of a study. Not being pre-emptive in entering the field will save time, and importantly may prevent undue demands upon participants. Identifying a well balanced and justified mix of methods to both collect and generate data with participants will result in a deeper and more complex data set that should allow for higher levels of conceptual analysis. Considering the importance of writing both as a method of analysis, and as a way to sharply identify research findings that are easily understandable and have 'grab' will provide an opportunity to make a difference in your chosen field.

---

**KEY POINTS**

- The choice of a methodology is strongly linked to the desired outcome of the study
- Flexibility in the use of qualitative methodologies is essential to create a best-fit with the research question, and to optimize the desired outcome
- Qualitative research methodologies map to a number of different themes of knowledge
- Methodology determines how the researcher thinks about and positions themselves in relation to a study
- Research methods are the strategies that are employed in the conduct of a study and include: identification and recruitment of data sources, data generation or collection, field-work, data recording, data analysis and the reporting of a study
- A number of critiques of qualitative methodologies have been posited and these are important to consider when planning a research design
- In qualitative research, the researcher is an instrument in the collection, generation and analysis of data
- Methods of data generation and collection generally include capturing records of interviews, audio-visual materials and physical objects, documents including surveys, observations, fieldnotes and memos
- Qualitative data analysis is based on the researcher's decision-making processes about evidence identified in the data set

- How would you define the terms 'methodology' and 'methods'? Consider how you would explain the difference to a colleague unfamiliar with the distinction.
- What is the relationship between philosophy, methodology and methods in a qualitative research study?
- Why do you think interviews have been so heavily relied upon in qualitative research? Are any of the strengths inherent in this method potentially available from other data gathering strategies?

## Suggested further reading

Saldaña, J. (2013) *The Coding Manual for Qualitative Researchers*. London: SAGE Publications.

'The Second Edition of Johnny Saldaña's international bestseller provides an in-depth guide to the multiple approaches available for coding qualitative data. Fully up to date, it includes new chapters, more coding techniques and an additional glossary. Clear, practical and authoritative, the book describes how coding initiates qualitative data analysis, demonstrates the writing of analytic memos, discusses available analytic software, and suggests how best to use *The Coding Manual for Qualitative Researchers* for particular studies. In total, 32 coding methods are profiled that can be applied to a range of research genres from grounded theory to phenomenology to narrative inquiry. For each approach, Saldaña discusses the method's origins, a description of the method, practical applications, and a clearly illustrated example with analytic follow-up. A unique and invaluable reference for students, teachers, and practitioners of qualitative inquiry, this book is essential reading across the social sciences' (SAGE Publications, 2013).

## References

Adams, C.A. and Thompson, T.L. (2011) 'Interviewing objects: including educational technologies as qualitative research participants', *International Journal of Qualitative Studies in Education*, 24: 733–750.

Baker, C., Wuest, J. and Stern, P.N. (1992) 'Method slurring: the grounded theory/phenomenology example', *Journal of Advanced Nursing*, 17: 1355–1360.

Birks, M. and Mills, J. (2011) *Grounded Theory: A Practical Guide*. London: SAGE Publications.

Birks, M., Chapman, Y. and Francis, K. (2007) 'Probing data and processes', *Journal of Research in Nursing*, 12: 1–8.

Birks, M., Chapman, Y. and Francis, K. (2008) 'Memoing in qualitative research: probing data and processes', *Journal of Research in Nursing*, 13: 68–75.

Borbasi, S., Jackson, D. and Wilkes, L. (2005) 'Fieldwork in nursing research: positionality, practicalities and predicaments', *Journal of Advanced Nursing*, 51: 493–501.

Brulle, R.J. and Benford, R.D. (2012) 'From game protection to wildlife management: frame shifts, organizational development, and field practices', *Rural Sociology*, 77: 62–88.

Carter, S.M. and Little, M. (2007) 'Justifying knowledge, justifying method, taking action: epistemologies, methodologies, and methods in qualitative research', *Qualitative Health Research*, 17: 1316–1328.

Cleary, M., Mackey, S., Hunt, G.E., Jackson, D., Thompson, D.R., and Walter, G. (2012) 'Reputations: a critical yet neglected area of scholarly enquiry', *Journal of Advanced Nursing*, 68: 2137–2139.

Creswell, J. (2003) *Research Design: Qualitative, Quantitative and Mixed Methods Approaches*. Thousand Oaks, CA: SAGE Publications.

Creswell, J. (2013) *Qualitative Inquiry and Research Design: Choosing Among Five Approaches*. Thousand Oaks: SAGE Publications.

Emerson, R., Fretz, R. and Shaw, L. (2001) 'Participant observation and fieldnotes', in P. Atkinson, A. Coffey, S. Delamont, J. Lofland and L. Lofland (eds), *Handbook of Ethnography*. 1st edn. London: SAGE Publications, pp. 352–368.

Favero, L.W. and Heath, R.G. (2012) 'Generational perspectives in the workplace: interpreting the discourses that constitute women's struggle to balance work and life', *Journal of Business Communication*, 49: 332–356.

Hammersley, M. (2008) *Questioning Qualitative Inquiry: Critical Essays*. Los Angeles; London: SAGE.

Hoare, K.J., Buetow, S., Mills, J., and Francis, K. (2012) 'Using an emic and etic ethnographic technique in a grounded theory study of information use by practice nurses in New Zealand', *Journal of Research in Nursing*, doi: 10.1177/1744987111434190

Holloway, I. and Biley, F. (2011) 'Being a qualitative researcher', *Qualitative Health Research*, 21: 968–975.

Janesick, V. (2004) *'Stretching' Exercises for Qualitative Researchers*. Thousand Oaks, CA: SAGE Publications.

Kincheloe, J. (2001) 'Describing the bricolage: conceptualizing a new rigor in qualitative research', *Qualitative Inquiry*, 7: 679–692.

Lincoln, Y., Lynham, S. and Guba, E. (2011) 'Paradigmatic controversies, contradictions, and emerging confluences, revisited', in N. Denzin and Y. Lincoln (eds), *Handbook of Qualitative Research*. 4th edn. Thousand Oaks: SAGE Publications, pp. 97–128.

Merriam, S. (2009) *Qualitative Research: A Guide to Design and Implementation*. San Francisco: Jossey-Bass.

Morse, J.M. (2011) 'Molding qualitative health research', *Qualitative Health Research*, 21: 1019–1021.

Munir, F., Kalawsky, K., Lawrence, C., Yarker, J., Haslam, S., and Ahmed, S. (2011) *Cognitive Intervention for Breast Cancer Patients Undergoing Adjuvant Chemotherapy: A Needs Analysis*. Available at: http://ovidsp.ovid.com/ovidweb.cgi?T=JS&PAGE=reference&D=ovftl&NEWS=N&AN=00002820- 201109000-00007.

Nelson, A.M. (2008) 'Addressing the threat of evidence-based practice to qualitative inquiry through increasing attention to quality: a discussion paper', *International Journal of Nursing Studies*, 45: 316–322.

Paterson, B., Bottorff, J. and Hewat, R. (2003) 'Blending observational methods: possibilities, strategies, and challenges', *International Journal of Qualitative Methods*. Available at: http://www.ualberta.ca/~iiqm/backissues/2_1/html/patersonetal.html.

Richardson, L. (1994) 'Writing: a method of inquiry', in N.K. Denzin and Y.S. Lincoln (eds), *The Handbook of Qualitative Research*. 1st edn. Thousand Oaks, CA: SAGE Publications, pp. 516–529.

SAGE Publications (2013) *The Coding Manual for Qualitative Researchers: Second Edition*.

Saldaña, J. (2009) *The Coding Manual for Qualitative Researchers*. London: SAGE Publications.

Saldaña, J. (2013) *The Coding Manual for Qualitative Researchers*. London: SAGE Publications.

Sandelowski, M. (2002) 'Re-embodying qualitative inquiry', *Qualitative Health Research*, 12: 104–115.

Sandelowski, M. (2011) 'When a cigar is not just a cigar: alternative takes on data and data analysis', *Research in Nursing and Health*, 34: 342–352.

Sandelowski, M. and Barroso, J. (2002) 'Finding the findings in qualitative studies', *Journal of Nursing Scholarship*, 34: 213–219.

Schwandt, T. (2007) *The Sage Dictionary of Qualitative Inquiry*. Thousand Oaks, CA: SAGE Publications.

Seale, C. (2003) 'Quality in qualitative research', in Y. Lincoln and N. Denzin (eds), *Turning Points in Qualitative Research: Tying Knots in a Handkerchief*. Thousand Oaks, CA: SAGE, pp. 169–184.

Shah, S. (2006) 'Sharing the world: the researcher and the researched', *Qualitative Research*, 6: 207–220.

Silverman, D. (1998) 'The quality of qualitative health research: the open-ended interview and its alternatives', *Social Sciences in Health*, 4: 104–118.

Silverman, D. (2007) *A Very Short, Fairly Interesting and Reasonably Cheap Book About Qualitative Research*. London: SAGE Publications.

Stake, R. (2010) *Qualitative Research: Studying How Things Work*. New York: The Guilford Press.

Wolcott, H. (1994) *Transforming Qualitative Data: Description, Analysis, and Interpretation*. Thousand Oaks: SAGE Publications.

# PART II

# 4
# Action Research

Bob Dick

┌─ **Learning objectives** ─────────────────────────────────────────┐

After reading this chapter, you should be able to:

- outline the history and development of action research and some of the influences that have impacted on it
- discuss the importance in action research of involving participants in the research and being flexible and responsive to the research situation
- defend sources of quality and rigour in action research, in recognition that it seems to violate many of the traditional evaluation criteria
- discuss action research as an empowering research philosophy
- examine action research as a cyclic process for researching change as it happens
- describe the ways in which information is collected, analysed, utilized and reported in action research

## Introduction

Action research is distinguished from other research methodologies by three characteristics in conjunction. It is action oriented, intended to produce research-informed change to address live issues. Those affected by the change are involved as participants in the research, often as a deliberate moral commitment to empowerment, or for the benefits of creating knowledge and action collaboratively (Reason and Bradbury, 2008; Wadsworth, 2011b). In the interests of flexibility and responsiveness to a changing situation, action research is iterative, cycling through steps of planning, action and review. Many action researchers including Reason (2006) and Torbert (1999) add multiple ways of knowing to this trilogy. This chapter will explore the history and philosophical underpinnings of action research as a basis for discussing practical application of the methodology.

## History of the methodology

The three primary emphases identified above were already present from the beginning. They can be found for example in the work of Kurt Lewin (1946), usually credited with the development of action research. To his work with groups in a variety of industrial and community situations, Lewin brought his eclectic interests in group dynamics and change. The same emphases are to be found in Collier's (1945) ventures as an activist working with Native Americans. Lewin's association with the Tavistock Institute in London brought action research to Britain (Trist, 1990).

The characteristics of action research attracted practitioners, who took it into different fields and different parts of the globe. As Selener (1998) has noted, action research was adopted by education, organizational change, community change, and farmer research. Each of these influenced action research in return. Different national traditions have also made their contribution. So have many of the different varieties of action research, including the applied anthropology of such researchers as William Foote Whyte (1991) and those who followed him.

Education has been a substantial contributor to the action research literature. Early formulations of action research drew on the prior writing of such educators as Dewey (1916). In the 1940s, the educator Paulo Freire worked with the poor and disadvantaged in Brazil. His work became more widely known later through his book *Pedagogy of the Oppressed* (1972) and other works. Freire's work then led to an increased emphasis on empowering the disadvantaged and confronting the power of the advantaged. Within this tradition, Fals Borda (1987) has been prominent in developing action research and in documenting its history in Latin America.

In the anglophone world, educational action research accounts for a greater amount of published literature than any other field of action research. This was most evident during the 1950s, when action research was elsewhere side-lined by more traditional approaches to research. Authors such as Corey (1953) championed the use of action research for improving educational practice. The predominance of educational action research continues. Among many others, later authors include Stenhouse (1975), and (strongly influenced by the critical theory of Jürgen Habermas) Kemmis (2001).

Over the past half century a diversity of related approaches has blossomed, as Raelin (2009) and Coghlan (2010) have documented. Such diversity might have splintered the field of action research, and for a time threatened to do so. Three initiatives contributed to forestalling the threatened fracture. The 1997 World Congress of Action Learning and Action Research in Colombia, which Orlando Fals Borda perceptively titled 'Convergencia', was one. Then *The Handbook of Action Research* (Reason and Bradbury, 2001) and the Sage journal *Action Research* further reunited the varieties as a 'family of approaches' (Reason and Bradbury, 2008: 7) under the one label. Into this family, other processes – many with independent origins – have been invited and welcomed. These include action science (Argyris, Putnam and McLain Smith, 1985), action learning (O'Neil and Marsick, 2007), soft systems methodology (Checkland and Poulter, 2006), appreciative inquiry (Stratton-Berkessel, 2010), and the high-growth field of community-based participatory research (CBPR) (Minkler and Wallerstein, 2008). In turn, the newcomers have further enriched the field with concepts and tools.

The philosophical stance variously adopted is almost as disparate.

# Philosophical underpinnings

Lewin (1946) saw his own work as non-positivist and thus able to resolve real and important problems, though in style it was more quasi-experimental than is most current practice. Intended to resolve problems by integrating theory and practice, its philosophy has been characterized as 'pragmatic' (Greenwood and Levin, 2006: 150) in both the philosophical and common meanings of that word.

There has been a shift to postmodernism in qualitative research generally, and some action researchers have followed the trend. Constructivism, as Lincoln (2001) has noted, can fit well with a methodology that involves participants so fully. It sits less comfortably when the situation to be changed is viewed as 'real'. Tony Brown and Liz Jones (2001), for example, admit to being 'neither fulsome nor wholehearted' (p. 171) in their adoption of postmodernism.

For some action researchers such as McKernan (2006) and Winter and Munn-Giddings (2001) the critical realism of Roy Bhaskar (1978) has been an influential alternative. Critical realism assumes the world is real while acknowledging that we know it only imperfectly and indirectly. Further, it treats as real the beliefs and feelings of people, as these influence and are influenced by the material world. An approach that acknowledges that the world is real has appeal to researchers who wish to make a practical difference (French, 2009).

The many action researchers who are practitioners are more interested in changing the world than in discussing its philosophical status. To the extent that their discussion touches on philosophy, it is likely to be about the complexity of the world and therefore the value of non-reductionist systems approaches such as that of Burns (2007). Or it may be about values and ethics (that is, axiology) rather than the nature of the world (ontology) or our understanding of it (epistemology). Foremost among the values are those of participation and empowerment, with the researcher trying to engage participants as equals. Seldom achievable at the outset, this is sometimes more aspiration than reality. The implications for the position of the researcher can be substantial.

---

| Activity 4.1 | Commencing the change cycle |
| --- | --- |

Think of some social group (family, work team, club, etc.) that you know well but that has some aspect that you would like to change. If you weren't sure how to go about changing it, how might you approach it?

---

# Positioning the researcher

Different varieties of action research make use of different researcher roles. The differences can be conceptualized using Arnstein's (1969) ladder of participation. At one extreme lie varieties that some writers would not define as action research. For example, Sagor (2005) describes some educational action research in which an educator uses quasi-experimental methods to improve classroom practice without involving the learners. Some 'first-person action research' (Chandler and Torbert, 2003) augments participatory components with a less-participative self-reflection on the nature and role of the action researcher (Ragland, 2006).

Further along the continuum are points where researcher and participants have contrasting roles. The researcher is an expert who guides participants through the research. In what is sometimes termed technical action research (Carr and Kemmis, 1986) the issues addressed may be those of the researcher or derived from the literature. With some increase in collaboration, action research comes to resemble what is elsewhere (Schein, 1995) called process consultation. The research is *with* (not on) the participants, who choose the issues. Carr and Kemmis would name this practical action research.

In yet more collaborative forms the participants become co-researchers. They and the researcher together decide the issues to be studied, the processes used to study them, and the resulting actions to be taken. In Carr and Kemmis's terminology this is emancipatory action research. Probably, as Webb (1996) has asserted, emancipatory action research is more often espoused than actually achieved, at least initially. Beyond this on the continuum, participants drive the research completely. They perform the research and the improvement without external help. If emancipation is needed the participants emancipate themselves. This is 'do-it-yourself' research, as Wadsworth (2011a) calls it.

---

### Activity 4.2 — Identifying stakeholders

In the previous activity you chose a social group you would like to improve. List the 'stakeholders', the people who will be affected by or who can influence any change. For each, consider the extent of involvement that it would be useful for you to offer them.

---

## Aligning philosophy and methodology with purpose

The purpose of most action research can be summarized as participatory improvement in real and important issues through informed trial and error. The philosophy adopted by action researchers is less easily summarized. As described above, it can vary, even when their purposes or processes are similar. Coincidentally, for science generally, the pragmatist philosopher Rorty (1999) has said that despite differing philosophical positions scientists behave much the same in their laboratories. He doesn't believe that philosophy makes much difference.

The link between methodology and purpose is clearer, with different sets of tools serving different elements of the purpose. One set of action research tools engenders participation and therefore commitment to action. Another set produces good understanding, or theory. As in grounded theory, most of the theory is derived from the situation rather than being predetermined. When prior theory is used, it is expected to be in the *service* of practice. This is most evident in the case of practitioners, who deal with situations that are local and immediate. If they can't apply theory, especially academic theory, they ignore it (McKelvey, 2006).

Action researchers intend to generate both understanding of practical situations and action to improve them. As mentioned, involvement can promote commitment whether participation is adopted for ideological or pragmatic reasons. The diversity among participants (Crane and O'Regan, 2010) can provide more diverse information, and therefore a wider choice of solutions.

For novel or complex situations the iterative cycle of action alternating with reflection allows the flexibility of trial and error. Within each cycle, action and understanding are integrated. Theory in the form of understanding emerges from action and then informs and is tested in action. And if there are nested cycles the flexibility and integration can be enhanced. The innermost nested cycles may occupy only seconds or minutes as the participants try something, immediately notice the effect, and adjust behaviour as necessary. The outermost cycle may span an entire study or a substantial part of it.

The action–reflection cycle is important enough to warrant deeper examination. For Lewin (1946) the cycle had three steps: planning, action and evaluation. Kemmis and McTaggart (2005) offer the equivalent version of planning, action and observation, and reflection. Understanding and theory arise from the reflection, thus adding an implied fourth element. The theory component is explicit in the conceptually-similar experiential learning cycle of Kolb (1984): concrete experience, reflective observation, abstract generalization, and active experimentation.

Other tools are borrowed from other literatures. The author's own practice incorporates concepts and methods from organization development, community development, community engagement, facilitation, and several others. A similar eclecticism is displayed in the range of methods adopted by action researchers for data collection, analysis and interpretation.

## Data generation and collection

Data collection and analysis are often integrated, though to allow comparison with other chapters they are discussed here separately. As in grounded theory there are benefits in the integration. Formally or informally, within each action research cycle information is collected, analysed and interpreted. Information collection becomes more effective as understanding of the situation slowly builds and is acted on.

Informal data collection at a smaller scale often consists of discussion between participants. It may or may not be structured and there may or may not be a facilitator. The results of the discussion may be captured on a flip chart or whiteboard, or even as an audio record. Desirably, the discussion moves through a number of distinct stages. The nature of the data is agreed, and the information is exchanged and preferably captured. Later stages (see next section of this chapter) make sense of the information and derive a set of actionable conclusions from it.

Many different qualitative data collection methods are used. Observation is prevalent. Interviews and focus groups are common, often in combination. Surveys are sometimes employed, especially with larger participant groups and in community settings. Face to face surveys with small groups in the style of group feedback analysis (Heller and Brown, 1995) suit action research well. Participants in a CBPR study may embed a quasi-experiment in their research. There is a current tendency as in other qualitative research to make more use of visual methods. Examples include photovoice, especially with youth; see Foster-Fishman, Law, Lichty and Aoun (2010) for a detailed example. Participatory video (Wheeler, 2009) is being utilized in community interventions, especially with the disadvantaged.

An action research study may incorporate other intervention processes such as a search conference (Emery, 1999) or scenario planning (Volkery, Ribeiro, Henrichs and Hoogeveen, 2008), to name two of many. The usual data collection of the intervention process may then be adopted. Some versions of action research have their preferred methods for gathering data, for example rich pictures in soft systems methodology (Checkland and Poulter, 2006). As mentioned below, processes for data analysis can be adopted from other methodologies such as grounded theory.

## Analysis of data

The purpose of data analysis in action research is two-fold: to produce theory (or at least understanding) and to inform action. The critical reflection of the action research cycle builds collective understanding. As understanding increases, participants are able to devise more effective actions. This is an emergent process – as participants work to improve a situation their understanding of that situation slowly improves.

Because understanding is intended to inform action, action-oriented theoretical formulations are favoured. The neglect of academic theory may be due as much to its form as its content. Where immediate action is demanded, as in management (Sandberg and Tsoukas, 2011) for example, or nursing (McVicar, Munn-Giddings and Abu-Helil, 2012), theory perceived as impractical or locally inapplicable will be ignored. Practitioners want to know how to *act* in the specific situation they face. They would do well also to specify their assumptions about situation, outcomes and action. The assumptions can then be scrutinized when acted on. This form of theory was specified by Argyris and Schön (1974: 29) as follows:

In situation $S$, if you intend consequence $C$, do $A$, given assumptions $a_1 \dots a_n$

It may take trial and error to find actions that will work. Without effort to make learning explicit, understanding will often remain tacit. Schön (1983) advocated reflecting *while acting* as a way of enhancing learning. Such reflection-in-action, as he termed it, becomes easier if participants have specified their assumptions during the planning phase of the action research cycle. They can develop theory by making explicit their prior understanding of the situation, the desired outcomes and actions, and the associated assumptions (Dick, 2007).

There is a reasonably large literature about theory in action research. However, specific processes for developing theory are usually not well articulated. The handful of exceptions includes Huxham (2003), Stringer (2004) and Winter (1998). The processes of action science and soft systems methodology are also partially explicit about theory development. Otherwise, little guidance is provided. Some researchers (and many doctoral candidates) have responded by using grounded theory for data analysis. Teram, Schachter and Stalker (2005) have used such a combination successfully in sensitive health research. In the field of IT, Baskerville and Pries-Heje (1999) have used a combination that they term grounded action research.

---

| Activity 4.3 | Actions and outcomes |
| --- | --- |

Consider the example you used in Activities 4.1 and 4.2. Note down your responses to the following questions:

- What are the most important aspects of the situation?
- If you are correct about the situation, what outcomes are desirable?
- What actions would give you those outcomes in that situation?

For *each* of your answers, consider the rationale for your response. What evidence do you have and what assumptions have you made in deciding on these responses?

---

## Quality and rigour

Like qualitative research generally, action research is capable of exhibiting high quality and rigour, though not everyone agrees. There are writers such as Slavin (2002), for example, who believe that randomized control trials are the exemplar of good research even in natural settings such as classrooms. Others (Frost, Nolas, Brooks-Gordon, Esin, Holt, Mehdizadeh and Shinebourne, 2010) have been taught to value the characteristics of experimental research as criteria of quality, and may therefore recommend avoiding qualitative research and action research.

Without denying the virtues of experiment for teasing out causal relationships, the realities of practice make experiment difficult or impractical. At the beginning of a study, participants may have little more understanding than a vague sense that their present situation could be improved. They may not know enough to formulate a research question, let alone identify appropriate measures, identify relevant literatures, predict possible outcomes, or even know whom to involve. Action research must find its own sources of quality and rigour.

Fortunately there are many sources of rigour. Some, and two in particular, apply to all research. First, researchers of all flavours can maintain mindfulness and care throughout their research. At each step of the research process there are threats to quality as Maxwell (2012) contends. The alert researcher or participant seeks to become aware of these and acts to counter them. Second, all researchers can pay attention to the surprises: the information that doesn't fit their preconceptions. Better still, as Kidder (1981) recommends, they can actively seek out negative cases that challenge their emerging understanding.

Some sources of rigour are common to action research and qualitative research generally. For example, multiple sources of data and multiple collection methods can provide triangulation. Other sources of rigour capitalize on the distinguishing features of action research. Participatory action research involves participants as researchers. As they reconcile their different points of view they can deepen their understanding. In addition, the participants *act* on their understanding. In the whole study and in its every cycle the resultant actions challenge and test, pragmatically, the assumptions and learning supporting the actions. To paraphrase Greenwood (2002), this is a strong test of the understanding that informed the actions.

As a frequent topic of criticism, generalizability also deserves mention. It is commonly held that action research doesn't generalize, and many action researchers have accepted this. Baskerville and Lee (1999) contend that by neglecting different forms of generalizability we've given in too easily. There is an inevitable trade-off between global and local applications of theory. Global theories cannot be applied locally unless all and only the relevant variables apply in the theory and the situation. Local theories often attempt only to explain the specifics of the local situation. But if there were *no* generalizability there could be no learning. Experience in using action research would count for nothing.

One reason for choosing action research is that its flexibility and responsiveness allow it to engage with the uncertainties of a research situation. Yet we also expect that we can use what we learn from one situation in other similar situations. We can also draw on others' experience to identify where else we can use our new learning. We can accumulate understanding across multiple studies to turn the substantive theory (Glaser, 2001) from one study into something more like the formal theory that grounded theorists sometimes pursue.

In Box 4.1, Yoland Wadsworth (2005) provides a window into action research regarding the need for flexibility and responsiveness in an action research study.

BOX 4.1

## Window into action research

### Research for ...

The pilot study arose from a desire of service providers at the Arthritis Foundation to respond to a new group of sufferers from arthritis – young women. The professionals' inquiry began with looking at what other service providers did in comparable situations of housebound people, such as in aged services. From this, a proposal for a visiting volunteer program was developed, funded and commenced. The intention was that volunteers would be paired up with women to help them get out to local leisure activities. A volunteer coordinator was appointed to recruit volunteers and train them.

At the request of the funding body I, as an experienced evaluation consultant, and a woman with arthritis were appointed to oversee the evaluation and possible improvement of the program. We recommended consulting consumers about the name for the program, and also asking them for their feedback about whether the program was the best response to their needs. The consumer representative who was exerting continuing pressure to have consumers consulted was removed from the committee in order to reduce the pressure on staff. I required her reinstatement as a condition for my continuing on behalf of the funder and this was done. The coordinator then resigned.

### Research with ...

The advisory committee reiterated their commitment to consumers being consulted. A new coordinator with experience in action research and community development was appointed. Commencing with asking the young women about the program as conceived, and discovering that it seemed wide of the mark, she then conducted a more in-depth study of the views of 40 consumers to learn more about their whole experience of early onset of arthritis using very open-ended questions, and listening intently to their stories. She brought this information back to the advisory committee with some trepidation, as, with ten months of the twelve-month funding gone, and a target of a certain number of friendships to be formed, the program so far lacked a single successful matching being made.

### Research by ...

By now, in addition to myself as consultant, the coordinator, and the service manager, the committee consisted of four other members who all had the experience of arthritis. The action researcher brought to the committee the interview information, and it was examined in its complexity. It revealed the experience of being 'stuck at home', and the unshared emotional distress of the initial diagnosis, and additional distress at the loss of their normal working lives and friendships. Further – ironically, given the program's initial aim of helping the women – the women themselves expressed a need to be of help to others.

To address all of these, a telephone-based 'experiences exchange' was proposed. Interest was immediate. As the idea spread among the consumers, friendships spontaneously developed in an effortless way.

'Arthritis Phonelink', as the program was then named, became a long-lived and successful program.

# Presentation and dissemination of findings

Diversity of opinion has been a theme in this chapter, and again applies here. For writers such as Zuber-Skerritt (2001) public dissemination of results is one of the defining characteristics of action research. For others, dissemination need not proceed beyond the immediate participants in a study. The extent of formality and the reach of a given study may range from discussion among the participants and informal talks, to conference presentations, through to publication in peer-reviewed literature. In a working paper, Boaz, Ashby and Young (2002) have commented that the social science literature is fragmented and diverse, including such vehicles as the grey literature, practitioner journals, and a variety of reports. This is true of action research too, perhaps especially true because of the appeal of action research to practitioners. Many blogs and informal web pages also exist.

For those who seek peer-reviewed publications there are several specialist journals. They include *Action Research* (SAGE), *Educational Action Research* (Taylor & Francis), *International Journal of Action Research* (Hampp), and *Systemic Practice and Action Research* (Springer), each with its own nuance. In addition, *Action Learning: Research and Practice* (Routledge) caters for action learning, and *Progress in Community Health Partnerships* (John Hopkins University Press) for CBPR. Many qualitative research journals carry occasional action research articles, as do specialist journals in some of the more applied practitioner fields.

Whether or not publication is sought, there are benefits in the act of writing. It provides a different (and sometimes deeper) form of reflection that can be enhanced further by collaborative writing.

# Conclusion

In summary, action research appropriately combines and integrates action (that is, change) and research (that is, understanding). Most often, all those affected by the change are responsible for both the understanding and the action. These characteristics – action oriented, research-based, participative and cyclic – determine how the research is actually done, who is involved, how it is reported, and what outcomes are achieved.

---

**KEY POINTS**

- Most action research is participatory, emergent (it takes shape gradually), and action oriented. It is usually (though not necessarily) qualitative
- If a research study is intended to provide both a contribution to knowledge and practical improvement in a specific situation, action research may be a suitable choice of methodology

- There are many varieties of research process that are regarded as part of the action research family. They share a commitment to joint theory and action, and often a moral or epistemological commitment to participation
- Action research can draw on many sources of rigour and quality. Some, like care on the part of the researcher, and triangulation, it shares with other qualitative approaches
- Other outcomes, such as its testing in action of theory, are less common in other qualitative methodologies

## CRITICAL THINKING QUESTIONS

- Review the history of action research as discussed above. What influence has this had on how the researcher is positioned in respect of the study? Are the historical foundations evident in the alignment of the philosophical underpinnings and application of research methods?
- Consider the role of participants as co-researchers in action research. What are the strengths of this approach? What are the potential pitfalls?
- Action research is considered an empowering research philosophy. Why is this the case?

## Suggested further reading

Stringer, E. (2013) *Action Research*, 4th edn. Thousand Oaks: SAGE Publications.

'Community-based action research seeks to involve as active participants those who have traditionally been called subjects and is intended to result in a practical outcome related to the lives or work of the participants. No matter the setting – organizational, institutional, or educational – there are particular skills needed to conduct action research successfully. In *Action Research*, author Ernest T. Stringer provides a series of tools that assist the researcher in working through the research process. The Third Edition of this popular text provides a simple but highly effective model for approaching action research: * Look: Building a picture and gathering information * Think: Interpreting and explaining * Act: Resolving issues and problems' (SAGE Publications, 2013).

## References

Argyris, C. and Schön, D.A. (1974) *Theory in Practice: Increasing Professional Effectiveness*. San Francisco, CA: Jossey-Bass.

Argyris, C., Putnam, R. and McLain Smith, D. (1985) *Action Science: Concepts, Methods and Skills for Research and Intervention*. San Francisco, CA: Jossey-Bass.

Arnstein, D.R. (1969) 'A ladder of citizen participation', *Journal of the American Planning Association*, 35: 216–224.

Baskerville, R.L. and Lee, A.S. (1999) 'Distinctions among different types of generalizing in information systems research', in N.L. Introna, M. Myers and

J. DeGross (eds), *New Information Technologies in Organizational Processes: Field Studies and Theoretical Reflections on the Future of Work*. New York: Kluwer, pp. 49–65.

Baskerville, R.L. and Pries-Heje, J. (1999) 'Grounded action research: a method for understanding IT in practice', *Accounting, Management and Information Technologies*, 9: 1–23.

Bhaskar, R. (1978) *A Realist Theory of Science*. Brighton: Harvester Press.

Boaz, A., Ashby, D. and Young, K. (2002) 'Systematic reviews: what have they got to offer evidence based policy and practice?', Working Paper 2. University of London, ESRC UK.

Brown, T. and Jones, L. (2001) *Action Research and Postmodernism: Congruence and Critique*. Buckingham, UK: Open University Press.

Burns, D. (2007) *Systemic Action Research: A Strategy For Whole System Change*. Bristol: The Policy Press.

Carr, W. and Kemmis, S. (1986) *Becoming Critical: Education Knowledge and Action Research*. London: Falmer Press.

Chandler, D. and Torbert, B. (2003) 'Transforming inquiry and action: interweaving 27 flavors of action research', *Action Research*, 1: 133–152.

Checkland, P. and Poulter, J. (2006) *Learning For Action: A Short Definitive Account of Soft Systems Methodology and Its Use For Practitioners, Teachers, and Students*. New York: Wiley.

Coghlan, D. (2010) 'Seeking common ground in the diversity and diffusion of action research and collaborative management research action modalities: toward a general empirical method', *Research in Organizational Change and Development*, 18: 149–181.

Collier, J. (1945) 'United States Indian Administration as a laboratory of ethnic relations', *Social Research*, 12: 265–303.

Corey, S.M. (1953) *Action Research to Improve School Practices*. New York: Bureau of Publications, Teachers College Columbia University.

Crane, P. and O'Regan, M. (2010) *On PAR: Using Participatory Action Research to Improve Early Intervention*. Canberra: Australian Government, Department of Families, Housing, Community Services and Indigenous Affairs.

Dewey, J. (1916) *Democracy and Education*. New York: Macmillan.

Dick, B. (2007) 'What can grounded theorists and action researchers learn from each other?', in A. Bryant and K. Charmaz (eds), *The Sage Handbook of Grounded Theory*. Thousands Oaks, CA: SAGE, pp. 370–388.

Emery, M. (1999) *Searching: The Theory and Practice of Making Cultural Change*. Amsterdam: Benjamins.

Fals Borda, O. (1987) 'The application of participatory action research in Latin America', *International Sociology*, 2: 329–347.

Foster-Fishman, P.G., Law, K.M., Lichty, L.F. and Aoun, C. (2010) 'Youth ReACT for social change: a method for youth participatory action research', *American Journal of Community Psychology*, 446: 67–83.

Freire, P. (1972) *Pedagogy of the Oppressed*. London: Penguin Books.

French, S. (2009) 'Action research for practicing managers', *Journal of Management Development*, 28: 187–204.

Frost, N., Nolas, S.M., Brooks-Gordon, B., Esin, B., Holt, A., Mehdizadeh, L. and Shinebourne, P. (2010) 'Pluralism in qualitative research: the impact of different researchers and qualitative approaches on the analysis of qualitative data', *Qualitative Research*, 10: 441–460.

Glaser, B.G. (2001) *The Grounded Theory Perspective: Conceptualization Contrasted With Description.* Mill Valley, CA: Sociology Press.

Greenwood, D.J. (2002) 'Action research: unfulfilled promises and unmet challenges', *Concepts and Transformation*, 7: 117–139.

Greenwood, D.J. and Levin, M. (2006) *Introduction to Action Research: Social Research for Social Change.* Thousand Oaks, CA: SAGE.

Heller, F.A. and Brown A. (1995) 'Group feedback analysis applied to longitudinal monitoring of the decision making process', *Human Relations*, 48: 815–836.

Huxham, C. (2003) 'Action research as a methodology for theory development', *Policy and Politics*, 31: 239–248.

Kemmis, S. (2001) 'Exploring the relevance of critical theory for action research: emancipatory action research in the footsteps of Jürgen Habermas', in P. Reason and H. Bradbury (eds), *Handbook of Action Research: Participative Inquiry and Practice.* London: SAGE, pp. 91–102.

Kemmis, S. and McTaggart, R. (2005) 'Participatory action research: communicative action and the public sphere', in N. Denzin and Y. Lincoln (eds), *The Handbook of Qualitative Research.* 3rd edn. Thousand Oaks, CA: SAGE, pp. 559–603.

Kidder, L.H. (1981) 'Qualitative research and quasi-experimental frameworks', in M. Brewer and B. Collins (eds), *Scientific Inquiry and the Social Sciences.* San Francisco, CA: Jossey-Bass, pp. 226–256.

Kolb, D.A. (1984) *Experiential Learning: Experience As The Source Of Learning And Development.* Englewood Cliffs, NJ.: Prentice-Hall.

Lewin, K. (1946) 'Action research and minority problems', *Journal of Social Issues*, 2: 34–46.

Lincoln, Y.S. (2001) 'Engaging sympathies: relationships between action research and social constructivism', in P. Reason and H. Bradbury (eds), *Handbook of Action Research: Participative Inquiry and Practice.* London: SAGE, pp. 124–132.

Maxwell, J.A. (2012) *A Realist Approach for Qualitative Research.* Thousand Oaks, CA: SAGE.

McKelvey, B. (2006) 'Van de Ven and Johnson's "engaged scholarship": nice try, but...', *Academy of Management Review*, 31: 822–829.

McKernan, J.A. (2006) 'Choice and quality in action research: a response to Peter Reason', *Journal of Management Inquiry*, 15: 204–206.

McVicar, A., Munn-Giddings, C. and Abu-Helil, C. (2012) 'Exploring the development of action research in nursing and social care in the UK: a comparative bibliometric review of action research designs in social work (2000–2010)', *Action Research*, 10: 79–101.

Minkler, M. and Wallerstein, N. (2008) *Community-Based Participatory Research for Health: From Process to Outcomes.* San Francisco, CA: Jossey-Bass.

O'Neil, J. and Marsick, V.J. (2007) *Understanding Action Learning: Theory into Practice.* New York: Amacom.

Raelin, J. (2009) 'Seeking conceptual clarity in the action modalities', *Action Learning: Research and Practice*, 6: 17–24.

Ragland, B.B. (2006) 'Positioning the practitioner-researcher: five ways of looking at practice', *Action Research*, 4: 165–182.

Reason, P. (2006) 'Choice and quality in action research practice', *Journal of Management Inquiry*, 15: 187–203.

Reason, P. and Bradbury, H. (2001) *Handbook of Action Research: Participative Inquiry and Practice*. London: SAGE.

Reason, P. and Bradbury, H. (2008) *The Sage Handbook of Action Research: Participatory Inquiry and Practice*. Thousand Oaks: SAGE.

Rorty, R. (1999) 'The phony science wars', *[Review of]* Hacking, Ian, *The Social Construction of What? Atlantic Monthly*, 284: 120–122.

SAGE Publications. (2013) *Action Research*. 3rd edn. Available at: http://www.sagepub.com/books/Book229055 - tabview=packages.

Sagor, R. (2005) *The Action Research Guidebook: A Four-Step Process for Educators and School Teams*. Thousand Oaks, CA: Corwin.

Sandberg, J. and Tsoukas, H. (2011) 'Grasping the logic of practice: theorizing through practical rationality', *Academy of Management Review*, 36: 338–360.

Schein, E.H. (1995) 'Process consultation, action research and clinical inquiry: are they the same?', *Journal of Managerial Psychology*, 10: 14–19.

Schön, D.A. (1983) *The Reflective Practitioner: How Professionals Think in Action*. New York: Basic Books.

Selener, D. (1998) *Participatory Action Research and Social Change*. Ithaca, NY: Cornell Participatory Action Research Network, Cornell University.

Slavin, R.E. (2002) 'Evidence-based education policies: transforming educational practice and research', *Educational Researcher*, 31: 15–21.

Stenhouse, L. (1975) *An Introduction to Curriculum Research and Development*. London: Heinemann.

Stratton-Berkessel, R. (2010) *Appreciative Inquiry for Collaborative Solutions: 21 Strength-based Workshops*. San Francisco: Pfeiffer.

Stringer, E.T. (2013) *Action Research in Education* 4th edn. Upper Saddle River, NJ: Pearson.

Teram, E., Schachter, C.L. and Stalker, C.A. (2005) 'The case for integrating grounded theory and participatory action research: empowering clients to inform professional practice', *Qualitative Health Research*, 15: 1129–1140.

Torbert, W. (1999) 'The distinctive questions developmental action inquiry asks', *Management Learning*, 30: 189–206.

Trist, E. (1990) 'Historical overview: the foundation and development of the Tavistock Institute'. In E. Trist and H. Murray (eds), *The Social Engagement of Social Science, Volume I: The Socio-Psychological Perspective*. London: Free Association Books, pp 1–34.

Volkery, A., Ribeiro, T., Henrichs, T., and Hoogeveen, Y. (2008) 'Your vision or my model? Lessons from participatory land use scenario development on a European scale', *Systemic Practice and Action Research*, 21: 459–477.

Wadsworth, Y. (2005) 'How can professionals help people to inquire using their own action research?', *Action Research Case Studies # 2*.

Wadsworth, Y. (2011a) *Do It Yourself Social Research*. San Francisco, CA: Left Coast Press.

Wadsworth, Y. (2011b) *Building in Research and Evaluation: Human Inquiry for Living Systems*. San Francisco, CA: Left Coast Press.

Webb, G. (1996) *Understanding Staff Development*. Milton Keynes, UK: SRHE/Open University Press.

Wheeler, J. (2009) '"The life that we don't want": using participatory video in researching violence', *IDS Bulletin*, 40: 10–18.

Whyte, W.F. (1991) *Participatory Action Research*. Newbury Park: SAGE.

Winter, R. (1998) 'Managers, spectators and citizens: where does "theory" come from in action research?', *Educational Action Research*, 6: 361–376.

Winter, R. and Munn-Giddings, C. (2001) *A Handbook For Action Research In Health And Social Care*. London: Routledge.

Zuber-Skerritt, O. (2001) 'Action learning and action research: paradigm, praxis and programs', in S. Sankaran, B. Dick, R. Passfield and P. Swepson (eds), *Effective Change Management Using Action Learning and Action Research: Concepts, Frameworks, Processes, Applications*. Lismore, NSW, Australia: Southern Cross University Press, pp. 1–20.

# 5
# Discourse Analysis

Marianne LeGreco

┌─ **Learning objectives** ─────────────────────────────────┐

After reading this chapter, you will be able to:

- Navigate the multi-disciplinary and sometimes fragmented history of analysing discourse
- Distinguish between the *technical* and *situated* sides of discourse analysis
- Develop research questions and protocols for analysing discourses and discursive practices
- Identify different techniques of gathering discursive data for micro, meso and/or macro levels of analysis
- Select appropriate venues for sharing and distributing the results of research studies that use discourse analysis

└───────────────────────────────────────────────────────────┘

## Introduction

Discourse analysis as a qualitative methodology has a complex history that owes much to a wide range of disciplinary areas. This chapter examines the various forms of discourse analysis and discusses the implications of engaging in either macro-level or micro-level discourse analysis. The process of discourse tracing is introduced and worked examples of this method provided. Criteria to assure the quality and rigour of discourse analysis are provided and explained. In conclusion, key points in the effective dissemination of findings from a discourse analysis are identified.

## History of the methodology

The analysis of discourse is at the heart of many forms of qualitative social research. Because people are beings who communicate, the words that individuals and groups choose and how they speak profoundly shape and are shaped by relationships, institutions, and larger systems of practice. Scholars in communication, socio-linguistics, psychology, media studies, rhetoric, and health sciences are increasingly interested in the role of discourse in contemporary society. In the following window into discourse analysis, Karen Tracy explains why she has used various forms of discourse analysis to study phenomena including community meeting practices Tracy (2007) and face-attacks at a 9-1-1 call centre (Tracy and Tracy, 1998).

---

**BOX 5.1**

## Window into discourse analysis

For as long as I can remember I have been fascinated with the inferences people make about others based on small aspects of their language and other features of their talk. Over the years this fascination has led me to tape record and create transcripts of people participating in a variety of institutional practices, including school board meetings, 9-1-1 calls, and most recently, legislative hearings about same-sex marriage. People frequently ask me how I came to be interested in a particular practice. My answer has two pieces. First, there is usually an event that has touched me personally, even if in only a small way. For instance, I decided to study calls to 9-1-1, when a boy was beaten to death at a fast-food restaurant by teens from a neighboring school. The event occurred in the city I grew up in – Philadelphia – and the boy's death was attributed to the slow arrival of police even in light of 20 people calling 9-1-1. This event led me to want to understand better how 9-1-1 call-taking worked and how it could go awry.

Second, I am attracted to interactional scenes that involve tension and conflict among parties or that put speakers in situations where they experience contradictory goals. My attraction to sites of dilemmas has led to my current study of citizens speaking at legislative hearings in which a bill to change a state's marriage law is being considered. In these hearings, citizen speakers aim to persuade elected officials against the backdrop of a legislative context that assumes democratic values, including the partly contradictory right of citizens to express their religious views and their right to expect church and state decision-making to be separated. Such value tensions affect how people talk and this is exactly the kind of issue I seek to understand in my discourse studies.

---

Although the prevalence of discourse analyses has certainly increased, this does not necessarily mean that scholars have developed a unified approach to discourse analysis – or even a unified definition of discourse, for that matter (Cheek, 2004). Indeed, definitions of discourse and approaches to discourse analysis are wide and varied, a point in which many discourse scholars take some degree of pride (Fairhurst and Putnam, 2004). Considering that part of the richness of discourse analysis lies in the diversity of approaches to it, the purpose of this chapter is not to propose a unified theory of discourse or method for its analysis. Rather, this chapter begins by historicizing the definitions and methodologies associated with discourse analysis as a way of opening up deeper discussion in later sections.

Discourse analysis owes much of its history to related theoretical–methodological traditions including rhetoric and structuralism with their emphases on textual analysis, the interpretive turn in the social sciences, and the advancement of critical theory. These perspectives helped to create the conditions to study language, in use, through spoken and written words. Subsequently, discourse analysis became the umbrella

**Table 5.1**  Handbooks and introductory texts for discourse analysis

| Title | Author(s) | First Print | Publisher |
|---|---|---|---|
| Handbook of Discourse Analysis (4 volume series) | Teun van Dijk | 1985 | Academic Press |
| Approaches to Discourse | Deborah Schiffrin | 1994 | Blackwell |
| Discourse Studies: A Multidisciplinary Introduction | Teun van Dijk | 1997 | SAGE |
| An Introduction to Discourse Analysis: Theory and Method | James Paul Gee | 1999 | Routledge |
| Methods of Critical Discourse Analysis | Ruth Wodak Michael Meyer | 2001 | SAGE |
| Discourse Analysis | Barbara Johnstone | 2002 | Wiley–Blackwell |
| The Handbook of Discourse Analysis | Deborah Schiffrin Deborah Tannen Heidi Hamilton | 2003 | Wiley–Blackwell |
| Handbook of Discourse Processes | Arthur Graesser Morton Ann Gernsbacher Susan Goldman | 2003 | Lawrence Erlbaum Associates |
| The SAGE Handbook of Organizational Discourse | David Grant Cynthia Hardy Clifford Oswick Linda Putnam | 2004 | SAGE |
| The Routledge Handbook of Discourse Analysis | James Gee Michael Hanford | 2011 | Routledge |

term to describe various research techniques that are used to study everything from local language practices (Mirivel, 2007, 2008; Tracy and Ashcraft, 2001) to larger systems of socially-constructed meaning (Nahon-Serfaty, 2012; Wodak and Fairclough, 2010).

Navigating the complex history of discourse analysis means first understanding the resources that are available for learning what it is and how it's done. The first handbook that focused on discourse analysis appeared in 1985 (van Dijk, 1985). This four-volume series focused on topics including dialogue and conversation, discourse analysis as a cross-discipline, and dimensions of context. Even more so, van Dijk forecast that approaches to discourse analysis would experience some integration; however, discourse analysis would also 'differentiate into inevitable specialization' (1985: 9). Since that publication, discourse has become an increasingly well-documented object of study. Table 5.1 provides a summary of major handbooks and primers that detail the history of discourse analysis with greater precision.

The proliferation of handbooks and introductory texts has certainly contributed to the complexity of perspectives on discourse analysis – especially considering that this list does not include chapters about discourse analysis written in disciplinary-specific handbooks (Putnam and Fairhurst, 2001; Tracy and Mirivel, 2009), or the numerous journals and peer-reviewed articles that have been published since that first hand-book. At the same time, these texts have allowed for points integration. For example, most scholars who identify as doing discourse analysis are interested in a) some form of language, usually labelled as talk and text; b) some position on context, either the need to bracket it out or make it part of the analysis; and c) some use of discourse analysis as a methodological approach to make claims about interpretive and/or critical theories.

Although the history of discourse analysis in qualitative research cues us in to some of the key concepts and points of integration, the question still remains: what exactly is discourse and what does it mean to analyse it? To best address this question, an understanding of the philosophical underpinnings of discourse analysis is necessary.

## Philosophical underpinnings

Discourse can be a tricky object of study. Different scholars subscribe to different definitions of discourse, and the limits of this term are often debated in academic circles. Alvesson (2004), for example, worried that the term was becoming a 'catch-all' concept to describe any study that dealt with terms like language, dialogue, and text. The danger being that if discourse is everything, then the term really has no meaning. Despite the debate over what counts as discourse, some clarity and definition is still possible. In a very basic sense, discourse is talk and text. However, most scholars require a more precise definition than just talk and text, and two definitions of discourse tend to dominate.

For most research that is labelled discourse analysis, the first definition of discourse is focused on how individuals and groups use language in social settings. Talk is most often framed as naturally-occurring conversation and dialogue, or talk that is not influenced by a researcher (Tracy and Mirivel, 2009). Texts are often formal and informal documents that serve as written accounts of interaction. Because this definition of discourse favours local interactions – and sometimes even just short passages from a single conversation – this view has been characterized as micro-level discourses (Alvesson and Karreman, 2000; Conley and O'Barr, 1998), or 'little d' discourse (Gee, 1999).

A second definition of discourse addresses what some have called macro-level discourses or 'Big D' Discourses (Gee, 1999). Drawing from more critical and post-structural traditions (Fairclough, 1995; Foucault, 1972), this approach frames discourse as indicative of broader social patterns and practices. For example, discourses of 'nutritionism' (Rapoport, 2003) are evident in advertising strategies and public health policies that encourage people to construct a diet based on individual nutrients – like protein and carbohydrates – as opposed to actual foods – like meat and potatoes. They are embedded in nutrition curriculum and social institutions, like the US Department of Agriculture, and reproduced in social practices of dieticians and food writers. These macro-discourses are often positioned as enduring patterns of talk and text across contexts.

To add another layer of complexity, certain researchers also identify a meso level of discourse (Alvesson and Karreman, 2000). The meso level treats discourse as instances of talk and text that stitch together the connections between micro and macro discourses. In doing so, the meso level helps to illustrate how micro discourses scale up to the macro level, as well as how macro discourses bear down on the micro level (Cheney, Christensen, Conrad, and Lair, 2004). For some scholars, this emphasis on the meso level also means an opportunity to focus more directly on the concept of discourses as discursive practices, or the routine uses of talk and text to coordinate actions across contexts (LeGreco, 2012; LeGreco and Tracy, 2009).

These different approaches and definitions of discourse have been particularly useful for engaging in social research from interpretive and critical perspectives. At the heart of these perspectives, is the argument that language constructs, illustrates, and defines reality (Hoijer, 1954). In the field of nursing, for example, Crowe (2005) posits that discourse analysis provides a suitable alternative to more positivistic forms of research – especially for those scholars who are interested in asking interpretive research questions related to identity, language, social relationships, and power. As an illustration, she shows how a critical discourse analysis can be used to examine the power relationships that constitute the Diagnostic and Statistical Manual IV (DSM-IV) and its definition of mental illness. This analysis demonstrates the implications that this text had for authoritative statements and media representations about mental health.

Likewise, scholars from communication, sociology, and psychology have suggested that interpretive and critical perspectives are strengthened by the study of discourse (Tracy, Martinez-Guillem, Robles and Casteline, 2011; Le, Short and Le, 2011; Wodak, 2011). Because these perspectives focus on phenomena like the social construction of lived experiences and power relations in organizations, they are in need of methodologies that can 'get at' the complex interactions that language plays a part in constructing. Discourse analysis, with its emphasis on the use of talk and text in social settings, makes a more than sufficient match.

## Positioning the researcher

An important part of research design is deciding where to put the researcher. As with most questions about the doing of discourse analysis, the answer is always, 'it depends'. In terms of positioning the researcher, it depends on how that researcher works with talk and/or text (Chilton and Schäffner, 2002; Hodge and McHoul, 1992). Before digging into those differences, though, a more useful starting point might be the more common ways in which researchers who engage in discourse analysis are positioned. Tracy and Mirivel (2009) are quick to remind the reader that discourse analysis is a largely interpretive, and sometimes critical, endeavour. To keep in line with those theoretical perspectives, the general methodological position of the researcher is that of a human instrument (Lincoln and Guba, 1985). In this capacity, they are better able to collect data at multiple levels, react and adapt to situations in the field, and verify data with greater immediacy.

Another point of convergence is work with human subjects. While some scholars focus exclusively on texts, most researchers who do discourse analysis are usually working with people. Different research designs will approach working with human subjects in different ways, some of which are outlined later in this section. At the same time, all research protocols that call for interactions with people require some sort of ethics approval process. This process is meant to ensure the fair and ethical treatment of the individuals or groups who choose to participate in our research. For most studies, this usually means routing an application through a college or university's ethics committee or institutional review board. Additionally, scholars who do research in schools or health care services are sometimes required to do a separate application through that institution's ethics committee. Even independent scholars are encouraged to follow the same processes before implementing a study (Lindlof and Taylor, 2010).

Beyond those generalities, however, there are some fairly specific differences related to discourse analysis. Initially, researchers identify their position based on how they define instances of talk. For those who study discourse labelled at the micro level, capturing instances of talk in social settings is of particular importance. As such, the preference is for methods that record naturally occurring speech, from human subjects, and the researcher does his or her best not to influence how that speech develops. As a consequence, researchers must often position themselves as unobtrusively as possible, especially during the data collection process.

Additionally, researchers also position themselves within discourse studies based on how they approach texts (Hodge and McHoul, 1992). Although the preference in discourse analysis is for some type of human interaction, it is well within a researcher's position to focus exclusively on textual representations of language (Fernandez-Sola, Garnero-Molina, Manrique, Castro-Sanchez, Hernandez-Padilla, and Marquez-Membrive, 2012). The obvious difference is the absence of human subjects; however, this difference frames how researchers orient themselves to their research design. By emphasizing text over talk, researchers often adopt a position very similar to the way that rhetoricians approach their design (Cheney et al., 2004). These researchers expose a certain life in their chosen texts; however, their position is still somewhat distanced from the origination and production of those texts.

Finally, many researchers who study both talk and text – especially those who do so across micro, meso, and macro definitions of discourse – take much greater liberties with how they position themselves in the research process. Talk is conceptualized in a broader sense and might include naturally occurring speech, as well as interviews and observations where the researcher is more immersed in the field. Talk is also understood in relation to text, which focuses much more on drawing those connections across micro, meso, and macro levels. Some of the most provocative examples of these studies come from organizational communication (Buzzanell, Berkelaar and Kisselburgh, 2011; Fairhurst and Cooren, 2004; Putnam and Fairhurst, 2001). From this position, discourse analysis is more embodied and engaged (Scott and Trethewey, 2008) and sometimes even participatory (Groscurth, 2011).

As human instruments, researchers often interact directly with their participants through data collection procedures, as well as through the very design and analysis of the project itself. For example, Tracy (2000) served as a full participant in her critical discourse study of emotion labour on board a cruise ship. Additionally, Renn (2006) introduced the concept of co-operative discourse as a way to facilitate research on environmental management policies. His model treats researchers, everyday citizens, and environmental experts as peers who work to design and evaluate policy texts and research procedures. Thus, the term discourse has been used to define multiple approaches to analysing talk and text, allowing researchers several options regarding how they position themselves as a human instrument.

## Aligning philosophy and methodology with purpose

In order to translate the philosophical underpinnings and definitions of discourse into methodologies that inform the analysis of it, scholars have developed different traditions and practices. While it might seem like an easy choice to label one set of practices 'micro-discourse analysis' and the other set of practices 'macro-discourse analysis', such a distinction oversimplifies some of the methodological decisions that researchers actually make when designing a study. Moreover, setting up this distinction does not take into consideration the emergence of methodologies that emphasize practical approaches (Craig and Tracy, 1995; Tracy, 1995) or meso-levels of analysis that show connections across contexts (LeGreco and Tracy, 2009).

From a practical perspective, it is useful to frame the analysis of discourse as either more technical or more situated. Methods that favour the more technical side of discourse analysis align closely with what scholars traditionally refer to as Discourse Analysis with capitals, DA. To 'do' Discourse Analysis means to follow a strict code of methodological practice. Tracy and Mirivel (2009) outlined the practice of DA as having five key components:

1. Recording interaction
2. Transcribing the tape
3. Repeated study of the tape
4. Formulating claims about the conversational moves, structures, and strategies demonstrated in the interaction
5. Building an argument with transcript excerpts that are analysed

Their approach to DA will provide the reader with examples of the technical side as we work through the remaining sections of this chapter. DA scholars define discourse as 'language use in social settings' (Tracy and Mirivel, 2009: 153), with clear rules about what counts as data and how to transcribe naturally occurring speech. For example, Discourse Analysis is a close cousin to Conversation Analysis (CA), which is another method of studying verbal and non-verbal interaction in practice. These forms of qualitative research are related in terms of the precision that they employ in transcribing the tape. CA uses a Jeffersonian style of transcription, which is outlined in Table 5.2. This particular method of transcription

**Table 5.2** Basic transcription notation for conversation analysis

| Symbol | Name | What it Means |
| --- | --- | --- |
| . | Period | Falling pitch or intonation |
| ? | Question Mark | Rising pitch or intonation |
| , | Comma | Temporary rise or fall in pitch or intonation |
| - | Hyphen | An abrupt stop or interruption in speech |
| = | Equal Sign | A break followed by the continuation of speech |
| (#) | Timed Pause | The time in seconds of a pause in speech |
| (.) | Micropause | A brief pause, usually 0.2 of a second or less |
| : : | Colons | Prolonging a sound |
| beautiful | Underline | Stressed syllable or word |
| WORD | All Caps | Loud speech |
| °word° | Degree Symbol | Whisper or quiet speech |
| →word← | More Than/Less Than | Faster speech |
| ←word→ | Less Than/More Than | Slower speech |
| [word] | Brackets | Overlapping speech |
| (word) | Parentheses | Unclear speech or transcriptionist doubt |
| (     ) | Empty Parentheses | Non-transcribable speech |
| ((action)) | Double Parentheses | Description of a non-speech action |
| hhh | | Audible exhalation |
| .hhh | | Audible inhalation |

is quite precise – with symbols for overlapping speech, timed pauses, and audible breaths (Atkinson and Heritage, 1999). While there are several acceptable transcription methods for Discourse Analysis, the most common is some variation of the Jeffersonian system. By taking a very strict and technical approach to the management of data, DA studies are able to make very detailed observations and claims about dialogue structures, discursive practices, and conversation strategies in social settings.

Methods of situated discourse analysis suggest that the ways we use words are bound up in context. These types of analyses are more familiar in critical and post-structural studies (Fairclough, 1995; Foucault, 1972; Tracy et al., 2011), and have become particularly popular in organizational communication approaches to discourse (Fairhurst and Putnam, 2004; Zoller, 2003). By adopting the term 'situated', the intent is to focus not just on what constitutes a context, but also on what features of discourse coordinate practices across contexts. In other words, what exactly 'situates' a discourse? What organizes contexts across micro, meso, and macro levels?

To mobilize research questions like these, scholars have options ranging from critical (Fairclough, 1995), practical (Craig and Tracy, 1995), and post-structural (Foucault, 1972) traditions. These forms of discourse analysis emphasize concepts such as power, agency, and materiality. For example, Probyn's (2005, 2008) commentary on fat as a feminist issue invokes a Foucaultian language of discourse analysis. Not only does she draw attention to the lack of sophistication in the ways that scholars have studied the materiality of discourse, she highlights the political consequences that methodological choices have in terms of the body as discourse, the understanding of human subjectivity, and the need for better arguments that critique discourses of eating.

In order to provide a practical approach that attends to this situated, contextual, and critical side of discourse analysis, LeGreco and Tracy (2009) developed a methodology called discourse tracing. Their four-part approach focuses on the following features:

1. Research Design
2. Data Management
3. Data Analysis
4. Evaluation

Discourse tracing provides an example of implementation that will move us through the remaining sections of this chapter, especially as it highlights the situated decisions that researchers must make.

The labels of 'technical' and 'situated' do not suggest that technical discourse analysis isn't interested in context and situated discourse analysis isn't interested in details. On the contrary, some discourse studies that employ a very technical level of Discourse Analysis are also incredibly attentive to the role that context plays in local language use (Tracy and Tracy, 1998). In other words, most discourse studies incorporate some level of technical precision in the collection and transcription of naturally occurring speech; at the same time, they also take a position on context and the different levels of talk and text related to it.

The labels of 'technical' and 'situated' do suggest, however, that there are different decision processes that researchers will go through, depending on how they approach the technical or situated elements within their study. More technical studies tend to favour micro-instances of discourse that emerge without facilitation from the researcher; whereas situated studies lean towards embodied and participatory methods that draw out discursive connections across contexts. The next section provides concrete and practical illustrations of the technical and situated decisions surrounding discourse analysis by focusing on methods of data collection.

## Data generation and collection

If discourse analysis offers a methodology that turns our focus on talk and text, then its related methods of data collection are almost exclusively qualitative and include recordings of naturally occurring speech, interviews, observations, and relevant texts. Scholars who undertake discourse analysis have done a particularly good job engaging in conversations about what counts as data and how to collect it. The challenge becomes the capturing of these instances of discourse in a way that can be analysed in a systematic way to make claims about the social and critical construction of meaning.

For researchers interested in capturing the technical aspects of discourse through a more formal Discourse Analysis, data generation and collection initially focuses on 1) recording interaction and 2) transcribing the tape (Tracy and Mirivel, 2009). As mentioned throughout this chapter, the preference in discourse studies is for some form of talk in social settings. Naturally occurring speech might be generated in a dialogue between a doctor and a patient, a meeting among policymakers, or casual conversation between friends. Data collection procedures for this type of data emphasize two features: audio or video recording of these interactions in the least obtrusive way possible, and keeping the researcher from influencing the interaction. In other words, people might interact differently when they know they're being watched; therefore, researchers should try to reduce their presence during data collection. Being unobtrusive to minimize influence can sometimes be mistaken for deception, especially if the researcher is vague about how he or she intends to record the actual interactions between participants. As such, a preference for naturally occurring speech means that researchers must take great care with their research design to ensure an ethical process of capturing actual speech.

Once speech is captured on tape, the researcher is tasked with transcribing that tape. Certainly, the Jeffersonian style of transcription outlined in Table 5.2 is one option for achieving the technical precision required to do Discourse Analysis. Although less formal methods of transcription are also welcome in DA studies, Tracy and Mirivel (2009) suggested that most research using DA follows a fairly strict method of transcription. In doing so, the transcription can account for verbal and non-verbal cues, turn taking, conversation structures, and other discursive practices that are not always evident in a simple transcription of the words that were spoken.

---

### Activity 5.1 ⎯ Practising precise transcription

Learning to transcribe recorded interaction can be a challenging but useful skill to develop. Take a 2–4 minute excerpt from an audio or video-taped interaction. You can always record one of your classroom discussions, with classmates' permission, if you do not have easy access to a taped interaction. Using the Jeffersonian method of transcription outlined in Table 5.2, practice transcribing the 2–4 minute interaction. If you need more practice, visit the following tutorial developed by Emanuel Schegloff to see and hear how an interaction is transcribed using Jeffersonian methods:

http://www.sscnet.ucla.edu/soc/faculty/schegloff/TranscriptionProject/index.html

Now, take it a step further: have classmates and fellow researchers practise transcribing the same 2–4 minute interaction using the Jeffersonian method. Compare and contrast each transcription to see the similarities and differences in each individual's interpretation of the rules.

**Table 5.3**  Possible data across different levels of analysis

| Level | Data Type | Sample Data Sources | Example |
|-------|-----------|---------------------|---------|
| Micro | Observations | Field notes from participant observation at local sites | LeGreco's (2012) study of school meal policy included field notes from observations of local school meal programs, recordings and transcriptions of face-to-face interviews, and field notes from local policy meetings to capture micro-level instances of discourse. |
| | | Recordings and transcriptions of naturally occurring speech or interaction in local contexts | |
| | Interviews | Recordings and transcriptions from a face-to-face, semi-structured interview | |
| | | Recordings and transcriptions from focus group or small group interviews | |
| | Formal and Informal Texts | Personal records like report cards, electronic medical records, or annual reviews | |
| | | Individual journals, internet blogs, or other documentation of personal narrative | |
| Meso | Observations | Field notes from participant observations at regional, national, or international sites | McClellan's (2012) study of city planning processes looked at public participation and the city of Golden, Colorado. She used newsletters, City Council resolutions, membership lists, and a public review forum to show connections across contexts. |
| | | Recordings and transcriptions of naturally occurring speech or interaction across contexts | |
| | Formal Texts | Policy documents and public codes/laws | |
| | | Training manuals | |
| | Media Texts | Press Releases | |
| | | Newsletters | |
| Macro | Formal Texts | Archival documents that provide a historical perspective and context | Nestle's (2007) commentary on the creation of the USDA Food Pyramid included data from federal policy documents, historical and archival texts, and food advertisements to show a history of discourses that encouraged people to eat more. |
| | | National/global policies, treaties, or initiatives | |
| | Media Texts | News from television, newspapers, magazines | |
| | | Internet news and online media | |
| | Pop Culture Texts | Documentaries and other films | |
| | | Popular books and entertainment-education sources | |

Another way to approach data generation and collection is to consider the more situated side of discourse analysis. Data management strategies in small discourse analysis often borrow from other qualitative practices – including ethnography, participatory action research, and grounded theory. For example, discourse tracing offers researchers methods for studying multi-level discursive practices from critical, participatory, and post-structural traditions (LeGreco and Tracy, 2009). In terms of data collection, discourse tracing focuses on both research design, and data management. Research design helps discourse tracers define their case. Borrowing language from Foucault (1972), data starts with a rupture in the discourse. Sometimes, a rupture point marks a moment of significant change – like a new policy text – sometimes, it is simply a point of departure. By defining a rupture point in the discourse, researchers can outline what counts as micro, meso, and macro levels of data.

This focus on multiple levels of analysis leads directly into practices of data management. Because discourse tracing and other situated approaches are interested in examining discourse across macro, meso, and/or micro levels, a diverse – and often quite large – set of data is required. In other words, it takes a lot of data in order to make claims about how discourses get situated. Table 5.3 outlines different ways to conceptualize multiple levels of data illustrated by three examples (LeGreco, 2012; Nestle, 2007; McClellan, 2012). In order to follow the connections across these multiple levels, discourse tracers are asked to examine naturally-occurring speech, as well as interviews, observations, direct participation, formal and informal texts, and multiple forms of media.

Rather than focus on the precision of talk in social settings, like those who carry out Discourse Analysis, discourse tracing requires a different type of precision – that of managing rather large and diverse data sets. One way in which discourse tracers accomplish this control is through the chronological ordering of data. Chronological ordering is not intended to draw out causal processes, but to recognize that discourses have a history. At the end of the data collection process, discourse tracers will have access to transcriptions of naturally occurring speech, transcriptions of interviews, field notes, policy texts, manuals, newspaper articles, and other texts, all organized in terms of when they were spoken or written. In doing so, chronological ordering prepares discourse-tracing data for further analysis.

---

| Activity 5.2 | Finding the best data |

Think about a research question that you are interested in studying, or choose one of the following topics and write a research question:

- You have been assigned to observe an Emergency Room at a hospital in a major metropolitan city. You want to study how discursive practices and structures developed between doctors, nurses, and staff might lead to problematic outcomes like conflicts, tensions, shortcuts, or mistakes.
- You are interested in studying how discourses that support 'local' economies are invoked to organize individual and community-level eating practices. You are volunteering for a community-based food program that hosts an urban farm and a farmer's market, and you started working with them to collect data about this topic.

Based on the information found in Table 5.3, what are the *ideal* sources of data that you can use to answer your research question? If you cannot gain access to *ideal* data, what are the *sufficient* sources of data that you can use to answer your question? Is the most appropriate data found at the micro level? The meso level? The macro level? Is it found across levels? How about between levels?

# Analysis of data

Good discourse analysis requires sufficiently prepared and organized, or packaged data. As outlined in the previous section, the packaging process might look different for someone doing a more technical DA than it does for someone doing a more situated discourse tracing. Regardless of the approach, the researcher will move into the methods of analysis with a textual representation of the data to be analysed – be it a transcription of an interaction or interview, the copy of a policy text, or a set of field notes.

As with methods of data generation and collection, most methods of analysing discourse favour a qualitative approach. For those researchers whose questions require the more technical side of Discourse Analysis, analytic techniques are covered in the third and fourth of Tracy and Mirivel's (2009) activities: repeated study of the audio or videotape, and formulating claims about the conversational moves, structures, and strategies demonstrated in the interaction. Often, both of these activities are covered during what DA researchers call a data session. During a data session, individuals repeatedly listen to a taped interaction and read the transcript. Then, small groups of researchers gather to develop analytic claims about the structures and strategies at play on the tape. These data sessions usually include researchers, their assistants, and experts about the topic being studied. Practices of small groups will vary depending upon their makeup. For example, if a group is comprised of researchers who also have training in ethnography and grounded theory, their analytic practices might also include open and axial coding (Corbin and Strauss, 2007), which involves developing conceptually-based terms, applying them to the transcribed interaction, and organizing and drawing connections between data based on those codes. Thus, working through data sessions using grounded theory methods gives researchers the opportunity to draw analytic connections between pieces of data and make claims about how discourses operate in everyday social settings.

Additionally, discourse tracing offers another set of techniques for those researchers whose questions require methods of analysis examining how discourses get situated across micro, meso, and macro levels. Discourse tracing borrows techniques from its closest methodological cousin – process tracing (George and Bennett, 2005). Process tracing concentrates on tracing causal processes across different historical cases using a method called structured–focused comparison (George, 1979). While discourse tracing isn't interested in causal processes, the method of structured–focused comparison does provide a useful language for tracing how discourses scale up and bear down across micro, meso, and macro levels.

Structured–focused comparison involves developing questions that a researcher asks of their data. These questions might be more philosophical in nature (e.g., what is the purpose of policy?) or very practical in nature (e.g., which stakeholders were invited to develop a policy text?). Each question is applied across a chronologically ordered data set in order to trace connections between the different levels of discourse. For example, LeGreco and Tracy (2009) illustrate how policy changes in school meal programs for one school district could trace onto changes for another school district, thereby identifying policy texts as a meso-level discourse that connected school districts across contexts. Not only do these questions help discourse tracers illustrate what is present in the data, they also help researchers clarify what is missing from, or obscured by, discursive data. As such, the structured–focused questions are a particularly useful technique for discourse analysts.

## Quality and rigour

Discourse scholars have multiple ways to demonstrate the quality and rigour of their work. At the heart of these options are the concepts of reflexivity (Richardson, 2000) and transferability (Lincoln and Guba, 1985). These concepts are not unique to discourse analysis but represent standards that have been developed and applied across qualitative circles of research. Reflexivity refers to the constant looking back upon the data to consider theoretical and practical implications, ethical contributions, and the role of the researcher as a human instrument. Transferability refers to the ability to apply research findings in other contexts, often on a case-by-case basis.

Beyond these core concepts of quality, most qualitative methods of discourse analysis include a form of reflection about rigour. For example, the final step of LeGreco and Tracy's (2009) discourse tracing methodology is evaluation, which encourages the researcher to collaborate with participants to consider the theoretical and practical implications of their work, as well as the appropriateness of their research design in capturing their object of study. Tracy (2010) took this commentary a step further by developing eight 'big-tent' criteria for evaluating the quality and rigour of qualitative work (see Chapter 13). The following list considers how her general qualitative criteria can be adapted specifically to discourse analysis:

1. Worthy topic: select a timely and significant topic that addresses micro, meso, and/or macro levels of discourse
2. Rich rigour: sufficient and appropriate samples of talk and text, use of concepts like discursive practices, and data analysis techniques to make claims about discourse
3. Sincerity: self-reflexivity and transparency about choices made regarding the technical and situated sides of discourse analysis
4. Credibility: use of thick descriptions, excerpts from recorded interactions, and triangulation of data to show rather than tell how discourses operate
5. Resonance: evocative representations of findings and transferable implications that show how discourses connect across contexts

6. Significant contribution: adds to our understanding of concepts related to discourse, methods of DA and other discourse analyses, and/or discursive practices and strategies
7. Ethical: follows appropriate procedures (like human subjects) and culturally-sensitive ethics throughout the research process
8. Meaningful coherence: final products and reports reflect what the study set out to accomplish, and researchers connect the goals of their study with their choices of literature, research questions, methods, and evidence

These are useful criteria that apply to both the technical and situated sides of discourse analysis. Scholars and participants are well served to consider these criteria not only at the end of the research process, but in the very early stages of research design.

## Presentation and dissemination of findings

At the completion of any discourse study, the researcher faces the daunting task of finding the best outlet or outlets to disseminate the findings. The final activity in Tracy and Mirivel's (2009) DA process, after all, is building an argument that uses specific excerpts from the analysed data. As such, researchers need to consider carefully where and how they will share their conclusions about the substantive discourse studied. Fortunately for scholars, the opportunities to share research findings about discourse are growing in academic, community, and individual settings. As outlined in Table 5.1 the proliferation of handbooks devoted to various types of discourse analysis demonstrates that discourse scholars have produced an increasingly large body of research. The suggested further reading at the end of this chapter lists journals that represent some of the key outlets for peer reviewed academic research that use some form of discourse analysis.

This list is certainly not exhaustive; however, it provides a starting point for scholars who are interested in peer-reviewed discourse publications. Moreover, journals with a disciplinary-specific focus are beginning to feature more and more discourse analyses. In public health, for example, the *American Journal of Public Health* has started to create a space for discourse and communication as part of their aim and scope (Brownson, Chriqui and Stamakis, 2009; LeGreco and Canary, 2011). And in communication studies, the Journal of Applied Communication Research has opened up a conversation about the applied study of discourse (Scott and Trethewey, 2008; Zoller, 2003; Zoller, 2012). As a whole, opportunities to disseminate discourse research through peer-reviewed, academic journals are wide and varied. At the same time, discourse analysts must also consider how to share their results with communities and individuals.

The notion of communicating research results with participants and the wider community is nothing new. Qualitative scholars have long debated how research should benefit our participants (Fine, Weis, Weseen, and Wong, 2000; Trethewey, 2002), and one possible way to do that is to share our research results directly with the individuals and communities who generated data. Researchers and participants can host community forums where the research is presented through formal and informal presentations. They can also work with local news affiliates to share information through broadcast and print media. Another option is to collaborate to develop communication and promotion materials that are culturally appropriate to the community being served. These materials might include pamphlets and resource guides, websites and online blogs, or even community performances.

Researchers can also turn to Tracy and Mirivel (2009) one more time for a novel methodological practice that can help discourse analysts share their research and participants reflect on their use of talk and text. They advocate the use of focused reflection (Mirivel, 2006), which is a methodological training ground similar to a data session. Researchers work with students, participants, lay experts, and community members to review the audio or video recordings. In doing so, these individuals have the opportunity to learn how to analyse a tape, and have a chance to reflect upon how the data connects to their own experiences. As such, focused reflection has the potential to offer some provocative insights about how researchers connect their research with the larger community.

Throughout this process, researchers should remember the importance of mining the data and sharing their results through multiple outlets. Discourse analysis provides researchers and participants with a unique opportunity to study how individuals, groups, and communities use talk and text in everyday interactions. By paying close attention to the technical and situated sides of discourse analysis, the differences between approaches like Discourse Analysis and discourse tracing, and strategies for collecting and analysing data, researchers can continue to develop a more precise language that describes what we do. Discourse is an important object of study, and reflecting upon how we analyse it is equally important.

---

**KEY POINTS**

- Discourse analysis is based in theory from interpretive social science, structuralism and post-structuralism, rhetoric, and critical-cultural studies. This approach is evident in research from Communication, Socio-Linguistics, Psychology, Media Studies, and even health-related fields like Nutrition and Nursing
- Rooted in interpretive and critical philosophies that focus on concepts like talk and text in social settings, approaches to discourse analysis are based on how the researcher defines discourse
- The position of the researcher depends on how the researcher works with talk and text
- Aligning philosophy and methodology with purpose requires researchers to consider technical and situated sides of research design
- Data collection involves collecting speech, interviews, observations, archival data, and other relevant texts to show the multiple levels of discourse
- In discourse analysis, data analysis involves reviewing the tape and engaging in small group data sessions in order to make claims about discursive strategies and practices
- In discourse tracing, data analysis involves using structured-focused questions to lift themes and arguments out of the data and make connections between discursive practices

- Quality and rigour aligns with general criteria for quality and rigour in qualitative research. Chief among them are the concepts of reflexivity and transferability
- Opportunities to share research results include through peer-reviewed journals and directly with individuals and communities who can benefit

## CRITICAL THINKING QUESTIONS

Think about a research project that you are currently working on or that you plan to start in the near future.

- What are some of the strategies that you might implement to encourage increased participation and community engagement, beyond simply serving as a research subject?
- What are some ways in which participants and a larger community can get engaged in your research project about discourse?
- Which individuals and organizations should be involved in the conversation?
- At what stage in the research project should they be invited to participate? Should they be a part of the design process itself? Or should they enter into the conversation during data sessions and focused reflection sessions?
- Which individuals and organizations would be the most helpful in translating your research results into actual resources for members of the community?
- Consider contacting one of the individuals or organizations that you identified as part of this activity. Discuss your topic and ask for feedback on your project. How might you incorporate this feedback into your research plans?

# Suggested further reading

## Journals

*Discourse & Society:* A multi-disciplinary journal that creates a space for research at the boundaries of discourse analysis; calls largely for the use of qualitative methods.

*Discourse Studies:* An international journal that concentrates on the study of talk and text; calls for both qualitative and quantitative research from a mostly interpretive, social science approach.

*Discourse Processes:* An interdisciplinary journal that focuses on the structure and function of discourse; calls for original experimental and theoretical essays and leans towards quantitative analyses.

*Discourse Analysis Online:* A web-based journal that promotes online collaboration about objects of study and questions pertaining to discourse; calls for research using a wide range of discourse-related methodologies.

*Critical Discourse Studies:* An interdisciplinary journal that creates a space for critical research and social change.

*Textual Practice:* An international journal that focuses on radical literary studies, as well as the history and significance of the study of texts.

*Qualitative Inquiry:* An international, multi-disciplinary journal that concentrates largely on qualitative research in general; has developed a history of publishing interpretive and critical discourse research.

## Book

Grant, D., Hardy, C., Oswick, C., et al. (2004) *SAGE Handbook of Organizational Discourse.* 1st edn. Thousand Oaks: SAGE Publications.

'The SAGE Handbook of Organizational Discourse is the definitive text for those with research and teaching interests in the field of organizational discourse. It provides an important overview of the domains of study, methodologies and perspectives used in research on organizational discourse. It shows how discourse analysis has moved beyond its roots in literary theory to become an important approach in the study of organizations. The editors of the Handbook, all renowned authors and experts in this field, have provided an invaluable resource on the application, importance and relevance of discourse to organizational issues for use by tutors and researchers working in the field, as well as providing important reference material for newcomers to this area. Each chapter, written by a leading author on their subject, covers an overview of the existing literature and also frames the future of the field in ways which challenge existing preconceptions' (SAGE Publications, 2013).

## References

Alvesson, M. (2004) 'Organizational culture and discourse', in D. Grant, C. Hardy, C. Oswick, & L. Putnam (eds), *The Sage Handbook of Organizational Discourse.* Thousand Oaks, CA: SAGE, pp. 317–335.

Alvesson, M. and Karreman, D. (2000) 'Varieties of discourse: on the study of organizations through discourse analysis', *Human Relations*, 53: 1125–1149.

Atkinson, J.M. and Heritage, J. (1999) 'Jefferson's transcription notation', in A. Jaworski and N. Coupland (eds), *The Discourse Reader.* New York: Routledge, pp. 158–166.

Brownson, R.C., Chriqui, J.F. and Stamakis, K.A. (2009) 'Understanding evidence-based public health policy', *American Journal of Public Health*, 99: 1576–1583.

Buzzanell, P.M., Berkelaar, B.L. and Kisselburgh, L. (2011) 'The mouths of babes: exploring families' career socialization of young children in China, Lebanon, and the United States', *Journal of Family Communication*, 11: 148–164.

Cheek, J. (2004) 'At the margins? Discourse analysis and qualitative research', *Qualitative Health Research*, 14: 1140–1150.

Cheney, G., Christensen, L., Conrad, C., and Lair, D. (2004) 'Corporate rhetoric as organizational discourse', in D. Grant, C. Hardy, C. Oswick, & L. Putnam (eds), *The Sage Handbook of Organizational Discourse.* Thousand Oaks, CA: SAGE, pp. 79–103.

Chilton, P. and Schäffner, C. (2002) *Politics as Text and Talk: Analytic Approaches to Political Discourse*. Amsterdam: John Benjamins Publishing Co.

Conley, J. and O'Barr, W. (1998) *Just Words: Law, Language, and Power*. Chicago: University of Chicago Press.

Corbin, J.M. and Strauss, A.L. (2007) *Basics of Qualitative Research: Techniques and Procedures for Developing Grounded Theory*. Thousand Oaks, CA: SAGE.

Craig, R.T. and Tracy, K. (1995) 'Grounded practical theory: the case of intellectual discussion', *Communication Theory*, 5: 248–272.

Crowe, M. (2005) 'Discourse analysis: towards an understanding of its place in nursing', *Journal of Advanced Nursing*, 51: 55–63.

Fairclough, N. (1995) *Critical Discourse Analysis: The Critical Study of Language*. Harlow, UK: Pearson Education.

Fairhurst, G.T. and Cooren, F. (2004) 'Organizational language in use: interaction analysis, conversation analysis, and speech act semantics', in D. Grant, C. Hardy, C. Oswick, & L. Putnam (eds), *The Sage Handbook of Organizational Discourse*. Thousand Oaks, CA: SAGE, pp. 131–152.

Fairhurst, G.T. and Putnam, L. (2004) 'Organizations as discursive constructions', *Communication Theory*, 14: 5–26.

Fernandez-Sola, C., Garnero-Molina, J., Manrique, G.A., Castro-Sanchez, A.M., Hernandez-Padilla, J.M., and Marquez-Membrive, J. (2012) 'New regulation of the right to dignified dying in Spain: repercussions for nursing', *Nursing Ethics*, 19: 619-628

Fine, M., Weis, L., Weseen, S., and Wong, L. (2000) 'For whom? Qualitative research, representations, and social responsibility', in N. Denzin & Y. Lincoln (eds), *Handbook of Qualitative Research*. 2nd edn. Thousand Oaks, CA: SAGE, pp. 107–132.

Foucault, M. (1972) *The Archaeology of Knowledge*. New York: Pantheon Books.

Gee, J.P. (1999) *An Introduction to Discourse Analysis: Theory and Method*. New York: Routledge.

George, A. (1979) 'Case studies and theory development: The method of Structured, Focused Comparison', in P.G. Lauren (ed), *Diplomatic History: New approaches*. New York: Free Press, pp. 43-68.

George, A. and Bennett, A. (2005) *Case Studies and Theory Development in the Social Sciences*. Cambridge, MA: MIT Press.

Grant, D., Hardy, C., Oswick, C., et al. (2004) *SAGE Handbook of Organizational Discourse*. 1st edn. Thousand Oaks: SAGE Publications.

Groscurth, C.R. (2011) 'Paradoxes of privilege and participation: the case of the American Red Cross', *Communication Quarterly*, 59: 296–314.

Hodge, B. and McHoul, A. (1992) 'The politics of text and commentary', *Textual Practice*, 2: 189–209.

Hoijer, H. (1954) 'The Sapir-Whorf hypothesis', in H. Hoijer (ed.), *Language in Culture Conference on the Inter Relations of Language and Other Aspects of Culture*. University of Chicago Press, pp. 1–8.

Le, T., Short, M. and Le, Q. (2011) *Critical Discourse Analysis: An Interdisciplinary Perspective*. Hauppauge, NY: Nova Science Publishers, Inc.

LeGreco, M. (2012) 'Working with policy: restructuring healthy eating practices and the Circuit of Policy Communication', *Journal of Applied Communication Research*, 40: 44–64.

LeGreco, M. and Canary, H.E. (2011) 'Enacting sustainable school-based healthcare: a communication-centered approach to policy and practice', *American Journal of Public Health*, 101: 431–437.

LeGreco, M. and Tracy, S.J. (2009) 'Discourse tracing as qualitative practice', *Qualitative Inquiry*, 15: 1516–1543.

Lincoln, Y.S. and Guba, E.G. (1985) *Naturalistic Inquiry*. Beverly Hills, CA: SAGE.

Lindlof, T.R. and Taylor, B.C. (2010) *Qualitative Communication Research Methods*. Thousand Oaks, CA: SAGE.

McClellan, S.E. (2012) 'Planning for a postmodern era: storytelling, public participation, and the limits of ordinary democracy', unpublished doctoral dissertation. University of Colorado at Boulder.

Mirivel, J.C. (2006) 'Getting "nipped and tucked" through talk: a communication take on cosmetic surgery', unpublished doctoral dissertation, University of Colorado at Boulder.

Mirivel, J.C. (2007) 'Managing poor surgical candidacy: communication problems for plastic surgeons', *Discourse & Communication*, 1: 309–336.

Mirivel, J.C. (2008) 'The physical examination in cosmetic surgery: communication strategies to promote the desirability of surgery', *Health Communication*, 23: 153–170.

Nahon-Serfaty, I. (2012) 'The disruptive consequences of discursive fragmentation in the organization and delivery of health care: a look into diabetes', *Health Communication*, 21: 506–516.

Nestle, M. (2007) *Food Politics: How The Food Industry Influences Nutrition and Health*. Berkeley, CA: University of California Press.

Probyn, E. (2005) 'Sex and power: capillaries, capabilities, and capacities', in C. Calhoun, C. Roject and B. Turner (eds), *The Sage Handbook of Sociology*. London: SAGE, pp. 516–529.

Probyn, E. (2008) IV. 'Silences behind the mantra: critiquing feminist fat', *Feminism & Psychology*, 18: 401–404.

Putnam, L.L. and Fairhurst, G.T. (2001) 'Discourse analysis in organizations: issues and concerns', in F. Jablin and L. Putnam (eds), *The New Handbook of Organizational Communication: Advances in Theory, Research, and Methods*. Thousand Oaks, CA: SAGE, pp. 78–136.

Rapoport, L. (2003) *How We Eat: Appetite, Culture, and the Psychology of Food*. Toronto: ECW Press.

Renn, O. (2006) 'Participatory processes for designing environmental policies', *Land Use Policy*, 23: 34–43.

Richardson, L. (2000) 'Writing: a method of inquiry', in N. Denzin and Y. Lincoln (eds), *Handbook of Qualitative Research*. 2nd edn. Thousand Oaks: SAGE Publications, pp. 923–948.

SAGE Publications. (2013) *The SAGE Handbook of Organizational Discourse*. Available at: http://www.sagepub.com/books/Book217666?siteId=sage-us&prodTypes=any&q=handbook+of+discourse&fs=1.

Scott, C.W. and Trethewey, A. (2008) 'Organizational discourse and the appraisal of occupational repertoires, heedful interrelating, and identity at work', *Journal of Applied Communication Research*, 36: 298–317.

Tracy, K. (1995) 'Action-implicative discourse analysis', *Journal of Language and Social Psychology*, 14: 195–215.

Tracy, K. (2007) 'The discourse of crisis in public meetings: case study of a school board's multi-million dollar error', *Journal of Applied Communication Research*, 35: 418–441.

Tracy, K. and Ashcraft, C. (2001) 'Crafting policies about controversial values: how wording disputes manage a group dilemma', *Journal of Applied Communication Research*, 29: 297–316.

Tracy, K. and Mirivel, J.C. (2009) 'Discourse analysis: the practice and practical value of taping, transcribing, and analysing talk', in L. Frey and K. Cissna (eds), *Routledge Handbook of Applied Communication Research*. New York: Routledge, pp. 153–177.

Tracy, K. and Tracy, S.J. (1998) 'Rudeness at 911: reconceptualizing face and face-attack', *Human Communication Research*, 25: 225–251.

Tracy, K., Martinez-Guillem, S., Robles, J.S., and Casteline, K.E. (2011) 'Critical discourse analysis and (US) communication scholarship', *Communication Yearbook*, 35: 241–286.

Tracy, S.J. (2000) 'Becoming a character for commerce: emotion labor, self-subordination, and discursive construction of identity in a total institution', *Management Communication Quarterly*, 14: 90–128.

Tracy, S.J. (2010) 'Qualitative quality: eight "big tent" criteria for excellent qualitative research', *Qualitative Inquiry*, 16: 837–851.

Trethewey, A. (2002) 'Forum introduction', *Management Communication Quarterly*, 16: 81–84.

van Dijk, T.A. (1985) *Handbook of Discourse Analysis*. London: Academic Press.

Wodak, R. (2011) 'Commentary: discourse, context, and interdisciplinarity', *Communication Yearbook*, 35: 287–296.

Wodak, R. and Fairclough, N. (2010) 'Recontextualizing European higher education policies: the cases of Austria and Romania', *Critical Discourse Studies*, 7: 19–40.

Zoller, H.M. (2003) 'Health on the line: identity and disciplinary control in employee occupational health and safety discourse', *Journal of Applied Communication Research*, 31: 118–139.

Zoller, H.M. (2012) 'Communicating health: political risk narratives in an environmental health campaign', *Journal of Applied Communication Research*, 40: 20–43.

# 6
# Critical Ethnography

Urmitapa Dutta

## Learning objectives

After reading this chapter, you will be able to:

- Outline the evolution of critical ethnography
- Discuss the philosophical assumptions underlying ethnographic approaches
- Identify the links between epistemological positions and specific methods
- Describe the critical role of the ethnographer in the research process
- Explore key ethical and validation issues in ethnographic research
- Identify the range of methods available for data collection, analysis, and dissemination of ethnographic research

## Introduction

The term ethnography is derived from the Greek *ethnos* meaning nation or people and *graphia*, meaning writing. In the classical tradition, ethnography refers to the descriptive study of 'other' (usually non-western) cultures through a researcher's immersion in that culture. However, as with many other research methods, ethnography has come to mean different things in different historical and political contexts. History is perspectival and the standpoint of the historian is embedded in the historical rendering, therefore one is bound to find several differing narratives concerning the history of ethnography (Burawoy, 2000; Denzin and Lincoln, 2011; McCall, 2006). In this chapter, ethnography is presented as a methodology rooted in the humanistic and social justice commitments of qualitative enquiry (Denzin and Lincoln, 2011). The historical development of traditions of ethnography will be discussed with a focus on critical theory as an important philosophical underpinning of this methodology. Examples of how critical ethnography is enacted in the field are provided to illustrate how the researcher can position themselves in relation to participants and the data both generated and collected through observation and interviews. Methods of data analysis are examined, with an emphasis on the re(presentation) of data as findings that can be considered reflective of a dialogic process.

# Historical overview

Ethnography, as both method and product has multiple intellectual traditions, located in diverse disciplinary, and even regional contexts (LeCompte and Schensul, 2010). The origins of ethnographic approaches may be traced to classical anthropological efforts to understand and elaborate culture. However, as a methodology it has permeated multiple academic disciplines over the past two centuries. Despite the dominance of ethnography in anthropology, anthropologists themselves do not have a unified notion of what constitutes this methodology (Hymes, 1996). Tracing the various intellectual lineages and trajectories of multiple ethnographic research designs is beyond the scope of this chapter. Instead, this section offers a historical sketch of ethnography, highlighting shifts that have been crucial to the evolution of contemporary critical ethnographic practices.

Participant observation, the dominant method of data generation in ethnography can be traced far back to the ancient Greek period, but ethnography as a social science methodology evolved mainly during the nineteenth and twentieth centuries. During the mid-to-late nineteenth century, anthropologists increasingly recognized the need for experientially gained knowledge of cultures, knowledge acquired through direct participation (Tedlock, 2000). The development of ethnography as the dominant methodological approach in anthropology is often linked with the work of two anthropologists – Franz Boas and Bronislaw Malinowski. Their contribution to ethnography lies in establishing fieldwork at the centre of ethnographic practice (Rabinow, 1985; Tedlock, 2000). Boas and Malinowski were both committed to a comprehensive understanding of culture through participant observation carried out over extended periods of stay in the field.

Starting in the 1920s, the Chicago School of Ethnography developed in the Department of Social Sciences and Anthropology at the University of Chicago. Scholars in this school changed the focus of ethnography from the culture of foreign lands towards the urban landscape (e.g., Robert Park, John Dewey, and Herbert Blumer). During the 1960s and 1970s, ethnomethodologies (Garfinkel, 1967) and symbolic and interpretive anthropologies (Turner, 1967; Geertz, 1973) also became two major influences on ethnography. *The Interpretation of Cultures* by Clifford Geertz (1973) introduced the term 'thick description' to the language of qualitative research, with its emphasis on the need to understand and elaborate the symbolic import of what is observed and systematically documented during fieldwork. These approaches added an interpretive element to ethnography in an effort to enhance the quality of ethnographic texts.

The investigation of culture, non-western cultures in particular, continued to be the most distinctive aim of ethnographies conducted at this time. The aim of ethnographic studies began to alter in the 1980s, when ethnography became a site of politicization with the influence of feminist, critical, indigenous, and postmodern approaches impacting on the process and outcomes of this research design (Lassiter and Campbell, 2010). The colonial and imperialist perspectives of classic ethnographic approaches, in which power asymmetries are implicit were questioned and critiqued. This unmasking of ethnographic authority and the deconstruction of culture were integral to the growth of more collaborative ethnographic approaches (Bourgois, 2006). There was a distinct shift towards studying existing social suffering and inequities, galvanized by contemporary moves in anthropology to carve out more activist, civic, and public agendas (Angel-Ajani, 2006; Burawoy, 2000; Hale, 2008).

# Philosophical underpinnings of ethnography

Much of nineteenth century ethnography is anchored in the philosophy of realism, the idea that reality exists independent of the researcher (Hammersley, 2002). The goal of research at this time was to produce as accurate an account of that reality as possible. Ethnography, through its emphasis on long-term contact and participation, was considered an appropriate methodology through which the reality of different cultures and communities could be elaborated. Another competing epistemology in ethnography was that of social constructivism, which argues that people construct social worlds through their interpretations and the actions stemming from such interpretations. In the context of ethnography, such a view would imply that the research product is something co-constructed by the researcher and participants.

Philosophical issues in ethnographic approaches are not limited to the apparent contradiction between realist and constructivist epistemologies. The range of epistemologies influencing ethnography is varied, which is in turn reflected in the complex and variegated ethnographic approaches. Ethnography has also been influenced by structuralism, functionalism, pragmatism, symbolic interactionism, hermeneutics, phenomenology, feminism, Marxism, post-structuralism and post-modernism (Tedlock, 2000). Over the past few decades, critical, collaborative performance, and activist ethnography with their explicit social justice agendas have begun to assume a vital place in the landscape of qualitative research (Lassiter, 2005; Madison, 2005, 2012; Sanford, 2006; Tedlock, 2011). While critical theories undergird these more recent approaches, they also reflect in part an altered conceptualization of fieldsites, which have become increasingly multi-sited and cannot be bracketed easily (Marcus, 1995). It should be noted that not all ethnographers are equally committed to understanding the philosophical underpinnings of ethnography, preferring to make the practice and production of ethnographies the foci of their inquiry (Hammersley, 1992). Nevertheless, as the next section illustrates, philosophical assumptions crucially shape research questions and the methods employed to address those questions.

---

**Activity 6.1** | **Ethnographic concepts in qualitative research**

Consider what you know about qualitative research generally and other qualitative methodologies specifically. Make a list of the philosophical and methodological concepts of ethnography that are evident in other approaches to qualitative research.

# Aligning philosophy and method with purpose

Different philosophical positions or assumptions lie at the core of methodological choices made throughout the ethnographic process, including that of writing. As ethnographers set about their study, it is important to develop a critical awareness of the philosophical underpinnings or paradigmatic stances that inform the research design. Whether the researcher acknowledges it or not, epistemological issues remain embedded in methodological deliberations. It is therefore worthwhile to reflect on why ethnography is the methodology of choice and why certain specific ethnographic approaches are privileged over others. A researcher working from a critical standpoint is likely to attend to inequities and oppression, explicating the connections between structural inequities and intimate suffering. Influences of critical–ideological standpoints are seen in critical and performance ethnographic practices (Denzin, 2008; Madison, 2005, 2012; Saldaña, 2005), in collaborative ethnography (Lassiter, 2005) as well as in relatively recent trends of public and activist anthropology with its emphasis on civic engagement and activism (Angel-Ajani, 2006; Hale, 2008). Denzin and Lincoln state:

> Ethnography is more than the record of human experience. The ethnographer writes tiny moral tales, tales that do more than celebrate cultural differences or bring another culture alive. The researcher's story is written as a prop, as a pillar that, to paraphrase William Faulkner (1967), p. 724, will help men and women endure and prevail in the opening years of the 21st century. (Denzin and Lincoln, 2011: xiii)

Similarly, in *Critical Ethnography*, Madison (2005) argues that this research design 'begins with an ethical responsibility to address processes of unfairness or injustice within a particular *lived* domain' (p. 5). This kind of work is grounded in the recognition that conditions of existence within a particular context and for specific subjects are not what they should or could be, which entails a moral and ethical responsibility of the researcher to intervene. Critical ethnographic research then involves disrupting the status quo and challenging those institutions and regimes that limit choices, constrain resources and marginalize identities. Committed to the construction of knowledge that privileges the perspectives of those who have been subjugated, critical ethnographic approaches simultaneously examine axes of race, class, culture, gender, and history. Regardless of the specific methods employed to further the action agenda, the goal of critical ethnography is to offset colonial models of ethnographic research, striving towards greater civic engagement, advocacy, activism, and collaboration. Through attempting to decolonize and democratize research, critical ethnographic approaches can potentially expand ethnographers' repertoire of engaging more meaningfully and critically with their research and practice contexts.

# Positioning the researcher

In addition to philosophical assumptions, researchers also bring their own world-views and biographies to their research endeavours. As researchers, we are located at the intersections of particular socio-political milieu, culture, and history. These intersections comprise the horizon wherein we are embedded and wherefrom we act. Positionality refers to the explication of the horizon in which we stand as researchers. A cornerstone of ethnography is the researcher's deep immersion in the community or context of the study, which makes issues surrounding positionality all the more critical. Positionality compels us to engage with our own power, privilege, and life histories and the biases and insights stemming from them (Madison, 2005). It is necessary to delineate how our positionality impacts our research relations, and the texts we produce, in order to remain firmly anchored in the empirical world of the other (Vahali, 2009). Attention to emotional and structural positionality is also critical to studying others without rendering their otherness in terms that reproduce hegemonic relationships and representations.

There is no singular ethnographic identity that can be predetermined and bracketed (Denzin and Lincoln, 2011). Instead the ethnographer has to continually contend with the question of *'when, where, how* am I?' (Trinh, 1991: 157). This complex question is tied to reflexivity, which is the practice of continually examining and evaluating our roles in specific social contexts (Finlay, 2002). A self-reflexive stance involves thinking critically about how our identities as researchers intersect with the research context. Depending on the research context, one can be faced with rather fraught situations that compel us to confront important methodological and ethical questions. In the following window into ethnography (Box 6.1), Gayatri Moorthi illustrates how taking a reflexive stance means researchers are accountable for their research paradigms, their own positions of authority, and their ethical responsibilities relative to representation and interpretation.

---

**BOX 6.1**

### Window into ethnography

It was during one of those cold winter mornings in Delhi, while I was walking towards my field site, that these challenging questions of participation, ethics and ethnography came to the fore. In 2008, I was working with a non-governmental organization (NGO) called Ashray, which provides harm reduction services to injecting drug users and HIV positive clients in one of the poorest and most marginalized communities of the city. Sudhir an elderly client stopped me, *'Can you help Amitabh, didi (sister)? His condition is very bad and these people (Ashray) are not doing anything to help. He will surely die.'* Amitabh, a

*(Continued)*

---

client of Ashray, had severe abscesses in his groin as a result of injecting drugs. He had been lying on the road for the last few days refusing all help. I promised Sudhir that I would talk to the NGO staff about Amitabh. The NGO's response however left me disturbed. They reported that Amitabh was approached previously, but had refused any kind of help. The NGO's position was clear: *'We are here to give the client choices, but we can't force them (to accept our help).'* Added to this was the unspoken but harsh reality that there were hundreds of equally desperate, but willing clients who vied for the NGO's attention. Despite the odds stacked against them, Ashray did make one last effort with Amitabh, who after much insistence agreed to go to the hospital. But he died en route.

The staff, unlike me, had come to accept such deaths with equanimity and would seek to normalize the event by citing 'fate', choice and a lack of resources. My own 'participation' had come very late and one could argue was minimal. I juggled with the ideas of intervention as opposed to participation as an ethnographer and questioned balancing research ethics with humanistic concerns. *Could I make Amitabh's 'ordinary' death extraordinary by laying bare the dynamics that lead him to make such a 'choice'? Was that the extent of my role as a participant observer?* As ethnography seeks to find a place in a rapidly changing social milieu we must ask of ourselves these questions as we return to the field each time.

Reflexive use of autobiography can also serve as a critical tool for establishing inter-subjectivity in research (Roth, 2005). Ethnographers can utilize relevant life events, experiences, memories, and structural positioning to expand out of the context of their own experiences to understand the issue being studied. For example, the author's 'fieldsite' is also her hometown. Critically reflecting on her own struggles around the experience of home and belonging have crucially shaped her understanding of the emotional nuances of ethnic conflict in Northeast India. She integrates auto-ethnographic material into her critical ethnography of ethnic conflict in Northeast India in a number of ways. This integration is influenced by the tradition of interpretive interactionism (Denzin, 2001), which takes a narrative approach to understand lived experience as it is enacted and performed. Interpretive interactionism utilizes epiphanic moments, that is, moments of heightened self-awareness of the situated self that emerge from crises of identity/representation (Denzin, 2001). She employed such moments, locating them in larger discursive spaces in an attempt to provide a more holistic reading of the complex geopolitics of Northeast India and the identity struggles of the people who live there. Auto ethnographic material also includes discursive self-reflexive insights, musings, anecdotal information, alternative discourses, and her emotional responses connected to the project. These are offered as 'thick descriptions' (Geertz, 1973) and at times as insights into her reflexivity in relation to the project (Davies, 1999). Thus narrative functions as an integral part of data utilized in this project. Such an approach was crucial not only because of the local, cultural understandings that the researcher brought to the work; but also because the lens through which she views this research is inextricably intertwined with her life history. By dissolving conventional boundaries between ethnography, oral history, testimonials, and storytelling, it is possible to open up discursive spaces in which to explore alternative frames and meanings, especially for those in marginalized locations.

## Data generation and collection

Fieldwork is a cornerstone of ethnography typically involving the researcher's participation in a community or setting over an extended period of time. The level and type of immersion or involvement varies widely across philosophical paradigms and ethnographic genres. From the point of view of data collection, fieldwork may be conceptualized as a phase of deep immersion in a particular setting, which allows the ethnographer to gather available data to illuminate the research questions or issues being explored. As with other qualitative research methodologies, ethnographic research too requires a design that charts the pragmatics of the research process. This includes developing core research questions or goals, being mindful of the paradigms that frame the questions, ethical and methodological deliberations, and an optimal timeline across which to execute the project. Crucially though, ethnographic research, from its very conception to dissemination is an iterative, rather than linear process.

Research questions animating an ethnographic project can have multiple starting points. One could be interested in a specific issue or problem and design an ethnographic project to understand those issues. For example, Duneier's (1999) interest in, and concern for, people on the margins of urban societies led him to study the lives of individuals who make their livelihoods on the sidewalks of Greenwich Village in New York. Alternatively, a researcher could be invested in a particular community, with the issues pertaining to that community forming the basis of their questions.

Sampling in ethnographic research is usually criterion-based and purposeful, that is, participants are selected to provide the most information-rich data possible. Two modes of sampling often employed in ethnographic research are snowball sampling and theoretical sampling. In snowball sampling, existing participants who have been interviewed are used to recruit further participants. This technique is particularly useful while working with at-risk populations or populations that are difficult to access. Theoretical sampling is the process of selecting 'incidents, slices of life, time periods, or people on the basis of their potential manifestation or representation of important theoretical constructs' (Patton, 2002: 238). The goal of theoretical sampling is to arrive at a nuanced understanding of emerging theoretical concepts (Glaser and Strauss, 1967). Thus considerations such as sample size may be decided iteratively as data collection progresses.

Ethnographic data span the spectrum of information that could potentially illuminate the research questions at hand. Specific methods employed to gather data may include formal and informal interviews, conversations, observations, surveys, focus groups, performances, and collection of archival data. Data can take the form of texts such as ethnographic fieldnotes, interview transcripts, documents, artifacts, and images. Methods of data collection may be used singly or in creative combinations to secure multiple perspectives and span multiple levels of analysis. For instance, the author of this chapter employed focus groups to elicit the perspectives of marginalized youth in her ethnographic research based in Northeast India. This decision stemmed from the recognition that youth are more comfortable having a discussion with their peers rather than responding individually to interview prompts, which was the method of choice while interviewing more powerful stakeholders.

Classic forms of ethnography entail studying everyday or already existing conditions. However, critical ethnographers, working within a social justice framework, are ethically bound to both intervene and address issues of inequity and injustice (Madison, 2005). The following window into the author's fieldwork illustrates how social action can be conceptualized within fieldwork using a participatory action research framework.

---

**BOX 6.2**

### Window into critical ethnographic

In the course of her fieldwork in the Garo Hills region of Northeast India, the author learned about a workshop planned for the region by a national level not-for-profit, nongovernmental organization based in Delhi. The workshop was proposed as part of this group's endeavour to represent the aspirations of the Indian civil society with special attention to grassroots activism. The author became an informal member of the local coordinating body that was constituted to attend to the logistics at the local level. Originally, her involvement in this group was animated by a desire to examine how multiple interests and agendas unfold in the course of the collaboration between the non-profit organization and the local community. In the course of her participation though, she learned that the workshop was planned as a large-scale community event that would bring together diverse audiences. Recognizing the potential of such a space for inclusion and assertion of youth voices, she leveraged her ongoing community involvement and longstanding credibility in the community to propose a youth panel as one of the items on the workshop agenda. The panel was proposed as an effort to articulate local youth perspectives. For the participating youth, this project was broadly framed as an opportunity for them to talk about what *they* view as issues of concern within the community, to engage with those issues, investigate them, and then share their understandings with a diverse audience at the workshop. While a major goal was to engage the perspectives of young people in Garo Hills and create a legitimate space for their voices to be taken seriously, an equally important focus was on facilitating participation across ethnic lines. In practical terms, this meant the creation of a third space, a *safe space* that would enable all members to participate in their local community.

---

Ethnographic research typically entails partnerships and relationships with individuals, organizations, agencies, and/or communities over a sustained period.

Relationships are paramount and can critically shape how the ethnographic project unfolds over time. Today many ethnographers recognize how power and history influence the ethnographic process with a consequential shift towards ethnographic processes that prioritize dialogue, intersubjectivity, and collaboration (Marcus and Fischer, 1986; Lassiter, 2005). An entire treatise could be devoted to the subject of relationships in ethnographic research and still fail to exhaust the vicissitudes and complexities that establishing connections like these entail. What is crucial to remember at the outset is however, that like any relationship, ethnographic relationships also evolve and shift over time, and require nurturing that is context-dependent.

During fieldwork and data collection, ethnographers can be faced with multiple, competing demands across a number of domains – personal (e.g., time constraints, life circumstances), professional (e.g., rules and standards imposed by professional organizations, politics of evidence), ethical (e.g., institutional review boards), and economic (e.g., funding agencies). While regulatory ethics as codified by ethics committees or institutional review boards and professional societies provide some basic guidelines, it is ultimately the researcher's responsibility to ensure that the methods used do not unwittingly perpetuate the marginalization of oppression of participants (Bradley, 2007; Cahill, 2007). Setting out into the field, one also has to be mindful of the fact that ethical issues and conundrums often remain inextricably tied to methodological decisions. In other words, decisions about sample and site selection, as well as the kinds of questions asked can have far reaching consequences in relation to meeting the aims of the study.

## Data analysis

The goal of analysis is to seek patterns as well as irregularities, examining data for explanations of the phenomenon being studied. Ethnographic data typically take textual forms although images and artifacts are increasingly becoming more popular. The first step in data analysis is usually coding, which is the process of organizing data into meaningful units or categories. Coding can be inductive or deductive. In practice though, coding tends to be informed by theoretical predilections as well as emergent understandings in the field. Ethnographers can draw upon a range of analytic approaches depending on their epistemological foundations, theoretical orientation, and research objectives. Approaches to data analysis can include: cultural analysis (Quinn, 2005; D'Andrade, 2005; Strauss, 2005), thematic analysis (Boyatzis, 1998), narrative analysis (Bruner, 1986; Clandinin and Rosiek, 2007; Loseke, 2007; Strauss and Corbin, 1997; Charmaz, 2006), content analysis (Hsieh and Shannon, 2005; Neuendorf, 2002), and discourse analysis (Potter, 2003; Wetherell, 1998). These approaches are not mutually exclusive and it is possible to combine several strategies to highlight different facets of the issue being studied and thus arrive at a more in-depth understanding.

---

**BOX 6.3**

**Innovative methodological combinations for more contextualized understandings**

A recent monograph entitled 'How socialization happens on the ground: Narrative practices as alternate socializing pathways in Taiwanese and European-American families' demonstrates an instance of combining multiple methods of data gathering and analysis. The authors sought to examine the nature and role of personal storytelling in everyday socialization processes. Aiming to develop a more in-depth, dynamic, and contextualized understanding of childhood socialization, the researchers effectively combined ethnographic fieldwork, interviews with parents, qualitative microanalysis of stories, longitudinal home observations, and baseline frequencies of occurrence. They also carried out comparative analyses, where they compared the two detailed and contextualized cases – that of Taipei and Longwood to underscore regularities and/or differences to address any potential cultural omissions. The researchers thus attended to both narrative and discursive practices. Through this innovative combination of methods, they were able to elucidate the similarities as well as differences in the ways in which practices of personal storytelling are configured in Taipei and Longwood, while maintaining the complexities and unique meanings characterizing each context; thus offering an enriched and culturally nuanced understanding of early socialization processes.

---

# Quality in ethnographic research

One of the criticisms often levied against ethnographic research is the perceived lack of boundaries between journalistic inquiry and ethnographic inquiry. Atkinson (1992) has responded to this charge by pointing out that superior quality work in these two fields shares some common elements, namely extensive research, ethical conduct, systematic review of literature or evidence, and coherent presentation of findings, mindful of their impact. Furthermore, the emergent and relatively less-structured qualities of ethnographic research often lead to the mistaken notion that using such a process is not systematic enough to ensure quality and rigour, both of which are traditionally established through validation. Validation processes are concerned with making *truth* claims in research. Yet, with poststructural and postmodern turns in the social sciences, we know that power is crucially implicated in what is constructed as *truth*, leading to a questioning of the authority wherein such claims are made. Such turns have resulted in methodological approaches that focus on *justice* rather than *truth* (Smith, 2005). The question then stands: are we doing justice to the narratives of our participants? This is complicated further when we try to account for multiple perspectives. Thus, we have to critically reflect on the implications of the story that gets told through our research in order to appraise its quality.

Critical ethnography demands a reinterpretation and reframing of traditional notions of validity. Elements of intersubjectivity and representation and how we identify, understand, and utilize each of these concepts are integral to appraising the quality of critical ethnographic research (Madison, 2005), rather than appealing to a predetermined set of authoritative norms (Lincoln, 1995). Validation processes are not simply individual cognitive acts; rather they are social and political practices that can have real life implications for different subject populations. It thus follows that validation processes in critical ethnographic research must attend to: the role/impact of macrosocial forces on the issue being studied, as well as their influence on the perceptions and experiences of people; how power operates at personal, relational, and larger structural levels; promotion of psychopolitical literacy; education and empowerment of participants to address social injustice at individual, community, and institutional levels; promotion of solidarity; and positionality and contingencies. We have to contend with these issues as part of ensuring quality and rigour of ethnographic research.

Validation is also tied to ethics and should be considered on an ongoing basis throughout processes of research and writing. There are a number of validation processes and principles that are particularly suited for critical ethnographic research. A few are discussed here. A validation principle that attends to some of the above considerations is *ontological authenticity* (Lincoln and Guba, 1986), that is, achieving a more sophisticated and enriched conception of reality that was not previously appreciated. Guba and Lincoln also argue that validation criteria should include how secure we feel as ethnographers to use our findings to inform or construct social policy and legislation (Guba and Lincoln, 2005). Prilleltensky (2003) talks about psychopolitical validity, offering a set of questions to guide and critically evaluate research in the service of understanding, resisting, and addressing forms of oppression. Two types of psychopolitical validity – epistemic validity that accounts for power dynamics operating at psychological and political levels in efforts to understand the phenomenon of interest, and transformative validity, the extent to which change towards liberation is effected in personal, interpersonal and structural domains are offered by this author. Validity in this formulation thus assesses the extent to which the critical ethnographic research disrupts the status quo.

## (Re)presentation and dissemination of ethnographic research

The end product of an ethnographic study is usually an ethnographic text. This scenario is changing as ethnographic approaches to data collection and analysis are increasingly employed in conjunction with other research methods such as performance. Even in cases where ethnography constitutes the dominant methodology, there has been a growing interest in exploring alternative modes of representation, wrought by the crisis of representation accompanying the postmodern turn (Denzin and Lincoln, 2011). This is evidenced by the emerging field of critical performance ethnography and ethnodrama (Conquergood, 1991; Denzin, 2008; Madison, 2012; Saldaña, 2005) each of which are anchored in the need to render visible the dynamic interactions between power, politics, and poetics. These shifts are animated by ethical concerns around voice and silencing, attempting to strike the delicate balance between the participants' voices and meaning and those of the ethnographer's interpretation and authority.

Ethnographic production is a complex process and entails more than simply 'writing up' one's research findings. It departs from many other research methods in that the processes of data analysis and production of the ethnographic text are iteratively intertwined. Interpretations and meaning making do not end with a formal phase of data analysis but continue throughout the writing process. Although ethnographic texts are typically authored by researchers they can also, to varying extents, be written collaboratively (Lassiter, 2005; Duneier, 1999). Lassiter (2005) makes the argument that if ethnographers acknowledge the intersubjective and collaborative processes involved in fieldwork, then the production of the ethnographic text should also reflect this dialogic process. While production of the ethnographic text is a major academic enterprise, the dissemination of ethnographic findings can take many forms, including non-academic avenues. For example, in an ethnography of the dietary and health practices of women in a rural Indian context that discovers critical gaps between health policies and practice leading to poor health outcomes, there is an ethical imperative to disseminate the findings among agencies involved in providing or overseeing healthcare in those settings. Depending on the implications of the findings, avenues such as news media, local agencies, policy recommendations, and grassroots activism can be used to complement, or as an alternative to, peer-reviewed publications.

---

**Activity 6.2** — **Production of the ethnographic text**

Select some examples of published ethnographic writing, including those related to your research area. Review these with an eye to the following domains:

i) narrative form and structure
ii) techniques and devices used to convey complexity
iii) use of 'I'
iv) expression of ethnographic voice and authority
v) expression of participants' voices
vi) presentation of multiple perspectives/voices
vii) description of method
viii) action potential or policy implications of the findings

As part of this process, consider the kind of ethnographic text you would like to produce. These ideas will undergo multiple iterations, but this is a good place to begin.

---

# Conclusion

Ethnography is a vast methodological field spanning multiple disciplines and epistemologies. Although this chapter discusses issues pertaining to more critical and activist ethnographies, in doing so, it does not necessarily invalidate other ethnographic approaches. Ultimately, there are key questions that determine the appropriateness of using particular ethnographic approaches. What are the major goals for this project (academic, personal, intervention)? What are the questions that the ethnographic research is trying to address? What specific methods are used? What modes of analysis are best suited for the particular questions as well the methods used? Is the analysis in consonance with the ideological framework guiding the project? Each of these questions should be revisited regularly over the course of the research process. Our identities and identifications as researchers seem to be as much in flux as our 'fields' and we have to be open to adapting inquiry as understanding deepens, thus providing the space to pursue new directions as they develop.

The primary goal of ethnography may not be that of 'generalization' in the more positivist sense of the term. Instead, the foci of ethnographers may be viewed as intensely 'local' in that it takes up the concerns of what would be considered a relatively small group of people in a particular part of the world. The local as it were, continues to be of intrinsic value in ethnography. Simultaneously though, there is an ethical imperative to examine how the local or micropolitical within a specific context exists in complex interplays with macrosocial national, transnational and global formations. As Tsing (2005) argues: 'To study a particular instance offers a window into the universal. The local enfolds into the global and the universal; our devotions must simultaneously know the local and its transcendence' (p. 97).

---

### KEY POINTS

- Classical ethnographic traditions involved descriptive studies of 'other', usually non-western cultures. The dominant method was that of participant observation. Influenced by critical, feminist, indigenous, and postmodern approaches, ethnography became politicized and led to the emergence of critical and activist ethnographic approaches
- Traditional ethnographic approaches were grounded in realist epistemologies. Ethnography has also been influenced by social constructivism as well as critical realism
- Different epistemological positions undergird the different ethnographic approaches. A critical–ideological standpoint underlies critical ethnographic approaches geared towards addressing social injustice and oppression through research
- As researchers we bring own worldviews and biographies into the research context. Positionality compels us to engage with our own power, privilege, and life histories and the biases and insights stemming from them. It is crucial to assume a self-reflexive stance, that is, thinking critically about how our identities as researchers intersect with the research context
- Sampling in ethnographic research is usually purposeful and criterion-based to provide the most information rich data possible. Sampling also depends on the depth and breadth of information needed to illuminate the issue at hand
- In the context of critical ethnography, validity assesses the extent to which the research offers a more discursively complex understanding of reality and disrupts the status quo

- What are our values and how do they inform the research process?
- How do we evaluate our own potential to do harm in ethnographic research – in both fieldwork and through presenting our findings? What can we do to anticipate unintended negative consequences and work to circumvent them?
- How is the 'local' connected to macrosocial forces and to the larger human condition?
- Whose voice(s) are we privileging in our ethnography? Why?
- What implications does the ethnographic project have for the stakeholders involved? Are there policy implications? How can those implications be disseminated?
- How can we strike a balance between rigour and ethics in ethnographic research?

## Suggested further reading

Madison, S. (2012) *Critical Ethnography: Methods, Ethics and Performance*. Thousand Oaks: SAGE Publications.

'The revised Second Edition of Critical Ethnography guides readers through theories, methods, and ethics of ethnographic research creating a confidence to complete fieldwork while demonstrating analytical and theoretical depth. This text highlights the productive links between theory and method and how both become more valuable as they interact through fieldwork. Theoretical concepts range from queer theory, feminist theory, and critical race theory to Marxism and phenomenology. The methodological techniques range from designing and asking in-depth interview questions and developing rapport to coding and interpreting data. The various theories and methods culminate in three fictional ethnographic case studies that guide readers on how to incorporate theoretical concepts with their interpretations and data analysis' (SAGE Publications, 2013).

## References

Angel-Ajani, A. (2006) 'Expert witness: notes towards revisiting the politics of listening', in V. Sanford and A. Angel-Ajani (eds), *Engaged Observer: Anthropology, Advocacy, and Activism*. New Jersey: Rutgers University Press, pp. 76–89.

Atkinson, P. (1992) *Understanding Ethnographic Texts*. London: SAGE Publications.

Bourgois, P. (2006) 'Anthropology in the global state of emergency', in V. Sanford and A. Angel-Ajani (eds), *Engaged Observer: Anthropology, Advocacy, and Activism*. New Jersey: Rutgers University Press, pp. ix–xii.

Boyatzis, R.E. (1998) *Transforming Qualitative Information: Thematic Analysis and Code Development*. London: SAGE Publications.

Bradley, M. (2007) 'Silenced for their own protection: how the IRB marginalizes those it feigns to protect', *ACME: An International E-Journal for Critical Geographies*, 6: 339–349.

Bruner, E.M. (1986) 'Ethnography as narrative', in V. Turner and E.M. Bruner (eds), *The Anthropology of Experience*. Champaign-Urbana: University of Illinois Press, pp. 139–158.

Burawoy, M. (2000) 'Introduction: reaching for the global', in Burawoy, M., Blum, J., George, S., Gille, Z., & Thayer, M. (eds), *Global Ethnography: Forces, Connections, and Imaginations in a Postmodern World*. Berkeley: University of California Press, pp. 1–40.

Cahill, C. (2007) 'Repositioning ethical commitments: participatory action research as a relational praxis of social change', *ACME: An International E-Journal for Critical Geographies*, 6: 360–373.

Charmaz, K. (2006) *Constructing Grounded Theory: A Practical Guide Through Qualitative Analysis*. Thousand Oaks: SAGE.

Clandinin, D.J. and Rosiek, J. (2007) 'Mapping a landscape of narrative inquiry: borderland spaces and tensions', in D.J. Clandinin (ed.), *Handbook of Narrative Inquiry: Mapping a Methodology*. Thousand Oaks, CA: SAGE, pp. 35–76.

Conquergood, D. (1991) 'Rethinking ethnography: towards a critical cultural politics', *Communication Monographs*, 58: 179–194.

D'Andrade, R. (2005) 'Some methods for studying cultural cognitive structures', in N. Quinn (ed.), *Finding Culture in Talk: A Collection of Methods, Culture, Mind, and Society*. 1st edn. New York: Palgrave Macmillan.

Davies, C.A. (1999) *Reflexive Ethnography: A Guide to Researching Selves and Others*. London: Routledge.

Denzin, N.K. (2001) *Interpretive Interactionism*. 2nd edn. Thousand Oaks: SAGE Publications.

Denzin, N.K. (2008) *Searching for Yellowstone: Race, Gender, Family and Memory in the Postmodern West*. Walnut Creek, CA: Left Coast Press.

Denzin, N.K. and Lincoln, Y.S. (2011) 'Introduction: the discipline and practice of qualitative research', in N.K. Denzin and Y.S. Lincoln (eds), *Handbook of Qualitative Research*. 4th edn. Thousand Oaks: SAGE Publications, pp. 1–20.

Duneier, M. (1999) *Sidewalk*. New York: Farrar, Straus and Giroux.

Faulkner, W. (1967) 'Address upon receiving the Nobel Prize for Literature', in M. Cowley (ed.), *The Portable Faulkner*. New York: Viking, pp. 723–724.

Finlay, L. (2002) '"Outing" the researcher: the provenance, process, and practice of reflexivity', *Qualitative Health Research*, 12: 531–545.

Garfinkel, H. (1967) *Studies in Ethnomethodology*. Engelwood Cliff: Prentice-Hall Inc.

Geertz, C. (1973) *The Interpretation of Cultures*. New York: Basic Books.

Glaser, B.G. and Strauss, A.L. (1967) *The Discovery of Grounded Theory: Strategies for Qualitative Research*. New York: Aldine.

Guba, E. and Lincoln, Y.S. (2005) 'Paradigmatic controversies, contradictions, and emerging confluences', in N. Denzin and Y.S. Lincoln (eds), *Handbook of Qualitative Research*. 3rd edn. London: SAGE, pp. 191–216.

Hale, C.R. (2008) *Engaging Contradictions: Theory, Politics, and Methods of Activist Scholarship*. University of California Press.

Hammersley, M. (1992) *What's Wrong with Ethnography?* London: Routledge.

Hammersley, M. (2002) 'Ethnography and realism', in A.M. Huberman and M.B. Miles (eds), *The Qualitative Researcher's Companion*. 1st edn. Thousand Oaks, CA: SAGE Publications, pp. 65–80.

Hsieh, H.F. and Shannon, S.E. (2005) 'Three approaches to qualitative content analysis', *Qualitative Health Research*, 15: 1277–1288.

Hymes, D. (1996) *Ethnography, Linguistics, Narrative Inequality: Toward an Understanding of Voice.* London: Taylor & Francis.

Lassiter, L.E. (2005) *The Chicago Guide to Collaborative Ethnography.* Chicago; University of Chicago Press.

Lassiter, L.E. and Campbell, E. (2010) 'What will we have ethnography do?', *Qualitative Inquiry*, 16: 757–767.

LeCompte, M. and Schensul, J. (2010) *Designing and Conducting Ethnographic Research.* Lanham: Rowman Altamira.

Lincoln, Y.S. (1995) 'Emerging Criteria for Quality in Qualitative and Interpretive Research', *Qualitative Inquiry*, 1: 275–289.

Lincoln, Y.S. and Guba, E.G. (1986) 'But is it rigorous? Trustworthiness and authenticity in naturalistic evaluation', *New Directions for Program Evaluation*, 73–84.

Loseke, D.R. (2007) 'The study of identity as cultural, institutional, organizational, and personal narratives', *Theoretical and Empirical Integrations. The Sociological Quarterly*, 48: 661–688.

Madison D.S. (2005) *Critical Ethnography: Method, Ethics, and Performance.* Thousand Oaks: SAGE Publications.

Madison, D.S. (2012) *Critical Ethnography: Method, Ethics, and Performance.* Thousand Oaks: SAGE Publications.

Marcus, G.E. (1995) 'Ethnography in/of the world system: the emergence of multi-sited ethnography', *Annual Review of Anthropology*, 95–117.

Marcus, G.E. and Fischer, M.M.J. (1986) *Anthropology as Cultural Critique: An Experimental Moment in the Human Sciences.* Chicago: University of Chicago Press.

McCall, G.J. (2006) 'The fieldwork tradition', in D. Hobbs and R. Wright (eds), *The Sage Handbook of Fieldwork.* Thousand Oaks: SAGE Publications, pp. 3–22.

Miller, P. and Fung, H. (2012) 'Introduction', *Monographs of the Society for Research in Child Development*, 77: 1–14.

Neuendorf, K.A. (2002) *The Content Analysis Guidebook.* Thousand Oaks: SAGE Publications.

Patton, M.Q. (2002) *Qualitative Research and Evaluation Methods.* Thousand Oaks: SAGE Publications.

Potter, J. (2003) 'Discourse analysis and discursive psychology', in P.M. Camic, J.E. Rhodes and L. Yardley (eds.), *Qualitative Research in Psychology: Expanding Perspectives in Methodology and Design.* Washington: American Psychological Association, pp. 73–94.

Prilleltensky, I. (2003) 'Understanding, resisting, and overcoming oppression: toward psychopolitical validity', *American Journal of Community Psychology*, 31: 195–201.

Quinn, N. (2005) 'Introduction', in N. Quinn (ed.), *Finding Culture in Talk: A Collection of Methods, Culture, Mind, and Society.* 1st edn. New York: Palgrave Macmillan, pp. 1–34.

Rabinow, P. (1985) 'Discourse and power: on the limits of ethnographic texts', *Dialectical Anthropology*, 10: 1–13.

SAGE Publications (2013) *Critical Ethnography: Method, Ethics and Performance*. Available at: http://www.sagepub.com/books/Book234498?q=ethnography&prodTypes=Books&pager.offset=0&fs=1.

Saldaña, J. (2005) *Ethnodrama: An Anthology of Reality Theatre*. Walnut Creek, CA: Altamira Press.

Sanford, V. (2006) 'Introduction', in V. Sanford and A. Angel-Ajani (eds), *Engaged Observer: Anthropology, Advocacy, and Activism*. New Jersey: Rutgers University Press, pp. 1–18.

Smith, L.T. (2005) *Decolonizing Methodologies: Research and Indigenous Peoples*. New York: Zed Books.

Strauss, A.L. and Corbin, J.M. (1997) *Grounded Theory in Practice*. Thousand Oaks: SAGE Publications.

Strauss, C. (2005) 'Analyzing discourse for cultural complexity', in N. Quinn (ed.), *Finding Culture in Talk: A Collection of Methods, Culture, Mind, and Society*. 1st edn. New York: Palgrave Macmillan, pp. 203–242.

Tedlock, B. (2000) 'Ethnography and ethnographic representation', in N. Denzin and Y.S. Lincoln (eds), *Handbook of Qualitative Research*. 2nd edn. Thousand Oaks: SAGE Publications, pp. 455–486.

Tedlock, B. (2011) 'Braiding narrative ethnography with memoir and creative nonfiction', in N.K. Denzin and Y.S. Lincoln (eds), *Handbook of Qualitative Research*. 4th edn. Thousand Oaks: SAGE Publications, pp. 331–340.

Trinh, T.M. (1991) *When the Moon Waxes Red: Representation, Gender and Cultural Politics*. New York: Routledge.

Tsing, A.L. (2005) *Friction: An Ethnography of Global Connection*. Princeton, NJ: Princeton University Press.

Turner, V.W. (1967) *The Forest of Symbols: Aspects of Ndembu Ritual*. Ithaca: Cornell University Press.

Vahali, H.O. (2009) *Lives in Exile: Exploring the Inner World of Tibetan Refugees*. New Delhi: Routledge.

Wetherell, M. (1998) 'Positioning and interpretative repertoires: conversation analysis and post-structuralism in dialogue', *Discourse & Society*, 9: 387–412.

# 7

# Grounded Theory

Jane Mills, Melanie Birks and Karen Hoare

---

**Learning objectives**

After reading this chapter, you should be able to:

- Discuss the historical, philosophical and methodological underpinnings of traditional, evolved and constructivist grounded theory
- Examine the position of the researcher and its relationship to philosophical and methodological alignment in a grounded theory study
- Identify various sources of data for use in grounded theory studies
- Outline the process of analysis used in grounded theory research

---

## Introduction

This chapter will discuss the history of grounded theory and the various philosophical positions that researchers can assume, which will influence their choice of which package of methodology/methods to adopt. For the purposes of this chapter, we identify three main genres of grounded theory: traditional, evolved and constructivist. Traditional grounded theory is underpinned by postpositivism, evolved grounded theory is founded on symbolic interactionism and constructivist grounded theory has its roots in constructivism. Differences between grounded theory methodologies will be outlined in relation to implementing a study, including the position of the researcher, processes of data generation and collection, and data analysis. The development of a modern day dissemination strategy for the findings from a grounded theory study will also be discussed in relation to impact and innovation.

## History of the methodology

Glaser and Strauss, the originators of grounded theory, began researching together in the 1960s at the University of California, San Francisco (UCSF). Their study of how terminal patients dealt with the knowledge that they were dying, and the reactions of hospital staff caring for these terminally ill patients (Glaser and Strauss,

1965), resulted in a new way of organizing and analysing qualitative data that they called grounded theory. Subsequent to this initial study, they published *The Discovery of Grounded Theory* (Glaser and Strauss, 1967), to explain how theory could be developed inductively from data, as opposed to being deductively tested and then accepted or refuted (Noerager Stern, 2009).

Glaser left the academy in the early 1970's to work as an independent researcher and author. In 1978 he published *Theoretical Sensitivity*, providing further explanation of the grounded theory methods initially described in *Discovery*. In particular, Glaser focuses on identifying the unit of analysis, core variables and a basic social or psychological process in the data (Charmaz, 2008; Noerager Stern, 2009). Importantly Glaser uses this text to explain in detail the use of 18 sociological coding families to assist with the process of integrating a grounded theory, as well as the concept of theoretical sensitivity. Since this time, Glaser has self-published a large number of texts (1978; 1992; 1998; 2001; 2004; 2005; 2007b; 2008) and journal articles (2002a; 2002b) about traditional grounded theory, establishing the *Grounded Theory Institute* (Rhine, 2012) to promote the work of this methodological approach.

Strauss published *Qualitative Analysis for Social Scientists* (1987) in which he writes about symbolic interactionism and grounded theory methods. Three years later Strauss co-authored *The Basics of Qualitative Analysis* (1990) with Juliet Corbin, in which they offer a number of very concrete strategies for using grounded theory methods, including accounting for the context of the study in the process of data analysis. It is this shift in focus that has led the work of Strauss and Corbin to be dubbed 'evolved grounded theory'. Unfortunately, Glaser viewed Strauss and Corbin's book as 'undermining his intellectual property' (Noerager Stern, 2009: 28), contending that their procedures contradicted the fundamental premise of inductive grounded theory by forcing data and analysis into pre-conceived categories (Glaser, 1992).

Strauss passed away in 1996 prior to the publication of the second edition (1998) of his and Corbin's popular, but controversial text. There are a number of changes in both the second and third edition (Corbin and Strauss, 2008) of this text, which reflect Corbin's continued influence on the development of evolved grounded theory over time. Of note, the conditional matrix originally conceived by Strauss and founded in his intellectual work as a symbolic interactionist has been amended with a decentring of action in this analytical heuristic.

During Strauss and Glaser's tenure at the UCSF they taught a number of research methods classes that were instrumental in further developing their individual thinking about grounded theory methods. Undoubtedly, there was a divergence of priority issues for consideration in their implementation of a grounded theory study that developed during this time, with Strauss' interest in action and context leading to evolved grounded theory, as compared to Glaser's focus on the emergence of theory from the data set collected, which is aligned with the thinking of traditional grounded theorists.

Of the students that Strauss and Glaser taught at UCSF, a number went on to become grounded theorists in their own right. Collectively this group of researchers are known as 'second generation grounded theorists' (Morse, Stern Corbin, Bowers, Clarke and Charmaz, 2009) and includes a number who have been particularly influential in contemporary thinking about this qualitative methodology. In particular, Charmaz's development of the genre of constructivist grounded theory (2006, 1995, 2000), marks the next stage in the history of this popular research design. Mentored by both Glaser and Strauss, Charmaz suggests that it was their profound influence that led to her rethinking the possibilities for grounded theory using a different philosophical approach.

Over time postmodern scholars have also challenged the tenets of traditional grounded theory as epistemologically naïve and mirroring a modernist philosophy. Adele Clarke, another second generation grounded theorist, is acknowledged as having brought grounded theory around the postmodern turn (2005) through a process she named situational analysis. Situational analysis uses three cartographic approaches that allow researchers to analyse complex situations of inquiry, namely: situational maps, social world/arenas maps and positional maps. Clarke's concern with power relations and context draws upon the work of Foucault who she compares, contrasts and links with Strauss' mandate to develop the analytic work of context and action (Strauss, 1993).

Stemming from these debates and developments has been the evolution of grounded theory in a methodological spiral (Mills, Chapman, Bonner and Francis, 2006) from its origins in postpositivism to now including a range of other methodological choices that can underpin the use of a common set of essential grounded theory methods. It is the choice of philosophy and methodology that determines how grounded theory methods can be used to different effects in a congruent research design (Birks and Mills, 2011).

## Philosophical underpinnings

The question of 'truth' or the nature of reality lies at the heart of a discussion about philosophical underpinnings of any qualitative research methodology. As Guba and Lincoln (2004) argue 'whether or not the world has a "real" existence outside of human experience of that world is an open question' (p. 202). The methodological schools of thought that shape the use of grounded theory methods are clearly divided on the question of reality. A traditional approach to grounded theory argues there is an objective reality that exists outside of human perception but that it is only ever imperfectly perceived. Evolved and constructivist grounded theorists generally assume what is called a relativist position, where reality is understood as 'relative to a specific conceptual scheme, theoretical framework, paradigm, form of life, society or culture ... there is a non-reducible plurality of such conceptual schemes' (Bernstein, 1983: 8).

Glaser, as a traditional grounded theorist, is influenced in his thinking by mid-twentieth century postpositivism (1978, 1992), which results in him seeking general explanation and prediction that is not context specific to a research site. While enrolled in his PhD at Columbia University, Glaser underwent rigorous quantitative research training under the tutelage of Paul Lazarsfield, which influenced his approach to the use of grounded theory methods. The concept of emergence has a strong presence in traditional grounded theory, with the idea that given time and the correct application of grounded theory methods, a theory will emerge from the data that is representative of an external reality.

Strauss studied and taught at the eminent Chicago School of Sociology at Chicago University and was a student of George Herbert Mead who first described the principles of symbolic interactionism, a theory later developed by one of his colleagues, Herbert Blumer (1969). Symbolic interactionism is a perspective that arises from the philosophy of pragmatism, and assumes society, reality and self are constructed through interaction – relying on language, communication and the social group in this process. Philosophically, pragmatism tentatively assumes that an objective reality does exist but that it has multiple natures and is open to many interpretations (Sandstrom, Martin and Fine, 2003).

It is this relativist position that becomes apparent in the work of Charmaz (2000) with its focus on developing and implementing a constructivist grounded theory methodology. For those new to this literature, a frequently asked question is the difference between constructivism and constructionism. The difference between the two perspectives is that constructivists suggest meaning is located within the mind of an individual, whereas constructionists place greater emphasis on defining meaning within relationships (Gergen, 2009). Raskin (2008) argues that constructivists and social constructionists are uneasy bedfellows, as constructivists may feel that social constructionists' rejection of individual construing is too extreme. Charmaz and Bryant (2011) discuss the epistemological elements of constructivist grounded theory, all of which hinge on the position of the researcher in relation to the participants and the data. 'Unlike earlier versions of grounded theory, constructivist grounded theory accepts the notion of multiple realities, emphasizes reflexivity, and rejects assumptions that researchers should and could set aside their prior knowledge to develop new theories' (p. 293).

## Position of the researcher

Originally, neither Glaser nor Strauss (1967) attended to how they influenced the research process, collected data or represented research participants. For a traditional grounded theorist who supposedly enters the field as a 'blank slate' (Glaser, 1978), data collection is straightforward, and data are self-evident with the analysis of these providing explanations and predictions. Participants' words and actions are data that need to be obtained in as objective a manner as possible (Strauss and Corbin, 1990; Glaser and Strauss, 1967; Glaser, 1978). In *Discovery*, Glaser and Strauss discuss how data can often be obtained by the researcher 'without the people he talks with, overhears or observes recognizing his purpose … he may obtain his data clandestinely in order to get it quickly, without explanations, or to be allowed to obtain it at all' (Glaser and Strauss, 1967: 75). Clearly, since this time, ethical requirements have become more stringent with the need for participants to provide informed consent considered an essential requirement of conducting rigorous research, however in the 1960s these tenets were not always adhered to as thoroughly as today, as is reflected in the previous quote.

There are some who argue that Strauss stood outside the various critiques of positivistic methods in the 1960s (Bryant and Charmaz, 2007), intensified as they were by the cultural ruptures experienced globally at this time (see Chapter 2). Rather than focusing on the implications of conducting a postpositivist traditional grounded theory, Strauss adopted a pragmatic study of action in his work and 'understood the methodological implications of symbolic interactionism' (p. 49) in relation to using grounded theory methods.

Regardless of their early lack of discussion about the epistemological nuances of evolved grounded theory, Strauss and Corbin (1994) do demonstrate a shift in how they view their interaction with participants over time, stating 'the interplay between researcher and the actors studied – if the research is intensive – is likely to result in some degree of reciprocal shaping' (p. 280). In their later text they clarify their definition of interplay as the 'researcher ... actively reacting to and working with data' (1998: 58). This, and the last edition of their text (Corbin and Strauss, 2008), acknowledges the co-construction of meaning between researcher and participant as implicit in the generation of data from unstructured interviews.

In relation to how an evolved grounded theorist might position themself, Strauss (1987) as a symbolic interactionist, clearly identifies that researchers' biographies exert influence on the use of grounded theory methods, and that there is a need for this to be accounted for during the research process. Strauss and Corbin (1998) later advocate that researchers keep a written record of their metaphorical journey, usually in the form of a reflective journal, with the aim of learning from their experiences.

Constructivist grounded theorists also acknowledge that they enter a field of inquiry with their own histories and theories, which require scrutiny during the research process. Charmaz's work (2006) identifies the researcher as author, reconstructing experience and meaning from data. Her important contribution to the evolution of grounded theory is that rather than being a distant expert, grounded theorists are instead implicit in the research process, co-constructing experience and meaning with research participants (Charmaz, 2008).

Constructivist grounded theorists do not assume that theory emerges from data; rather they believe researchers construct the analysis of the data and thus the categories and core category that eventually makes up a grounded theory. Explanations of data are presented in context and participants' voices are portrayed as integral to the analysis and presentation of findings. When engaging in evolved or constructivist grounded theory, researchers must think about what they themselves are doing, be explicit about how and why they are doing it and consider the effect they are having on the data and eventual findings. Memos are the most useful of grounded theory methods for this activity (Birks et al., 2009). As discussed in Chapter 2, reflexivity is of paramount importance in constructivist grounded theory, with the researcher at the same time striving to know the world from the viewpoint of the research participants.

Positioning yourself as anything other than a traditional grounded theorist requires a transformation of the participant/researcher relationship so the researcher prioritizes and analyses interactions occurring between the two. Epistemologically the great majority of evolved grounded theorists, and all constructivist grounded theorists, believe it is impossible to separate researcher from participant in the generation of data, however this is what taking a traditional position requires. Each methodological position places a different value on the contribution that various forms of data can make to a grounded theory, although grounded theory methods for analysing data remain the same – no matter what constitutes the data.

One such method that has direct relevance to the position that the researcher has in relation to their study is the need to possess theoretical sensitivity. As is discussed in the following section, a defining characteristic of grounded theory research is that it aims to develop theory that is grounded in data. Theoretical sensitivity is essential to the process. Theoretical sensitivity is defined as 'the ability to recognize and extract from the data elements that have relevance for your emerging theory' (Birks and Mills, 2011: 59). The experience that you bring to your research and the position that you take towards it will influence how theoretically sensitive you are to what you see in the data, how you analyse that data and the direction that you follow in response to this analysis.

## Aligning philosophy and methodology with purpose

Grounded theory is most appropriately employed in studies where little is known about a phenomenon of interest. The purpose of a grounded theory study whether traditional, evolved or constructivist, is to inductively generate theory from data. Theory can be defined as 'an explanatory scheme comprising a set of concepts related to each other through logical patterns of connectivity' (Schwandt, 2007: 292). Often this theory describes a process that is explicated through the use of grounded theory methods. There are two types of grounded theory discussed in the literature: substantive and formal. Substantive grounded theories are concerned with a delimited area of inquiry. Formal grounded theories take the core category of a substantive grounded theory as a starting point and then 'sampling more widely in the original substantive area and in other substantive areas and then constantly comparing with the purpose to conceptualize the general implications' (Glaser, 2007a: 100).

A number of studies purporting to be grounded theory may employ some of the essential grounded theory methods but never actually result in the generation of theory. As such we may regard them as employing a 'grounded theory approach' or using grounded theory methods. These studies never actually generate a theory that has the potential to explain a phenomenon, and therefore cannot be considered to be grounded theory research (Birks and Mills, 2011).

## Data generation and collection

You will see from the preceding discussion that your philosophical and methodological position dictates if you consider yourself an objective instrument of data collection *from* participants, or a subjective active participant in data generation *with* participants. There will be an opportunity for you to both generate and collect data depending on the source, however when it comes to human participants your philosophical position will determine how you interact with them in order to elicit data.

As is the case with other qualitative methodologies, interviews are a popular source of data in grounded theory research. Other sources of data include documents, literature and elicited material such as questionnaires and surveys. Materials produced by the researcher in support of the research process can also be used as sources of data. Field notes and memos are examples of such materials, with memos being a particularly important strategy in conducting grounded theory research as they provide an opportunity to log research activities, record decision-making processes and progress analytical procedures (Birks et al., 2009).

Grounded theory is characterized by concurrent data collection and analysis. This means that each data collection event is followed by analysis of the data that is generated or collected. Initially the researcher employs purposive sampling when commencing data collection in a grounded theory study. Following initial analysis, the researcher employs a technique called *theoretical sampling* to determine where, when and how to collect further data that will inform the developing theory. Through theoretical sampling, coupled with theoretical sensitivity, the researcher is able to ensure that the raw data is reflected, or grounded, in the final theory produced.

---

**Activity 7.1** ──── **Theoretical sampling in grounded theory**

Consider the concept of theoretical sampling and its purpose in grounded theory. How does the purpose of theoretical sampling align with the philosophical underpinnings of this methodology?

---

## Analysis of data

Grounded theory data analysis involves a number of strategic methods that facilitate the development of a theory that is grounded in the data. These methods include those referred to in the preceding discussion: concurrent data collection and analysis; theoretical sampling to direct data generation and collection; theoretical

**Table 7.1**  Types of grounded theory coding

|  | **Traditional** | **Evolved** | **Constructivist** |
|---|---|---|---|
| **Initial** | Open coding | Open coding | Initial coding |
| **Intermediate** | Selective coding | Axial coding | Focused coding |
| **Advanced** | Theoretical coding | Selective coding | Theoretical coding |

sensitivity to aid the identification of concepts relevant to the developing theory; and memoing as an important strategy in facilitating and recording analytical decision making. In addition, analysis in grounded theory research is reliant on a process of constant comparison in which each incoming segment of data is compared with existing data in the process of coding and category development.

The process of data analysis in a grounded theory study can be divided into three phases of coding – *initial*, *intermediate* and *advanced*. A convenient way of explaining the similarities and divergences between traditional, evolved and constructivist grounded theorists in relation to data analysis is to begin with a comparative table of terminology (Table 7.1, adapted from Birks and Mills, 2011), providing a reference point to which you can return throughout the following discussion.

## Initial coding

Traditional and evolved grounded theorists referred to the initial phase of coding as *open coding*, while constructivists use the term *initial coding* for this first stage of the coding process in grounded theory. As the process that commences analysis, initial coding begins with the first data generated or collected and involves the fracturing of data into smaller segments for the purpose of comparison with other data segments from the same or other data sources. Questions are asked of the data to ascertain its relevance to the study, the processes that are evident and what the data is saying (Glaser, 1978). Strauss and Corbin in their initial work (1990, 1998) propose the use of a coding paradigm (subsequently modified in Corbin and Strauss, 2008) to guide questioning of the data around condition, actions/interactions and consequences. Initial coding progresses into intermediate coding as categories start to take shape.

## Intermediate coding

Theory development occurs in grounded theory research through a process of gradual abstraction of concepts during the various stages of coding. Following initial coding, an intermediate phase of coding occurs. Intermediate coding is known as *selective*, *axial* and *focused coding* by traditional, evolved and constructivist grounded theorists, respectively. This process involves furthering theory generation through the development of categories, often around a core variable (Glaser,

1978) or category axis (Strauss and Corbin, 1990, 1998). Theory development is advanced through the identification of relationships between categories as analysis progresses. As intermediate coding moves to the advanced phase, the researcher looks to saturate categories. Saturation occurs when the process of theoretical sampling does add further to the development of categories that form the final theory. Throughout the intermediate coding phase, analysis may be aided by the use of diagramming (Birks and Mills, 2011).

### Advanced coding

During advanced coding, final theoretical integration occurs. Both traditional and constructivist grounded theorists refer to this stage as *theoretical coding*, while evolved grounded theorists use the term *selective coding*. Theoretical integration is aided by the use of techniques such as the writing of the *storyline*. The storyline technique was originally proposed by Strauss and Corbin in their 1990 text and was further developed as a tool for theoretical integration by Birks, Mills, Chapman and Francis (2009). The storyline provides both a narrative of the grounded theory and assists the researcher to identify gaps in the theory during the final phases of its development.

Once the storyline is developed, the grounded theory is finalized through the use of *theoretical codes*. Theoretical codes 'are advanced abstractions that provide a framework for enhancing the explanatory power of your storyline and its potential as theory' (Birks and Mills, 2011: 123). Glaser (1978, 2005) advocates the use of theoretical codes and describes a number of concepts drawn from sociology for this purpose. He does, however, advise the use of theoretical codes drawn from other disciplines and we encourage you to consider coding frameworks that may be drawn from your own discipline (Birks and Mills, 2011).

### Quality and rigour

Quality in grounded theory research is dependent on the researcher demonstrating rigour through the use of techniques such as those discussed in Chapter 13, including demonstrating an ability to conduct the research, ensuring philosophical and methodological alignment, and the correct application of essential grounded theory methods discussed in this chapter. Chief among these is the use of memoing. In addition to its use in aiding reflexivity and analytical processes, memoing enables the researcher to maintain an audit trail of the research process that will serve to reinforce and articulate quality activities in the conduct of the research (Birks and Mills, 2011; Birks, Chapman and Francis, 2008).

Traditional, evolved and constructivist grounded theorists have all developed criteria for the purpose of evaluating the outcomes of grounded theory research. These criteria are summarized in Table 7.2

**Table 7.2** Criteria for evaluating a grounded theory

| Traditional | Evolved | Constructivist |
|---|---|---|
| **Glaser and Strauss (1967):**<br>Does it *fit* with its intended use?<br>Is it *understandable* for those who will work with it?<br>Is it *general* enough for flexible application?<br>Does the user have *control* over its use? | **Strauss and Corbin (1990):**<br>Does the theory demonstrate *data quality*?<br>Is the *research process* adequate?<br>What evidence is there of *empirical grounding*? | **Charmaz (2006):**<br>Does the theory have *credibility*?<br>Does it demonstrate *originality*?<br>Does it have *resonance*?<br>What evidence is there of its *usefulness*? |
| **Glaser (1978):**<br>Does the theory *fit* the data?<br>Does it *work* in that it possesses explanatory and predictive power?<br>Is it *relevant*?<br>Is it *modifiable*? | **Strauss and Corbin (1998):**<br>Does the theory demonstrate *data quality*?<br>What judgements can be made about *theory quality*?<br>Is the *research process* adequate?<br>What evidence is there of *empirical grounding*? | |
| **Glaser (1992):**<br>Does the theory *fit* the data?<br>Does it *work* in that it possesses explanatory and predictive power?<br>Is it *relevant*?<br>Is it *modifiable*?<br>Does the theory demonstrate *parsimony*?<br>Does it have *scope* for broader application? | **Corbin and Strauss (2008):**<br>10 basic criteria for appraising theoretical outcomes<br>13 additional criteria for judging structure and process | |

(Adapted from Birks and Mills, 2011).

---

> **Activity 7.2** — **Philosophical alignment of evaluation criteria**
>
> Consider the evaluation criteria outlined in the above table in light of your knowledge of the three genres of grounded theory. Construct a simple table of your own indicating how these criteria reflect the philosophical underpinnings of each genre.

# Presentation and dissemination of findings

We have written in detail previously (Birks and Mills, 2011) about the four principles of presenting the findings from a grounded theory study:

1. Identify your audience
2. Decide what level of analytical detail is required

3. Choose an appropriate style of writing
4. Present your grounded theory as a whole. (p. 131)

Each one of these principles aims to increase the impact of your research through effectively disseminating your grounded theory findings. Research impact can be defined as 'an effect on, change or benefit to the economy, society, culture, public policy or services, health, the environment, or quality of life, beyond academia' (Cameron, 2012). This definition differs from others in that it asks the researcher to think beyond traditional methods of disseminating research findings such as peer reviewed journal articles and theses, and instead challenges them to think about how they can otherwise increase their exposure to community members, industry, policymakers and government. This is not to say however, that the importance of traditional methods of disseminating research findings are in any way lessened, with the metrics associated with measuring impact such as citation rates, and by association open access publishing, becoming increasingly important in evaluating your performance as a researcher.

Grounded theory findings are by their very nature amenable to knowledge translation and implementation, so it's important to capitalize on having such an easy product to sell. Terras (2012a) provides a witty and informative commentary on the potential for social media to develop your research profile. Using a combination of green open access (Harnad, Brody, Vallieres, Carr, Hitchcock, Gingras, Oppenheim, Stamerjohanns and Hilif, 2004), Twitter®, and blogging, Terras (2012b) demonstrates how combining social media with traditional peer-reviewed journal articles can dramatically increase exposure to your findings, and hopefully increase their impact long term.

Raising your profile though, is only one part of a dissemination strategy that needs to also focus on the potential contribution that your grounded theory study can make in respect of innovation and change. A recent report from Australia examines the growing international trend for governments to undertake impact and innovation assessments as part of their research funding strategy (ATNU/Group of 8, 2012), a topic we discuss at length in Chapter 14. The salutary message from this report for grounded theorists is to think about the challenges of communicating: 'what was done, why it was done, what difference it made and how the research made it happen' (p.19).

## Conclusion

Grounded theory as a research methodology has an interesting evolutionary path and a rich history in terms of philosophical development. Those researchers who favour a more structured approach to the qualitative research process often favour grounded theory. Grounded theory methods provide a suite of strategies for conducting an investigation into phenomena about which little is known. Attention to careful application of grounded theory methods in the conduct of a study ensures quality outcomes in the form of a theory with explanatory power that can make a significant contribution in terms of knowledge and potential practical application.

## CRITICAL THINKING QUESTIONS

- In your own words, define traditional, evolved and constructivist approaches to grounded theory.
- Think about a research study that you may be considering undertaking using grounded theory. Which of the philosophical positions described in this chapter do you think most closely align with your personal philosophy and the proposed aims of your research?
- Consider data generation and collection in grounded theory. How might the essential methods used in this approach to research influence the sources and treatment of data in grounded theory? How does this differ from other methodologies with which you are familiar?
- Grounded theory produces quite specific outcomes in the form of a theory that is grounded in the data. What impact might this have on the potential for dissemination and application of the research relative to other methodologies?

## Suggested further reading

Birks, M. and Mills, J. (2011) *Grounded Theory: A Practical Guide*. London: SAGE Publications.

'This is a highly practical book which introduces the whole range of grounded theory approaches. Unlike most existing books in this area, which are written from a particular philosophical standpoint, this text provides a comprehensive description of the strategies and techniques employed in this methodology. Birks and Mills' accessible and highly-readable text is driven by practical case examples throughout to help the reader get to grips with the process of doing grounded theory analysis for themselves. The book deploys a variety of educational activities to guide readers through both the principles and the application of grounded theory, making this an ideal starter text for those new to the approach. This is an ideal first introduction to grounded theory for any student or researcher looking to use grounded theory approaches in their analysis for the first time' (SAGE Publications, 2013).

# References

ATNU/Group of 8. (2012) 'Excellence in innovation: research impacting our nation's future – assessing the benefits'. Available at: http://www.atn.edu.au/newsroom/Docs/2012/ATN-Go8-Report-web.pdf.

Bernstein, R. (1983) *Beyond Objectivism and Relativism: Science, Hermeneutics, and Praxis*. Philadelphia: University of Pennsylvania Press.

Birks, M. and Mills, J. (2011) *Grounded Theory: A Practical Guide*. London: SAGE Publications.

Birks, M., Chapman, Y. and Francis, K. (2008) 'Memoing in qualitative research: probing data and processes', *Journal of Research in Nursing*, 13: 68–75.

Birks, M., Mills, J., Chapman, Y., and Francis, K. (2009) 'A thousand words paint a picture: the use of storyline in grounded theory', *Journal of Research in Nursing*, 14: 405–418.

Blumer, H. (1969) *Symbolic Interactionism: Perspective and Method*. Berkeley: University of California Press.

Bryant, A. and Charmaz, K. (2007) *Handbook of Grounded Theory*. London: SAGE Publications.

Cameron, F. (2012) *Research Impact*. Available at: http://www.arc.gov.au/media/arc_presentations.htm.

Charmaz, K. (1995) 'Grounded Theory', in J. Smith, R. Harre and L. Langenhove (eds), *Rethinking Methods in Psychology*. London: SAGE Publications, pp. 27–65.

Charmaz, K. (2000) 'Grounded theory: objectivist and constructivist methods', in N.K. Denzin and Y.S. Lincoln (eds), *The Handbook of Qualitative Research*. 2nd edn. Thousand Oaks, CA: SAGE Publications, pp. 509–535.

Charmaz, K. (2006) *Constructing Grounded Theory: A Practical Guide Through Qualitative Analysis*. Thousand Oaks: SAGE.

Charmaz, K. (2008) 'Constructionism and the Grounded Theory Method', *Handbook of Constructionist Research*. New York: The Guilford Press, pp. 397–412.

Charmaz, K. and Bryant, A. (2011) 'Grounded theory and credibility', in D. Silverman (ed.), *Qualitative Research: Issues of Theory, Method and Practice*. 3rd edn. London: SAGE, pp. 291–309.

Clarke, A. (2005) *Situational Analysis: Grounded Theory After the Postmodern Turn*. Thousand Oaks, CA: SAGE Publications.

Corbin, J.M. and Strauss, A.L. (2008) *Basics of Qualitative Research: Techniques and Procedures for Developing Grounded Theory*. Los Angeles: SAGE Publications.

Gergen, K.J. (2009) *An Invitation to Social Construction*. London: SAGE Publications.

Glaser, B.G. (1978) *Theoretical Sensitivity: Advances in the Methodology of Grounded Theory*. Mill Valley, CA: Sociology Press.

Glaser, B.G. (1992) *Basics of Grounded Theory Analysis*. Mill Valley: Sociology Press.

Glaser, B.G. (1998) *Doing Grounded Theory: Issues and Discussions*. Mill Valley, CA: Sociology Press.

Glaser, B.G. (2001) *The Grounded Theory Perspective: Conceptualization Contrasted With Description*. Mill Valley, CA: Sociology Press.

Glaser, B.G. (2002a) 'Constructivist grounded theory?', *Forum: Qualitative Sozialforschung/Forum: Qualitative Social Research*, 3. (accessed 15 September 2005).

Glaser, B.G. (2002b) 'Grounded theory and gender relevance', *Health Care for Women International*, 23: 786–793.

Glaser, B.G. (2004) 'Remodelling grounded theory', *Forum: Qualitative Sozialforschung/Forum: Qualitative Social Research*, 5. (accessed 21 January 2008).

Glaser, B.G. (2005) *The Grounded Theory Perspective III: Theoretical Coding*. Mill Valley, CA: Sociology Press.

Glaser, B. (2007a) 'Doing formal grounded theory', in A. Bryant and C. Charmaz (eds), *The Sage Handbook of Grounded Theory*. London: SAGE Publications, pp. 97–113.

Glaser, B.G. (2007b) *Doing Formal Grounded Theory: A Proposal*. Mill Valley, CA: Sociology Press.

Glaser, B.G. (2008) *Doing Quantitative Grounded Theory*. Mill Valley: Sociology Press.

Glaser, B.G. and Strauss, A.L. (1965) *Awareness of Dying*. New York: Aldine.

Glaser, B.G. and Strauss, A.L. (1967) *The Discovery of Grounded Theory: Strategies for Qualitative Research*. New York: Aldine.

Guba, E. and Lincoln, Y. (2004) 'Competing paradigms in qualitative research', in S.N. Hesse-Biber and P. Leavy (eds), *Approaches to Qualitative Research: A Reader on Theory and Practice*. New York; Oxford: Oxford University Press, pp. 17–38.

Harnad, S., Brody, T., Vallieres, F., Carr, L., Hitchcock, S., Gingras, Y., Oppenheim, C., Stamerjohanns, H., and Hilif, E. (2004) 'The green and the gold roads to Open Access', *Nature*, 17.

Mills, J., Chapman, Y., Bonner, A., and Francis, K. (2006) 'Grounded theory: the spiral between positivism and postmodernism', *Journal of Advanced Nursing*, 58: 72–79.

Morse, J.M., Stern, P.N., Corbin, J., Bowers, B., Clarke, A.E., and Charmaz, K. (2009) *Developing Grounded Theory: The Second Generation*. Walnut Creek, CA: Left Coast Press.

Noerager Stern, P. (2009) 'In the beginning Glaser and Strauss created Grounded Theory', in J.M. Morse, P.N. Stern, J. Corbin, B. Bowers, A.E. Clarke and K. Charmaz (eds), *Developing Grounded Theory: The Second Generation*. Walnut Creek: Left Coast Press.

Raskin, J. (2008) 'The evolution of constructivism', *Journal of Constructivist Psychology*, 21: 1–24.

Rhine, J. (2012) *Grounded Theory Institute*. Available at: http://www.groundedtheory.com.

SAGE Publications (2013) *Grounded Theory: A Practical Guide*. Available at: http://www.sagepub.com/books/Book233955?siteId=sage-us&prodTypes=any&q=birks&fs=1.

Sandstrom, K., Martin, D. and Fine, G. (2003) *Symbols, Self and Social Reality: A Symbolic Interactionist Approach to Social Psychology and Sociology*. Oxford: Oxford University Press.

Schwandt, T. (2007) *The Sage Dictionary of Qualitative Inquiry*. Thousand Oaks, CA: SAGE Publications.

Strauss, A.L. (1987) *Qualitative Analysis for Social Scientists*. New York: Cambridge University Press.

Strauss, A.L. (1993) *Continual Permutations of Action*. New York: Aldine De Gruyter.

Strauss, A.L. and Corbin, J.M. (1990) *Basics of Qualitative Research: Grounded Theory Procedures and Techniques*. Newbury Park, CA: SAGE Publications.

Strauss, A.L. and Corbin, J.M. (1994) 'Grounded theory methodology: an overview', in N.K. Denzin and Y.S. Lincoln (eds), *Handbook of Qualitative Research*. Thousand Oaks: SAGE, pp. 273–285.

Strauss, A.L. and Corbin, J.M. (1998) *Basics of Qualitative Research: Techniques and Procedures for Developing Grounded Theory*. Thousand Oaks: SAGE Publications.

Terras, M. (2012a) 'The Impact of Social Media on the Dissemination of Research: Results of an Experiment', *Journal of Digital Humanities*, 1.

Terras, M. (2012b) *Melissa Terras' Blog*. Available at: http://melissaterras.blogspot.com.au.

# 8
# Historical Research

Seán L'Estrange

┌─ **Learning objectives** ─────────────────────────────────────────────┐

After reading this chapter, you should be able to:

- Trace the roots of historical research
- Explore the diverse philosophical foundations that underpin historical research
- Reconcile the unique position of the historical researcher in relation to their inquiry
- Describe the implications for philosophical and methodological alignment when working with historical data sources
- Outline processes of data collection and analysis and dissemination of outcomes in historical research

└───────────────────────────────────────────────────────────────────────┘

## Introduction

'The past is a foreign country: they do things differently there.' These words capture a peculiarly modern attitude to the past, reflected in diverse aspects of culture from time-travel fantasies, costume dramas, to historical theme parks, and reinforced by institutions such as heritage industries, museums, archives, and the academic disciplines of history and archaeology (Lowenthal, 1985). It is also the prevailing attitude of the social sciences, crystallized in the overriding concern with the present that defines disciplines such as anthropology, economics, geography, political science and sociology, not to mention more applied academic fields such as business studies, criminology, education, health, and social policy. Nonetheless, the importance of studying the past has not been entirely overlooked by researchers. The myriad ways in which the past shapes the present, the lessons it may hold for us, and the ways in which it can be exploited as a source of data – all have inspired forms of historical enquiry within a wide range of disciplines. 'Historical research' is the umbrella term used to refer to these (often conflicting) research activities. What it involves, the varied forms it takes, and how it might be utilized in different research projects, is the focus of this chapter.

# History of the methodology

'History' as a form of chronicle, frequently aimed at recording and celebrating the great deeds of past rulers, has been around for millennia and has existed in varying forms in different societies, both literate and oral (Woolf, 2011). Modern historical research, however, traces its roots to the middle of the nineteenth century, when the constellation of academic and scientific disciplines we know today was beginning to emerge in an organized and professional form. In most accounts of this process, the name of Leopold von Ranke (1795–1886) stands out as one of the leading figures concerned with establishing historical enquiry as a distinctive discipline capable of holding its own among the other emerging natural, human, and social sciences. Largely, this task involved redefining the nature and purpose of historical enquiry, specifying the legitimate range and scope of historical source materials, establishing strict protocols for their use as evidence (including criteria for identifying documents, procedures for authenticating them, rules for their interpretation) and developing strong guidelines for how history was to be written (Iggers and Powell, 1990). Reinforced by Ranke's own example as a practicing historian in numerous works, this new model of how historical enquiry was to be conducted gradually came to establish itself as the dominant form of historiography practiced in Western universities by the close of the nineteenth century (Iggers and Wang, 2008). Though the fortunes of historical enquiry have fluctuated over the course of the past century as competing visions challenged its pre-eminent place within the discipline of history (Stern, 1973; Iggers, 1997), the 'Rankean' model remains strong to this day. Forming a component part of the training of most historians, the model has been codified in undergraduate textbooks (Elton, 2002 [1969]), and has vocal defenders Evans (1997; 2002)) capable of defending its lasting value against a wide range of critics and criticisms. Furthermore, as a conceptualization of the nature of history as a professional academic discipline, promoting the image of practicing historians digging for details in dusty archives, the Rankean model retains a strong grip on the contemporary imagination – including that of other researchers within the human and social sciences.

Perhaps partly for this reason, most researchers in the human and social sciences have eschewed historical enquiry. Thus despite the fact that many of the pioneers of today's social-scientific disciplines – such as Adam Smith (1723–90), Alexis de Tocqueville (1805–59), Karl Marx (1818–1883), and Max Weber (1864–1920) – routinely drew upon history in their work, historical research outside the confines of the discipline of history has remained very much a minority pursuit. In part a result of the differentiation of enquiry into distinct disciplines jealous of their boundaries and particular identities, the marginalization of historical enquiry is also a consequence of the enormous attraction of a particular image of science that has helped shape today's social-scientific disciplines (Lepenies, 1988; Fleck, 2011). Seduced by the prestige of the natural sciences and dazzled by methods such as experimentation and quantification, many researchers regarded the kinds of evidence available to historians (documents, artifacts, relics) as second-rate kinds of data that were simply too weak to support strong scientific claims. Thus in a now classic exchange between two eminent sociologists representing competing currents within the human and social sciences, Goldthorpe (1991) decried the turn towards history as forfeiting the rigour of quantitative methods and robust data sets, while Mann (1994) defended the integrity of historical data and criticized Goldthorpe for privileging one form of evidence at the expense of all others, thereby excluding the potential for historical perspective on the present and dismissing all forms of enquiry that did not adhere to an idealized notion of quantitative enquiry. Furthermore, the image of the historian as preoccupied with detailed descriptions of particular events and individuals – often distant in time or obscure in significance – discouraged present-centred researchers from engaging with their work. What, after all, could such isolated antiquarian details tell us about politics in a democratic age, social relationships in the era of the internet, economics in a world of global finance, or the problems of population and over-consumption in a world on the precipice of an unprecedented environmental crisis? History, it seemed to many, was little more than a well-honed craft for producing 'stories' – often interesting, sometimes entertaining, and occasionally morally or practically instructive, but of limited relevance to disciplines concerned with systematic explanation of the modern world.

This, at least, was the dominant attitude for much of the twentieth century. History was recognized as a respected scholarly discipline, but like the study of languages, law, literature and philosophy, it was not regarded as (even potentially) one of the social sciences. Nevertheless, and despite the fact that most historians were quite happy to keep their distance from the social sciences – many remained critical of the pretensions of social scientists and viewed the new disciplines with suspicion – there was a continual exchange of ideas, concepts, and research techniques across disciplinary boundaries and between the humanities and social sciences that resulted in an expansion of the repertoires of historical enquiry. This cross-fertilization of ideas led to a radical transformation of the discipline of history itself, with new fields such as economic history and social history – in which concepts and techniques from social-scientific research were put to use in investigating the past – emerging in the 1960s alongside political, diplomatic and military history as major fields of enquiry. Furthermore, it also led to the creation of hybrid fields such as historical demography, historical geography and historical sociology during the 1960s and 1970s, and from the 1990s onwards, the effects of feminism and postmodernism began to be felt within the discipline. In addition, the process of inter-disciplinary exchange led to the formation of networks and communities of researchers united by a shared sense of the reciprocal importance of history and the social sciences. The Social Science History Association, established in 1975, is one such association, publishing its own journal *Social Science History* in which the work of historical researchers in the social sciences has been published for almost forty years.

Today the established fields of historical enquiry are numerous – within, outside and alongside the discipline of history. As a result, the term 'historical research' refers to an ever-widening range of research activities whose scope extends far beyond that first formulated by Ranke and his contemporaries. The continued and progressive broadening of the notion of 'historical source materials', and the concomitant expansion of ways in which highly diverse and heterogeneous materials are utilized as evidence in historical enquiry, was central to this diversification and to the proliferation of different forms of historical enquiry. Fossils, bone fragments, and shards of pottery now figure as evidence in geology and archaeology, while countless types of documents, artifacts and relics are used as evidence in fields as different as art history, urban history, the history of everyday life, the history of sexuality, and the history of disease. Even good old-fashioned political history increasingly uses source materials other than official documents stored in archives. In short, all kinds of documents, artifacts and relics provide grist for today's expansive historical mill. Hence what constitutes 'historical research' as a distinctive methodology (if indeed it is one) remains intensely problematic. To be sure, adopting some of the research practices of historians and/or drawing upon historical source materials are distinguishing marks of historical research in the humanities and social sciences. Yet beyond that, divergent visions of the scholarly and scientific enterprise begin to interfere in attempts to define the varied kinds of historical research conducted under its auspices.

## Philosophical underpinnings

The uses of historical research within the humanities and social sciences are as diverse as the forms of historical enquiry that are practiced within, outside, and alongside the discipline of history. This renders it particularly difficult to articulate a single coherent philosophy that could unite all its practitioners under one banner. By way of illustration, consider the case of the aforementioned Social Science History Association. In 1998, the association organized two sessions of its annual conference to focus specifically upon the question of the links between history and the social sciences as part of seeking a clearer definition of the raison d'être of the association (Baker, 1999). The result was a series of papers presenting contrasting (and conflicting) visions of historical enquiry and the social-scientific enterprise. Thus Abbott (1999) celebrated the anarchic plurality of the association and suggested that the central challenge for historical social science lay in devising new genres of research and writing, while Wetherell (1999) bemoaned such a state of affairs and called for the re-instatement of formal theory and formal quantitative methods to their former position as cornerstones of the association. Kasakoff (1999) meanwhile critiqued many of the assumptions of the association's project and called instead for a greater appreciation of culture, time and temporality within the association, suggesting that this might be accomplished by researchers in different disciplines actively learning to practice the techniques of other disciplines in order to overcome the ingrained assumptions peculiar to each. Thus, despite sharing active membership of the association, and despite being dedicated practitioners of historical enquiry within the social sciences, agreement on the nature of scholarly and social-scientific investigation of the past proved elusive, if not illusory. Judging by recent issues of the association's journal, it remains so to this day.

The difficulty in arriving at a common philosophy stems in part from divergent visions of the scholarly enterprise. Like Wetherell (1999), some consider the scientific status of disciplines to rest upon the systematic use of formal theory and the construction and testing of formal hypotheses via strict (often quantitative) methods. Self-consciously emulating what they regard as the modus operandi of the natural sciences, these researchers tend to regard the past as primarily a rich and varied source of data – a vast storehouse of the multitude of things said, done, and created by human beings. Human history, therefore, tends to be conceived as a kind of 'natural laboratory' in which researchers can conduct tests, trials and experiments. Thus historical research may be undertaken to unearth crucial data against which a hypothesis might be tested, or to assemble data sources into a body of evidence from which a plausible generalization might be formulated, or to investigate the value or validity of some important concept or other by testing its applicability in specific historical contexts. In this conception of the scholarly enterprise, historical research is very much a 'handmaiden' to scientific disciplines.

Other historical researchers, however, regard their work as closer to that of the humanities, and though not averse to formal–theoretical ventures or systematic use of quantitative methods, such devices tend to have a subordinate position within the overall enterprise. What matters most in this vision of the place of historical enquiry in the scholarly enterprise is how historical research can contribute to a better understanding of human society, and consequently of the present. Stressing the fundamental role of the past in shaping the present, and highlighting the myriad ways in which past human activities continue to act upon the present, historical enquiry is undertaken to illuminate and explain important features of the contemporary world. However, the forms of historical enquiry utilized to this end are highly diverse and include many conflicting and incompatible stratagems. As a result, this second category is itself heterogeneous and without a unifying philosophy of its own. Thus the differences, say, between Foucault's studies of Greek and Roman sexual mores (1985, 1986), and Mintz's study of sugar production and the construction of the modern 'sweet tooth' (1985), are such that the two have little in common beyond the conviction that many contemporary practices are only fully intelligible through an appreciation of the historical legacies that continue to shape them. In terms of practical methodologies, source materials and styles of analysis, they are very different, yet they are united by their insistence that it is often necessary to understand the present *through* study of the past. Consequently, beyond broad agreement that the present is inextricably linked to past human activity – often quite distant in time – and that these often need to be factored into our understanding of the contemporary world, there is little basis for constructing a common framework.

In short, there is no common underlying philosophy for the use of historical research in the humanities and social sciences, nor is it likely that one could be formulated in such a way as to win over the majority of practicing historical researchers. Despite recurrent attempts to formulate a unified vision of historical enquiry as part of an integrated scientific enterprise – some of which stretch back as far as Marx and include Max Weber as a leading example – competing visions of historical enquiry and disagreements over the nature of the scholarly and scientific enterprise continue to frustrate attempts to forge a shared philosophy capable of uniting all its practitioners.

## Positioning the researcher

From the point of view of many researchers focused on contemporary issues, historical researchers have the unique (and undesirable) distinction of not being in a position to directly engage with their subject matter, much less generate customized data. Unless they are engaged in specialist kinds of historical research such as life-course studies, oral history, or biographical research (Miller, 2000, 2005) in which there is scope for interviewing, observing or measuring their subjects, they are at the mercy of previous societies' predilections for producing and preserving records and artifacts. Consequently not only are they not in a position to generate the kind of data their research might ideally like to use, but the very existence of any relevant data is sometimes in doubt. While some regard this as the Achilles' heel of historical research methods, others accept it as the fate of most research in the humanities and social sciences. For even the most zealous champion of quantification is socially precluded from conducting experimentation in the manner of the natural sciences and hence can't obtain proper experimental data. Archaeologists, meanwhile, have been restricted to the most basic kinds of evidence conceivable, yet coupled with sophisticated techniques and the right kind of creative scientific imagination, they have nevertheless enhanced our knowledge and understanding of prehistoric human life and otherwise 'lost' societies and civilizations. In short, provided one does not operate with too blinkered a notion of 'science', then the position of the historical researcher can be seen to be not as peculiar or as disadvantaged as is sometimes made out.

Nevertheless, there is a distinctive feature of historical research that poses particular questions for how a researcher conceives her position as a researcher: time. Or more precisely, the *passage* of time. For to the extent that historical enquiry extends further back into the past, there is not only a progressive diminution in the surviving stock of records and relics, but there is also the added challenge of learning how to use as evidence what are often quite foreign materials. Furthermore, with respect to most historical events and processes, researchers have the benefit of hindsight in knowing the outcome of that which they are studying. Each of these – distance and hindsight – present particular challenges to the historical researcher with respect to how she positions herself, vis-à-vis her materials and/or subject matter.

Distance in time can present different challenges. On the one hand, an archaeologist may be faced with trying to decipher fragments of writing of a long-since dead language, or identifying the significance of the particular architectural layout of a ruined castle or monastery. Here the challenge is straightforwardly one of interpretation – trying to make sense out of something that is not on the surface readily intelligible. Yet other artifacts may *appear* readily intelligible in virtue of their apparent similarity to items the researcher is already familiar with from their own experience. Ornate daggers may appear to be weapons, yet closer examination coupled with knowledge of the conditions in which they were produced, may reveal that they were exclusively ceremonial items – jewellery rather than armaments. The scope for *mis*interpretation is thus rife within historical enquiry and requires correction on the part of the researcher through being prepared to set aside and critically assess the taken-for-granted assumptions and presumptions of her own culture. Though simple enough in the case of a dagger-as-jewellery, it can become trickier when encountering apparently familiar and routine documents and artifacts from bygone eras, and quite perilous when encountering apparently identical concepts and language to that used by the researcher in their own life. Thus nineteenth century newspapers may resemble those of today (minus colour photography and glossy magazine supplements) but may serve a very different set of functions and cater to very different audiences than contemporary newspapers. A news report, advertisement, or letter to the editor, will consequently have quite different meanings and consequences when appearing in a nineteenth century local or regional newspaper that has limited circulation and is primarily aimed at a narrow strata of educated professionals within a predominantly agriculture and illiterate society, than a similar item in today's global, electronic mediascape. Nominally identical terms (such as 'the people', 'the nation', 'liberty', 'democracy', 'science', 'nature') may also have radically different meanings within these very different contexts, requiring great care on the part of the researcher to ensure that their pre-reflexive understandings of terms are not inadvertently foisted upon those who used them a couple of centuries (or more) ago. In short, critical reflexivity on the part of the researcher (both with respect to their own society, and that which they are investigating), is essential to avoid gross misinterpretation of their sources courtesy of projecting the assumptions of the present into the past – a tendency known as 'anachronism', and considered one of the greatest risks of historical research in much the same way that 'ethnocentrism' is considered the greatest danger typically faced by anthropologists encountering a foreign culture.

The perils of hindsight, however, are arguably an even greater challenge to historical researchers. While 'knowing how the story ends' may appear to be a great advantage to a researcher, it nevertheless often results in a disfigured understanding of the historical phenomenon under investigation. Variously referred to as 'the Whig interpretation of history' (Butterfield, 1973 [1931]) or as 'present-centred history' (Wilson and Ashplant, 1988), it is clearest and most prominent in the historiography of science, though prevalent in less obvious forms in many other subfields of historical research. In the case of history of science, researchers have the benefit of contemporary scientific knowledge when examining previous scientific activity and thus are in a position to identify what was correct, mistaken, flawed, or simply downright false in examining an episode in scientific history. They are consequently also in a position to be able to identify the 'heroes' and 'villains' of some dispute or controversy and therefore allow these prior assessments to shape their investigations, narratives, arguments and conclusions. However, many scholars within the field of science studies argue that such after-the-fact knowledge produces a lop-sided history of science and a distorted understanding of the nature of scientific change, innovation, growth and progress (Shapin and Schaffer, 1985; Shapin, 1996; Collins and Pinch, 1998). Instead, they argue, researchers must actively set aside their knowledge of how the story ends and investigate the issue as if they didn't know the outcome. Only then, they claim, can the actual processes and procedures of scientific activity and interaction be disclosed without the distorting effects of hindsight, resulting in a very different image of science and scientists and allowing very different kinds of explanations of its various successes and failures. Indeed, one such formulation encapsulated this demand for the reflexive positioning of the researcher by arguing that researchers must avoid the 'TRaSP' trap, i.e. suspend their judgements regarding Truth, Rationality, Success, and Progress when investigating scientific phenomenon – a formula that is exceptionally demanding upon the researcher (Collins, 1981). While not all areas of historical enquiry will be equally demanding, to the extent that hindsight can disfigure understanding as much as enhance it, similar kinds of demands may be placed upon the historical researcher in order to actively counteract its malign effects.

In sum: while most scholars and social scientists are engaged in studying aspects of the present (and usually the society with which they are most familiar), and while they are ordinarily in a position to generate customized data for their research projects, the position of the historical researcher is distinctive. Appropriate data may be hard to come by or may be available in forms that are far from ideal. In addition, the data may not only be scarce or awkward, but it may present significant challenges of interpretation (even intelligibility), or demand a measure of reflexivity on the part of the researcher that is not usually required by other methods. Some forms of data may be particularly prone to *mis*interpretation on account of their superficial resemblance to familiar contemporary phenomena, while whole fields of enquiry may be liable to systematic distortion through the silent workings of anachronism and/or the hidden effects of hindsight. Yet as the examples of archaeology and science studies demonstrate, such 'problems' are best regarded as challenges. Yes, they are inherent in historical research, but equally they are part of what makes historical research both a rewarding methodology to use and a valuable strategy for contributing to many areas of enquiry.

---

| Activity 8.1 | Distance in time in historical research |
| --- | --- |

What do you think of the suggestion that the historical researcher is at a disadvantage because of their inability to engage directly with their subject matter as a result of distance in time? Make a list of advantages and disadvantages that might result when a qualitative researcher is removed in time from the sources of their data.

# Aligning philosophy and methodology with purpose

The primacy of purpose, and the fundamental importance given to a substantive research interest, is a common characteristic of much historical research. Thus, notwithstanding those who consider the past as a repository of data to be used for testing a hypothesis, generating theory or trialling a concept, philosophy and methodology are typically subordinated to what the research question demands. An interest in women's experiences of, say, health care in late nineteenth century Europe, may require an examination of a large array of sources: medical records in a local hospital; surviving correspondence among women's advocates, nurses and/or midwives; diaries, memoirs and autobiographies of literate women; reports of government enquiries on public health; creative fiction in which the lives of women are represented in detail; records of political parties; documents of private health spas; advertisements for health products in the local press; pamphlets of charities; newsletters of religious groups; morbidity and mortality statistics; contemporary descriptions of medical practices; forms of clothing and styles of fashion; court records of unlicensed health practitioners prosecuted for malpractice – the list goes on, and is limited only by the imagination of the researcher.

Of course, that is not to say that all such sources are equally valuable (much less available and accessible), but it shows that when it comes to delineating potential sources for historical investigation, philosophical and methodological scruples tend to take second place to the underlying research interest. Refining that research interest into a focused research question shapes the enquiry and orients the researcher towards particular kinds of source materials. Crucially, such refinement also leads to a more precise formulation of the particular questions the researcher will put to her source materials, as any given set of documents or artifacts can be used in a multitude of ways. Thus the records of a Victorian hospital may not just tell us about the 'throughput' of patients, but may also contain information about the then prevailing working practices of medics, nurses, and orderlies; medical authorities' attitudes towards the poor; the relative extent of 'medicalization' and 'moralization' of individual ailments; the conceptual architecture of Victorian medicine; the management of gender within the hospital; and much more besides. Extracting information from such documents is thus largely a matter of asking the right questions of them. What questions are asked depends on the substantive interest of the enquiry. Thus the same set of documents will serve as evidence for someone interested in the operation of institutionalized health care as well as for someone researching the creation of modern medical hierarchies – the source materials in themselves do not specify how they may be used. Consequently, a well-defined research interest, clarity of purpose, and a precise set of research questions are typically more important than any given philosophy or methodology.

Nevertheless, there are also more systematic and theory-driven ways in which a historical research project may be designed and executed. The above-mentioned goals of hypothesis testing, generating theory, and trialling a concept are some. But a significant body of historical enquiry in the social sciences takes different forms again. These include variant forms of macro historical sociology in which the identification of long-term trends, processes, and/or dynamics is the express goal of examining a broad sweep of time. For example, Elias (1994[1939]) developed a distinctive form of sociology in which consideration of the long-term effects of what he called the 'civilizing process' were placed centre stage. By investigating changes in desired behaviour documented in European 'manners books' from the fourteenth to nineteenth centuries, he observed how the slow transformation of social rules regulating acts such as urination, defecation and fornication, as well as protocols governing how food was served and eaten, and how individuals interacted with one another in the court societies of the period, all tended towards the same goal – the constitution of the 'civilized', polite, restrained, and rational individual that provided the model of human being valorized in western society. A complicated process governed this slow gestation of the modern individual, including micro-level refinements in the education and socialization of individuals, as well as macro-level processes that saw the formation of large territorial states that progressively seized control over crime and conflict within its boundaries and asserted the exclusive right to the legitimate exercise of force through its police, penal systems and armies. Consequently, in this study Elias is on the one hand providing us with a 'story' – a grand narrative of long-term tendencies substantially corroborated by large swathes of evidence. Yet on the other hand, he is also delineating a fecund social theory and sociological research program in which the study of processes assumes central importance – in sharp (and deliberate) contrast to most present-centred versions of social science that tend to privilege ahistorical individuals, actions or social structures (Elias, 1978). Thus the study of manners books that proscribed urinating in the corner of the room while people were eating and prescribed spitting into one's handkerchief rather than onto the floor, formed part of a grandiose vision and interpretation of modern western history and society. The 'civilizing' of manners was thus the springboard for a sophisticated account of the historic rise of a whole civilization.

There are plenty of other examples within this genre, such as Hobden and Hobson's (2002) study of the emergence of the international system, Mann's multi-volume work on the rise of organized power networks in human society (1986, 1993, 2005), and Tilly's (1975, 1984, 1992) research on the formation of the modern state. What all these studies share is a desire to identify long-term trends, processes, dynamics, and/or mechanics of fundamental social changes within human society with researchers prosecuting this aim via a combination of articulate and sophisticated theory, strategic research design, and a systematic approach to evidence. In this endeavour these researchers are joined by others who opt for a more explicit comparative research design, in which the goal of isolating the conditions common to otherwise disjointed cases forms the stepping stone to the construction of testable theory, as for example in Eisenstadt's (1978) and Skocpol's (1979) classic studies of revolutions through a form of comparative–historical enquiry. Yet more common still are countless studies with more modest time frames, smaller geographic reach, and a more concentrated focus upon a single institution, practice, or policy. Many of these types of studies are oriented towards research on processes, investigating their unfolding through time (a strategy largely precluded by a focus upon the present), and typically with a view to identifying the genesis of some phenomenon or other, the particular (often irregular and non-linear) pathways and temporalities exhibited by a given process, and/or simply as a historical case study.

In short, for most historical researchers, substantive research interests rule. They give shape to the enquiry and research project in a way that places considerations of formal philosophy and methodology firmly within the context of a clearly focused research strategy. Philosophy and methodology are necessary for the coherence and cogency of a given project or research program, but they are not ordinarily allowed to specify preconditions for the form of enquiry to be undertaken.

## Data generation and collection

As noted above, one of the most pronounced differences between historical research and other forms of research is the relative incapacity of historical research to produce its own customized data. This is because the historical researcher relies upon a given society or culture to produce potential data sources (documents, artifacts, relics) and to collect and maintain them through such institutions as libraries, archives and museums. It is from these 'collecting institutions' that the researcher will then gather the raw materials that will come to constitute the project's data.

This, of course, leaves a fair deal to chance. Most human activity goes undocumented – even in the era of mass media, the internet, email and closed circuit television cameras – and the further back in time one proceeds, both the technological capacities for recording and documenting, and the cultural proclivities to preserve records for posterity, tend to diminish. Furthermore, most materials used for records and documents have a limited life-span – stone weathers, paper disintegrates, ink fades – and to compound matters, the vast majority of documents are destroyed once they have served their immediate function, with only a select minority deemed important enough to be preserved for future use. Many of these may in turn not be organized or properly archived, or may have restrictive conditions placed upon access by the public – a condition most common in private holdings of records by businesses, political parties, churches, civil society associations, and families. Consequently, historical researchers find themselves at the mercy of many (typically arbitrary) factors that conspire to reduce the scope of data available to them.

Nevertheless, the profusion of documents most researchers can access is still staggering, and necessitates a clearly-focused research question in order to delimit the prospective range of sources to be consulted and examined. This task, however, has been made much simpler and less time-consuming in the past two decades, courtesy of the ongoing digitization of many records and the increased accessibility of digitized archives via the internet. Furthermore, the development of sophisticated search engines has largely displaced the older techniques of (manual) indexing, cataloguing and physically ordering documents – immensely improving the researcher's capacity to locate relevant documentation. Today, for example, one can visit the website of many governments and search the records of parliamentary debates over many decades (e.g., http://www.hansard-westminster.co.uk, where the official report of the British Parliament, Hansard, is fully searchable online), when little more than ten years ago the task would have involved locating a library with a complete set of volumes in order to struggle with its index and engage in a laborious and often speculative trawl for the pertinent data. Digitization has consequently transformed a research task that previously could take days – as well as incurring significant travel and accommodation costs – into something that can be done from the comfort of the researcher's living room in a matter of minutes. Add to this the fact that physically scattered sources in multiple locations (and even different countries) can be brought together on two tabs of an internet browser, and it can be seen that a genuine revolution in the scope of historical research and the capacity of an individual researcher to access and utilize a multitude of previously inaccessible sources, is taking place. Thus notwithstanding the vagaries responsible for what finds its way into the 'collecting institutions' of libraries, archives, and museums, continual digitization of source materials is putting today's historical researcher in a position of enormous power when it comes to gathering an ever-increasing range of materials. While many potential source materials are still only accessible via old-fashioned note-taking in a dusty archive, the overall reach and repertoire of the historical researcher has been immeasurably enhanced courtesy of the internet.

## Analysis of data

Most data sources in historical research come in documentary form, although the vast majority of these were never designed to be utilized as evidence for future researchers. The task of analysis is consequently a matter of learning ways of making these documents 'speak', and getting them to provide the answers to the questions the researcher has set out to explore. As such, the analytic strategies are those that belong to any form of documentary research and include techniques such as content analysis, discourse analysis, narrative analysis, life-story analysis, biography, hermeneutics, deconstruction, as well as secondary analysis of historic data sets (Scott, 1990; Plummer, 2001; McCulloch, 2004; Prior, 2003, 2011). The main difference however, concerns the additional considerations that come with the historicity of the documents, which may require researchers to position themselves differently than if the materials were contemporaneous. Sensitivity to temporal context is therefore one of the main requirements in the analysis of historical documents, as their original meaning and function may be far removed from that which they assume today. Thus if email is conspicuously replacing the handwritten letter as a form of interpersonal communication, this is itself simply the latest in the evolution and transformation of the meaning and functions of letters from their role as carriers of news prior to the establishment of regular newspapers, to their function as purely interpersonal communications in the age of mass media, and their residual function today as formal and authoritative documents used primarily for official communications. In other words, an eminently familiar and long-established category of document, 'the letter', can be seen not to have a uniform use, function or meaning across time, and much the same can be said of the other types of documents commonly used in historical research. Consequently the historical researcher needs to be aware of the function of the documents used in the time in which they were composed, and thus become familiar with the custom and practice deployed in their construction – alongside the usual considerations accompanying (contemporaneous) documentary research. Once the nature of the documentary sources in question are thereby established, various kinds of extant techniques for analysing documents can be deployed, none of which can claim primacy within historical research. Nevertheless, some styles of documentary analysis are more appropriate to some fields of research than others. For instance, statistical analysis is especially prominent in economic history and historical demography, while both content analysis and discourse analysis are common in studies of politics and the media. Narrative analysis looms large in studies focused on processes of historic change while textualist techniques such as hermeneutics and deconstruction are often favored in the study of thought and ideas. Thus, depending on the substantive topic of enquiry of the researcher, decisions need to be made regarding what formal analytic technique is best suited to the data sources and topic, while ensuring it engages with the central questions driving the research.

Achieving such an outcome is not always a straightforward exercise. In Box 8.1, Russell Ó Raigáin's window into historical research provides an account of factors that impact on the analysis of data using an example drawn from his own work.

---

## BOX 8.1

### Window into historical research

Due to the non-complete nature of the surviving evidence, and the existence of a variety of academic disciplines dedicated to investigating the various categories of this evidence, any multidisciplinary approach to studying the past must deal with numerous conflicting narratives. My own research is concerned with colonialism in the Iron Age and medieval Ireland and Scotland, a topic that can be approached in a number of ways. The main avenues would be historical, archaeological, art historical, and linguistic, however, the varying narratives offered by each of these disciplines are problematic. The traditional historical narrative is that various population movements took place, i.e., Gaels from Ireland to Scotland, and later Vikings and Anglo-Normans into both areas to varying degrees. However, the archaeological evidence as it stands indicates that the scale of this activity was much smaller than purported textually. The fact that linguistic change took place, as evinced by onomastic evidence further complicates the picture, as indeed does the mixing

*(Continued)*

of art styles throughout the period. Moreover, contemporary received wisdom based on these narratives has proven important in the construction of regional, national, and in many ways my own identity: Gaelic in Ireland and western Scotland, the othering of the Vikings to provide a vehicle for identity constriction through contradistinction, and the imperialist tendencies of the Anglo-Normans and their successor dynasties – sometimes referred to as 'the first English Empire'.

The solution, for this researcher at least, has been a *via media* of sorts, taking the recent criticisms of textual and art historical sources into consideration, but assigning a more dominant role to the material record, and especially settlement, due to its constant, but dynamic, presence throughout the period in question, and also in reaction to the more usually textually dominated approaches. By taking this stance, one can guard against essentialism and, more importantly, it is possible to move beyond ontological/epistemological considerations to address issues such as the nature of the constant struggle for control over ideological, military, economic and political power resources, and social processes such as acculturation, hybridization, and realization.

# Quality and rigour

In Act 1, Scene 3 of *The Merchant of Venice*, William Shakespeare gives Antonio the line: 'The devil can cite Scripture for his purpose'. As this is also the danger inherent in all research drawing on large bodies of evidence, a raft of scientific protocols has been established in order to regulate how researchers use evidence, from detailed specifications of the research process that lay out step-wise procedures to be followed from beginning to end, to collective controls over the dissemination, publication and critical assessment of research such as double-blind peer reviewing and replication. Not all of these procedures and protocols, however, are easily applied to historical research and consequently questions arise over how quality and rigour can be ensured in historical enquiry.

With respect to the execution of an individual research project, the practice of historical enquiry is not reducible to a set of formal rules and procedures that can function as a formula to follow in conducting research, and that can also serve as a means of assessing the extent to which an individual piece of research was properly executed. In this sense, historical research is unlike large swathes of the natural sciences in which such protocols, procedures and prescriptions do exist to govern individual (and group) research activity. Rather, as the great historian Marc Bloch (1954) argued, historical research is very much a 'craft' – governed as much by the informal rules acquired in training and practice as by the formal protocols and procedures specified in methodological manuals. This condition of being a 'craft' – halfway between art and science – has a number of implications for assessing individual research projects. For a start, formulaic assessment of the correctness of the research project's procedures is precluded: there is no comprehensive 'check-list' that can be used to assess if all the necessary steps and procedures were followed correctly. In recognition of this, most historical research will therefore involve a detailed critical discussion of the sources utilized in the enquiry in order to ascertain the authenticity, reliability, representativeness, appropriateness and comprehensiveness of the body of sources that serve as the evidential base of the study. Detailed description of the precise procedures followed – from identification of sources to classification to coding to analysis – is rarely provided, but the practice of copious footnoting of sources is prevalent in order to demonstrate the relationship between the final text and its roots in data sources. As the evidential base of historical enquiry is ordinarily too large to permit the inclusion of appendices or extensive quotations as evidence (rather than as illustration), this practice serves not only to expose the underlying evidence, but it also shows how (in practice) it was utilized in assembling the component parts of the overall argument. The explanation of the research procedures used in the study is therefore integrated into the overall argument and final presentation, rather than a separable section serving as a prelude to a set of findings.

Yet this raises another important issue – that of the strict replicability of historical enquiry. While standardized research protocols in fields such as biochemistry, nuclear physics or medicine enable other researchers to replicate a particular study in order to corroborate or disconfirm it, or to isolate uncontrolled factors in the study, this is usually not possible for an individual historical study. Besides the craft-like research practice involved, requiring irreducible crucial critical judgements as part of the research process, it is also often the case that the sources used in the enquiry may not be readily accessible to others to inspect. Strict replication is therefore rendered difficult, if not impossible, in something like the same way that replicating an ethnographic study or one based on participant observation is not possible. However, it is here that the collective quality controls over research and enquiry take effect, as other scholars with comparable or cognate expertise (and perhaps with direct familiarity with some of the same data sources) subject the finalized work to critical appraisals through standard scholarly protocols of peer review and collective criticism, which in some cases may prompt another researcher to revisit the main sources underpinning the study, without trying to re-enact it wholesale.

Nevertheless, notwithstanding what may look like methodological deficiencies in historical research that question its rigour, quality in historical research is, as often as not, to be found in the syntheses it produces and its capacity to intelligibly reconstruct events, processes, actions, and trends, than in fealty to prescribed procedures. Indeed, in many cases, assessing the outcome of historical enquiry involves assessing the quality of the narrative it produces – its plausibility, coherence, insightfulness, respect for context and evidence, and its capacity to make better sense of some phenomenon or other than previous accounts have managed. Notwithstanding the more formalist deployments of historical methods, the quality of much historical enquiry consequently resides in the quality of the interpretation it provides – with all that that entails.

# Presentation and dissemination of findings

Historical research in the social sciences attracts many different audiences, from other historical researchers and professional historians, to social scientists, policy-makers and political actors. Yet the core constituency for any piece of historical research remains those most interested in the specific topic being investigated. Thus, for example, historical research on the topic of violence can be expected to attract the interest of historians, criminologists, psychologists, sociologists, government officials, peace movements, and media outlets. While such a multiplicity of interested parties presents formidable challenges in communicating one's findings to radically different audiences, the mode of presentation of historical research findings within the scholarly community depends also (and crucially) upon the particular kind of historical research undertaken. Thus a qualitative–descriptive study will assume a different form to one oriented more towards theory or model building which will in turn be different to one primarily concerned with quantitative data.

Take our example of the topic of violence. While many media outlets like to portray today's world as increasingly violent, different kinds of historical research can be undertaken to interrogate this perception, leading to different kinds of publications. For example, a study of long-term trends in violent crime, designed to assess whether in fact today's world really is much more violent than, say, that of two or three centuries ago, could include a series of tables, scatter diagrams, bar charts, and line charts to visually represent the quantitative findings of the study and display the fluctuations in violent crime over time and in different places – all with a view to identifying a long-term trend-line or 'central tendency' (Gurr, 1981; Eisner, 2003; O'Donnell, 2009). The main function of the written text in such a study is to critically assess the sources used as evidence, provide critical commentary on the assembled data, and critically engage with multi-disciplinary literature on the nature of violent crime – perhaps concluding with an assessment of the validity of popular (or media) wisdom.

On the other hand, a study concerned with understanding, and perhaps modelling, the processes and dynamics that produce violent actions, may take a much more elaborate and discursive form, drawing upon a welter of historical evidence alongside contemporary data to illustrate or corroborate the main claims of the work (Collins, 2008; Tilly, 2003). Here the form taken by the text is quite open – there is no one fixed formula for presenting such findings, and every textual resource from tables, charts, pictures, illustrations, and schematic diagrams are used to present and support the overall argument. In short, the mode of presentation is highly variable when it comes to presenting the results of historical research. Virtually all available forms of presentation are used, depending on the topic, the kind of historical research undertaken, the overarching purpose of the enquiry, and the main constituency of the work.

Much the same can be said about dissemination – it can take a wide variety of forms. Nevertheless, formats such as poster presentations or short conference presentations tend to favour quantitative kinds of research in which the main findings can be presented concisely and the description and discussion of the processes and procedures for arriving at them can be left compressed. While quantitative studies may be more 'media friendly' in that they can be more readily compressed into 'sound bites' than qualitative historical research, more at home in monograph book form, nonetheless, these (Pinker, 2011) can also find large audiences.

## Conclusion

'Historical research' is a large and lumpy category covering the wildly heterogeneous ways in which different researchers study the past. An extension of the research practices of historians, it has expanded to encompass an enormous range of methods utilized across and within virtually all disciplines in the humanities and social sciences. Though capacious enough to include purely quantitative approaches, methods and techniques, it is most commonly thought of, and practiced, as a qualitative research methodology, and, considered in terms of its chief source materials, it is most closely aligned with documentary research methods. Yet as the above illustrates, the use of historical research methods poses particular challenges to the qualitative researcher in terms of self-positioning vis-à-vis the particular past under investigation and the materials used in order to undertake such research. Furthermore, though often undertaken as an end itself, aimed simply at reconstructing the past 'as it was', it is increasingly used as part of wider interdisciplinary strategies for understanding the present. In this latter form historical research aims to dismantle the common perception of the past as a foreign country, showing not only how past and present are interlinked, but how understanding why 'they do things differently there' is essential to appreciating why *we* do things the way we do.

---

### KEY POINTS

- Historical research is an umbrella term for the use of various sources of data to explore the ways in which the past shapes the future
- Modern historical research traces its roots to the middle of the nineteenth century with various established fields of historical enquiry existing across numerous disciplines

*(Continued)*

*(Continued)*

- The uses of historical research methods within the humanities and social sciences is diverse, rendering it particularly difficult to articulate a single coherent philosophy that unites all practitioners under one banner
- Historical researchers have the unique distinction of not being in a position to directly engage with their subject matter, thus creating distance between researcher and data sources
- For most historical researchers, substantive research interests shape the enquiry and research project, placing formal philosophy and methodology in the context of the research strategy
- Historical researchers have access to a staggering amount of existing data that was generally not intended to be used for the purposes of research and thus the task of analysis is to make documents 'speak' to provide the answers to the questions the researcher has set out to explore
- Historical research attracts many different audiences and in many cases, the quality of historical enquiry lies in the quality of the narrative it produces

## CRITICAL THINKING QUESTIONS

- Consider the discussion of the historical foundations of historical research. How do these align with the philosophical foundations? How does the evolution of the methodology explain the diversity in philosophical orientation?
- Refer back to the discussion in Chapter 2 about the position of the researcher in qualitative inquiry. Reflect on the discussion in this chapter that explores this positioning in respect of historical research. How might the potential disadvantages of being divorced in time from the data source be reconciled when undertaking research using this methodology?
- Rapidly developing technology has increased the accessibility of the researcher to data sources. How might this result in a concurrent increase in the way in which the types and amount of data are collected, how they are analysed and how they are presented? Should we expect the advent of technology to change our expectations of historical research? Does history itself therefore impact on the nature of historical research?

## Suggested further reading

'*Using Documents in Social Research* offers a comprehensive, yet concise, introduction to the use of documents as tools within social science research. The book argues that documents stand in a dual-relation to human activity, and therefore by transmitting ideas and influencing the course and nature of human activity they are integral to the research process. Key features of the book include: alerts students to the diversity of social scientific research documents; outlines the various strategies and debates that need to be considered in order to integrate the study of documents into a research project; offers a number of examples where documents have been used within a variety of research contexts. The book is written in an easy and engaging style which makes it accessible to undergraduates and postgraduate students. It will be essential reading for students and researchers across a range of social science disciplines' (SAGE Publications, 2013).

# References

Abbott, A. (1999) 'Life cycles in social science history', *Social Science History*, 23: 481–489.

Baker, P. (1999) 'What is social science history, anyway?', *Social Science History,* 23: 475–480.

Bloch, M. (1954) *The Historian's Craft*. Manchester: Manchester University Press.

Butterfield, H. (1973 [1931]) *The Whig Interpretation of History*. Harmondsworth: Penguin.

Collins, H. and Pinch, T. (1998) *The Golem: What You Should Know About Science*. Cambridge: Cambridge University Press.

Collins, H.M. (1981) 'What is TRASP? The Radical Programme as a Methodological Imperative', *Philosophy of the Social Sciences*, 11: 215–224.

Collins, R. (2008) *Violence: A Micro-sociological Theory*. Princeton: Princeton University Press.

Eisenstadt, S.N. (1978) *Revolution and the Transformation of Societies: A Comparative Study of Civilizations*. London: Macmillan.

Eisner, M. (2003) 'Long-term historical trends in violent crime', in M. Tonry (ed.), *Crime and Justice: A Review of Research*. Chicago: University of Chicago Press, pp. 83–142.

Elias, N. (1978) *What is Sociology?* London: Hutchinson.

Elias, N. (1994 [1939]) *The Civilizing Process: The History of Manners and State Formation and Civilization*. Oxford: Blackwell.

Elton, G.R. (2002 [1969]) *The Practice of History*. Oxford: Blackwell.

Fleck, C. (2011) *A Transatlantic History of the Social Sciences: Robber Barons, the Third Reich and the Invention of Empirical Social Research*. Basingstoke: Bloomsbury.

Foucault, M. (1985) *The Use of Pleasure – Volume 2 of The History of Sexuality*. New York: Random House.

Foucault, M. (1986) *The Care of the Self – Volume 3 of The History of Sexuality*. New York: Random House.

Goldthorpe, J.H. (1991) 'The uses of history in sociology: reflections on some recent tendencies', *The British Journal of Sociology*, 42: 211–230.

Gurr, T.R. (1981) 'Historical trends in violent crime: a critical review of the evidence', *Crime and Justice: A Review of Research*, 3: 295–352.

Hobden, S. and Hobson, J.M. (2002) *Historical Sociology of International Relations*. Cambridge: Cambridge University Press.

Iggers, G.G. (1997) *Historiography in the Twentieth Century: From Scientific Objectivity to the Postmodern Challenge*. London: Wesleyan University Press.

Iggers, G.G. and Powell, J.M. (1990) (eds) *Leopold von Ranke and the Shaping of the Historical Discipline*. Syracuse, New York: Syracuse University Press.

Iggers, G.G. and Wang, Q.E. (2008) *A Global History of Modern Historiography*. Edinburgh: Pearson Longman.

Kasakoff, A.B. (1999) 'Is there a place for anthropology in social science history?', *Social Science History*, 23: 535–559.

Lepenies, W. (1988) *Between Literature and Science: The Rise of Sociology*. Cambridge: Cambridge University Press

Lowenthal, D. (1985) *The Past is a Foreign Country*. Cambridge: Cambridge University Press.

Mann, M. (1986) *The Sources of Social Power, Vol 1: A History of Power From the Beginning to AD 1760*. Cambridge: Cambridge University Press.

Mann, M. (1993) *The Sources of Social Power, Vol. 2: The Rise of Classes and Nation-States, 1760–1914*. Cambridge: Cambridge University Press.

Mann, M. (1994) 'In praise of macro-sociology: a reply to Goldthorpe', *The British Journal of Sociology*, 45: 37–54.

Mann, M. (2005) *The Dark Side of Democracy: Explaining Ethnic Cleansing*. Cambridge: Cambridge University Press.

McCulloch, G. (2004) *Documentary Research in Education, History and the Social Sciences*. London: RoutledgeFalmer.

Miller, R.L. (2000) *Researching Life Stories and Family Histories*. London: SAGE.

Miller, R.L. (2005) *Biographical Research Methods*. London: SAGE.

Mintz, S.W. (1985) *Sweetness and Power: The Place of Sugar in Modern History*. London: Penguin.

O'Donnell, I. (2009) 'The fall and rise of homicide in Ireland', in S. Body-Gendrot and P. Spierenburg (eds), *Violence in Europe: Historical and Contemporary Perspectives*. Springer, pp. 79–92.

Pinker, S. (2011) *The Better Angels of Our Nature: Why Violence Has Declined*. London: Penguin.

Plummer, K. (2001) *Documents of Life 2: An Invitation to Critical Humanism*. London: SAGE.

Prior, L. (2003) *Using Documents in Social Research*. London: SAGE.

Prior, L. (2011) *Using Documents and Records in Social Research*. London: SAGE.

Scott, J. (1990) *A Matter of Record: Documentary Sources in Social Research*. Cambridge: Polity Press.

Shapin, S. (1996) *The Scientific Revolution*. Chicago: University of Chicago Press.

Shapin, S. and Schaffer, S. (1985) *Leviathan and the Air-Pump: Hobbes, Boyle and the Experimental Life*. Princeton, NJ: Princeton University Press.

Skocpol, T. (1979) *States and Social Revolutions: A Comparative Analysis of France, Russia and China*. Cambridge: Cambridge University Press.

Stern, F. (1973) *The Varieties of History*. New York: Vintage Books.

Tilly, C. (ed.) (1975) *The Formation of National States in Western Europe*. Princeton: Princeton University Press.

Tilly, C. (1984) *Big Structures, Large Processes, Huge Comparison*. New York: Russell Sage Foundation.

Tilly, C. (1992) *Coercion, Capital, Capital and European States, AD 990–1992*. Oxford: Blackwell.

Tilly, C. (2003) *The Politics of Collective Violence*. Cambridge: Cambridge University Press.

Wetherell, C. (1999) 'Theory, method, and social reproduction in social science history: a short Jeremiad', *Social Science History*, 23: 491–499.

Wilson, A. and Ashplant, T.G. (1988) 'Whig history and present-centred history', *The Historical Journal*, 31: 1–16.

Woolf, D. (2011) *A Global History of History*. Cambridge: Cambridge University Press.

# 9
# Case Study

Allison Stewart

## Learning objectives

After reading this chapter, you should be able to:

- discuss the background and philosophical foundations of case study research
- outline the benefits and issues associated with using case study as a methodology
- describe the key requirements for collecting and analysing case study data
- demonstrate how case study research can be effectively presented and disseminated

## Introduction

Case studies are a ubiquitous component of qualitative research used in a wide variety of disciplines to answer many different types of questions. In this chapter, the history, philosophy, and practical considerations of case study research are introduced, with the intent of providing an overview of the methodology for new and experienced scholars.

A case study is defined as an intensive study of an individual unit of interest (Stake, 1995), with a focus on the developmental factors of that unit (Flyvbjerg, 2011). Case study is an exploratory form of inquiry, providing an in-depth picture of the unit of study, which can be a person, group, organization or social situation. The definition of what constitutes the 'unit', or case to be studied, is at the discretion of the researcher. Smith (1978) describes this process as defining the 'boundaries of the system under study' (p. 342), where the boundaries should be justified by 'commonsense' and should encompass a system of connection. By this definition, most qualitative studies are case studies, as qualitative research is usually used in cases where in-depth study of a phenomenon is required, as opposed to quantitative research in which a broad spectrum of examples can be gathered. In general, case studies are most appropriate for the purpose of answering questions about 'how' or 'why' a contemporary phenomenon occurs, in situations where the researcher has little or no control over the phenomenon of interest (Yin, 2003).

Case study research can have single or multiple sites, permitting examination of issues, problems and concerns faced by the phenomena under study and how these may be addressed. Case study research encompasses a wide variety of methods, including interviewing, observation, questionnaires, surveys or almost any other single or mixed method of qualitative or quantitative research. The characterization of a research approach as a case study therefore suggests that the research will focus on a small number of detailed observations, rather than a specific method of inquiry (Creswell, 1998). Examples of case study research presented in this chapter will provide an understanding of the potential use of mixed methods that is a common approach in this research design.

Preparing to undertake a case study requires a lot of planning and thinking up-front, before the research can begin. It is necessary to clearly understand the research questions to be investigated, how they will be addressed by the case study, how the case study is influenced by the position of the researcher, and how the findings will be analysed. The following sections will outline how to achieve these aims, given the historical and philosophical context of case study as a qualitative methodology.

## History of the methodology

The case study as a tool of methodological investigation has a very long history (Flyvbjerg, 2011), prevalent for the better part of the twentieth century in many fields of academic study. Smith (1994) suggests that Charles Darwin's biography from the early nineteenth century can be considered an example of a case study, and that case study as a research design may date back to even earlier times. Platt (1992) traces the origins of published case study research to social workers' 'case histories' in the early twentieth century, and then to the Chicago School of Sociology, from where the idea that case studies necessitate lengthy observation originates. Case studies such as these are generally attributed to the field of anthropology, in which researchers used lengthy visits to remote cultures as their research site. Two notable examples of sustained periods of observation and immersion in the field are Malinowski's (1913) study of Australian Aborigines and Evans-Pritchard's (1940) research on the African Nuer tribe. As a result of these origins, proponents of case study research have traditionally been associated with the practice of ethnomethodology, which aims:

> [t]o treat practical activities, practical circumstances, and practical sociological reasoning as topics of empirical study, and by paying to the most commonplace activities of daily life the attention usually accorded extraordinary events, seeks to learn about them as phenomena in their own right. (Garfinkel, 1967: 1)

While the core of this definition is often evident in contemporary case study research, the rigid requirements of anthropological investigation, including the requirement to spend extended periods of time 'in the field', are now not considered the only method of conducting a case study (Yin, 2003). Over time, other disciplines have adopted case study research designs, which have become a common method of investigation in the social sciences. Case study has been applied in many contexts, including both traditional academic disciplines such as economics, law, history, politics, and sociology (Latour and Woolgar, 1986), and practice-oriented fields like urban planning (Flyvbjerg, 1998), education (Merriam, 1988; Stake, 1995), and public administration (Yin, 2003). In each of these contexts a wide range of methods has been applied to investigating a 'unit' of interest, expanding the application of case study research to a much broader sphere than that of traditional sociology. As such, the definition of a case study retains a focus on the unit of investigation, rather than on the methodological execution of a particular set of methods.

For a long time, however, case study has been viewed with scepticism as a research methodology, with most arguments suggesting that the researcher's focus on a small sample of a given phenomenon, rather than a broad and wide-ranging sample including many different units, means that they are unsuitable for addressing the broader scientific test of generalizability (Yin, 2003). Case studies are often incorrectly defined as having limited value in and of themselves, since they provide only a few examples (Flyvbjerg, 2006) of the phenomenon under investigation. This common misconception stems from a functionalist viewpoint that discounts the benefits of in-depth understanding. Yin (2003) argues that the traditional meaning of generalizability is restricted to 'scaling up' from a small sample to a larger population, whereas the case study is generalizable to the extent that it can provide a clear illustration of the generalizability of a theoretical construct. Yin (1981) also challenges the view that the exploratory benefits of qualitative research should be considered less useful than quantitative research; by contrast, he suggests that qualitative methodologies, like case study research, require fewer up-front assumptions than quantitative research, which is by necessity focused on a narrow range of data. In the last twenty years, several respected researchers have come to the defence of case study, with both Eisenhardt (1989) and Flyvbjerg (2006) arguing for the value of this method of theoretical inquiry, with the result that it is generally considered an acceptable form of research as long as it is executed with sufficient rigour and quality.

Case study research is also of interest to quantitative researchers. In general, quantitative approaches use case studies to initially explore a topic area to inform later quantitative studies. In this way, surveys, questionnaires, or other quantitative data collection techniques can be directed to more specific questions of interest. This is a common and accepted use of case studies, however it should not be considered by any means to be the only use of case study research, which has a much broader and deeper tradition than is often presented in quantitative reports. Uzzi and Lancaster (2003) provide an interesting example of how case studies can inform social network analysis, an area of research that is typically highly dependent on quantitative data. As they state, their use of a case study approach seeks:

> [t]o establish a plausible basis for a theoretical framework that explains how knowledge transfer, learning, and social structure are related. Specifically, we rely on field methods, which furnish *rich and plausible* data for new theories about how different types of learning and knowledge transfer occur. (p. 384, emphasis added)

Fieldwork in this study consisted of 29 interviews at 11 research sites, thereby providing the researchers with several opportunities to test their hypotheses. Thus, the rich data garnered from qualitative studies can influence further studies into social network analysis. For more information on this approach, Krathwohl (2004) provides useful and detailed comparisons of the uses of quantitative and qualitative research in case studies, and how the two approaches can be combined using a mixed-methods strategy.

## Philosophical underpinnings

Burrell and Morgan's (1989) work on sociological paradigms is a useful starting point to understanding the building blocks of a researcher's *ontology* and *epistemology*. *Ontology* refers to the researcher's beliefs about the world around them on a spectrum ranging from realist, in which the world is entirely objective, to nominalist, in which the world exists only in one's interaction with it. *Epistemology* relates to the researcher's beliefs about the nature of knowledge, which ranges from positivist, in which researchers seek to explain and predict the social world's perspective, and anti-positivist, also known as interpretivist, in which the world is essentially relativistic. Burrell and Morgan (1989) suggest that the decision of which methodology to use is largely based on the researcher's ontological and epistemological beliefs: a realist/positivist would prefer highly quantitative study in which results clearly relate to hypotheses to be tested, while a nominalist/interpretivist would tend to use methods that can capture a range of individual observations and present the complexity of these in their findings.

Given the origins of the case study methodology in fields such as anthropology and sociology, it is not surprising that it is generally labelled a nominalist approach to research, in which the individual interpreting the subject of study is considered to be highly involved in the understanding of his or her observations (Burrell and Morgan, 1989). Therefore, case study in the classic anthropological sense assumes that the researcher is inherently implicit in the unit being studied, and that the observations and influences of that individual are therefore the lens through which any observations of the unit are reported.

However, Miles and Huberman (1994) suggest that in qualitative research, 'epistemologies have become blurred. Current perspectives such as pragmatism and critical theory have qualities of both interpretivism and postpositivism,' (p. 5). Furthermore, since the case study methodology is in fact a broad definition of a choice of research focus, it can be used with numerous methods and accompanying philosophical positions. A highly-interpretivist approach to case study may choose to emphasize participant observation in research methods, for example by conducting a field ethnography in a unit, while a more realist approach to case study could elect to conduct regular surveys of a particular research site. The most important consideration in case study methodology is to ensure that the researcher's selected methods correspond to their particular ontological and epistemological beliefs.

# Position of the researcher

There is no right or wrong philosophical perspective in research. Rather, it is up to each individual researcher to decide how they want to approach their study. Since the case study does not predispose a researcher to a particular method or philosophy, it is up to the researcher to decide what type of philosophical viewpoint they adopt when conducting their case study. As there are many different research philosophies, the range of methods that can be applied are equally numerous.

While some junior researchers may feel that deciding on one's perspective is not a good use of time, it is extremely difficult to use a method that does not correspond with one's beliefs about the world, and is likely to lead to frustration for the researcher, and a sub-optimal result. Therefore, it is important to consider one's beliefs about the world and about the nature of knowledge, and to reflect on how these affect one's approach to the study of the world and knowledge. Fortunately, case study is a broad approach that can encompass a range of beliefs, so it provides a good framework for a wide variety of beliefs.

---

**Activity 9.1** — **Philosophical positioning in case study research**

Consider your ontological and epistemological beliefs. What perspectives do you agree with? What implications might these have for the methods that you choose to use in your case study research? How might these be different if you were to investigate the same phenomenon from an alternative perspective?

---

# Aligning philosophy and methodology with purpose

It is important to note that there are many different options in case study research. One or multiple organizations, individuals, groups, or social situations can be researched. Eisenhardt (1989) suggests that two or more units must be studied to understand where they compare, and where they differ; however this comparative approach to case study may not fit the situation that has been selected. As noted above, the first step is to decide on a particular philosophical approach.

One of the most important considerations in aligning philosophy and methodology with the purpose of the research is the nature of the question that is being answered. Choosing a method before defining the research question is akin to selecting a route to get from point A to point B before deciding whether to take a train, bus, or boat; instead, the method of travel will determine the route that should be taken (it would be difficult to take a train along a waterway, or a boat on train tracks). Therefore, one should start by defining the area to be studied. Case studies are typically useful for answering 'how' and 'why' questions, because they allow for in-depth exploration and interaction with participants, compared to other methods which are focused on measurement.

Similarly, the study propositions can affect the study design selected. Typically, these propositions stem from theoretical constructs relevant to the chosen topic of study, which provides initial ideas about the expected outcomes of the study. Deciding on whether to have study propositions, and if so, what these will be, should also influence your choice of methods (Yin, 2003).

A further consideration in using a case study approach is the unit of analysis. Case studies can focus on any unit of study, from a person, for example the organ transplant patients in a hospital research by Fox and Swazey (1974), to an entire organization like Enron, as researched by McLean and Elkind (2003). These two excellent books also demonstrate the differences between single and multiple case studies: where Fox and Swazey (1974) used multiple cases of patients in a comparative research study, McLean and Elkind (2003) used a single case study. It is possible to change from single to multiple case studies during the course of a research study, or to expand the boundaries of the case that has been selected. For example, a particular department of a company could be the initial subject of a case, but upon discovering that the employees in that department work closely with those of another department, the case may then expand to include this department as part of an emergent design. However, these decisions should be made deliberately rather than opportunistically, and should always take the research question as the starting point for any decisions about the research context.

Finally, the plan for analysing and reporting the data should be considered up-front. If the research question and/or study propositions calls for a statistical regression analysis, this will have significant implications on what methods should be selected. Similarly, if extensive quotes will be used in the final analysis and write-up, it is a good idea to gather audio recordings of interactions, whether in interviews or observations, so that they can be reproduced accurately in the final report.

## Data generation and collection

Generating and collecting data for a case study requires detailed planning and preparation in order to be successful. This section will discuss how to negotiate access to a case study site, how to prepare for a case study, how to conduct case study research, and how to process the findings from case studies.

### Negotiating access

The first step to developing a case study is to determine how to get access to a particular case study site. If the unit for the case study is a person, that person will need to confirm that they agree to the interaction, sometimes repeatedly for a period of time if the research design so requires. If the research site is a larger unit, such as a department or company, permission is usually obtained through a contact inside that unit, commonly referred to as a 'gatekeeper'. The gatekeeper will assist in achieving the required permissions from the unit for the research. Permissions will usually involve obtaining the agreement of senior staff within the unit, and potentially require the signing of a legal document confirming what data will be permitted for use in the research study. A professional, usually from the sponsoring university or research institution, should always review legal documents before the researcher signs them. Failure to do so can result in significant problems with later publication of the research; therefore, it is in the best interests of the researcher to take the time needed to negotiate a clear contract about the use of information. It is far better to choose not to conduct research at a particular site if you cannot agree on the terms, than it is to finish the research and then find that it cannot be published.

If a research project plan calls for multiple case studies, this will require contacting gatekeepers at each of the organizations to be included, and potentially negotiating contracts with each organization. It is best to assume that this will be a time-consuming process with it sometimes taking months to negotiate access. Therefore, it is important to start planning the research sites as early as possible after the research design has been decided, as this is a process often requiring negotiations with multiple sites at the same time.

The best way to approach a gatekeeper is highly dependent upon the organization. If the researcher has had some prior contact with the unit, maybe to explore the initial idea of the research or if someone within the organization has suggested that the unit would be a good site for the research, this is usually a good place to start in the negotiations. While the person initially contacted might not be the person who acts as the gatekeeper, they usually set the tone for future interactions with the unit – so be nice to them!

Conducting a case study will almost invariably involve interaction with human participants, and will therefore need to be approved by the researcher's ethics board or institutional review board. The process of gaining ethical clearance should be taken very seriously, as researchers can benefit from the insights of their more experienced colleagues who supervise the approval process. Research participants have the right to provide informed consent, and it should not be the purview of one researcher to determine whether the research meets these standards. By thinking through the ethics process, the final research outcomes will be both morally and methodologically defensible.

---

**Activity 9.2** ⎯ **The role of the gatekeeper**

Put yourself in the shoes of a 'gatekeeper' at a potential research site. What would you want to know about the research project before agreeing to it? What would you be concerned about? Make a list of critical questions that you consider must be answered before you would permit access to the research site.

# Preparing for the research site

Once access to the research site has been negotiated, the plan for the methods to be used must be prepared. In a case study, almost any combination of qualitative and quantitative methods can be used to obtain the data from the research site. It is important to consider the implications of the methods that are to be used, and how to prepare for them. Will people in the unit be interviewed? If so, how many? What characteristics do they need to have (e.g., age, seniority)? What questions will they be asked? Will the unit be observed? If so, how? Will the researcher have a defined position within the unit, or will they be watching other people going about their work? How might this affect their behavior? (See Gillespie (1991), for an excellent review of the famous Hawthorne studies which originally proposed the connection between observation and improved performance.) It is always a good idea to run a pilot study, within the research institution, of any tools that will be used, such as interview schedules, to ensure that they do not contain leading or confusing questions. The following window into case study research written by Dr. Eamonn Molloy, provides an example of how important planning is for effective data collection and subsequent analysis.

---

### BOX 9.1

### Window into case study research

After months of to-and-fro, trying to set up an interview with the Chief Executive Officer (CEO) of a large multi-national fast moving consumer goods firm, a date and a time was finally fixed. A seasoned professional at interviewing senior people, I arrived in plenty of time, advised the CEO's personal assistant and took a seat in the reception area. I used the waiting time productively, re-reading the brief on the company, triple checking the batteries were charged on my tape recorder, reminding myself of the content of the interview schedule and making sure my tie was straight and shoe-laces were done up.

The CEO in question arrived punctually and we shook hands. My first impression was that he was a relaxed, informal and genuinely warm person. Initially, I kept to the formalities, introducing myself, explaining the background aims and objectives of the project, and emphasizing I would take no more than an hour of his time and outlined the details of the confidentiality arrangements. He seemed happy with this, and proceeded to answer my first question. The tape recorder was on, and I took notes. I was fascinated and absorbed as he told me about the organization, his role, how he maintained morale, his career aspirations and I was surprised about some seemingly candid revelations about internal politics.

As the interview progressed, I became increasingly impressed by this individual – he was intelligent, sharp-witted, informed and oozed charisma. I could see why he was a successful CEO. As the hour mark passed, I mentioned that I shouldn't take any more of his time, and he insisted I stay around longer. He took me to the marketing floor and showed me the company's new state of the art, live sales data feeds, eagerly watched by the various product sales teams. Amazing! When two hours was up, my professionalism kicked back in. I said I really must go, thanked him for a fascinating discussion and left the building convinced it was time for a career change. What a place to work! If he had offered me a job on the spot, I would have taken it.

Reflecting on the interview while making my way back to my car, the terrible realization slowly dawned on me that in two hours he had given me practically none of the information that I wanted. I had been hoodwinked. The lesson? When interviewing, go by the book. Have an interview schedule and stick to it.

## Conducting case study research

After preparing sufficiently for the research, the next step is to conduct the research. On the first day, the researcher should be as prepared for the site as one would be for the first day on a new job. The researcher should ensure that they know where they are going, who they are going to meet when they arrive, and when the site's staff expect them to arrive. The researcher should never show up without notice and expect to be admitted to the site; this is akin to showing up to a job without a contract.

Throughout the study, the researcher must ensure that information about the study is available for people who ask for it. Some people may be nervous about participating in the research, and a clear, one-page description of what the research entails and how the case study site fits into this will put many people at ease. Additionally, some researchers are faced with hostility or mistrust from participants who were not consulted about the study, especially if the gatekeeper is more senior in the unit than they are. Dealing with these difficulties is one of the challenges of conducting case study research.

Given that case study research is generally conducted over a period of time, it is important to keep track of the research methods used over the course of the study. For example, if the researcher is conducting interviews, they must keep a detailed record of who has been interviewed, what their level is in the unit, what date they were interviewed, and if the interviews are recorded, the name of the recording file. While this may seem obvious at the time, important details may be forgotten in the time between data collection and returning to the research institution to analyse and write up the findings.

## Processing the findings

Collecting data at the case study site is only the first step of the data preparation process. In many cases, there are other steps that must be taken before one can begin analysing the data. If the interviews were recorded, one will usually want to transcribe them before beginning the analysis. If surveys were completed, data collected in questionnaires will have to be entered into a spreadsheet before it can be analysed. Data processing can often take a substantial amount of time, and it is important not to forget about this crucial step when planning the research.

# Analysis of data

While some qualitative researchers prefer the 'unhampered freedom' (Krathwohl, 2004: 225) of sitting down and writing up findings immediately after data collection is complete, the analysis of case study data should be approached with as much rigour and need for process as the analysis of any other qualitative or quantitative data. A case study is not a short cut to reduce the time needed for analysis. It is not sufficient to spend time immersed in the case study site, return to one's desk, and simply allow the experiences to flow onto the pages as prose, as has been suggested by some researchers who have used case study to poor effect in their work. This section will outline how to decide on analysis procedures, how to carry out the analysis, and how to write up the findings.

## Choosing an analytical approach

The type of research method used will often dictate the analytical approach. Time is a major factor for many researchers, and if there is little time to complete the analysis, a method that requires less detail should be chosen. In interviewing, for example, some researchers use field notes taken during the interviews as their primary source of data, while others record their interviews and use qualitative software to analyse the transcripts of these interviews. If quantitative techniques like surveys were used, analysis may be relatively more straightforward; however, there are often decisions to be made as to the level of analysis, even in statistical research.

## Conducting the analysis

Once the analytical approach has been selected, the analysis should proceed in a systematic way. For case study research to be effective, it must use a logical process of analysis that accounts for bias on the part of the researcher. Someone reading the research paper should be able to follow the analysis and understand how the conclusions were reached. Therefore, detailed records of the steps that were followed when conducting the analysis should be kept. If not, the write-up may be hampered by an inability to remember what was done, or to explain why it was done.

For multiple case studies, it is also important to conduct the same analysis on data from the different cases. The primary advantage of conducting multiple case analysis is that it provides an opportunity for comparison across sites. However, if different approaches are taken in the generation/collection and analysis of data, this benefit is largely reduced. It is also important to account for and identify data sources that come from different sites, as this can be an important source of information in interpreting one's findings. Miles and Huberman (1994) provide an excellent perspective on qualitative data analysis, and this is a good book in which to refer to specific strategies for the chosen case study method.

## Writing up the findings

Researchers may choose to write up their findings after they have finished their analysis, or as they are undertaking their analysis. While the typical research process recommends a linear progression through analysis to writing up findings, there are both advantages and disadvantages to writing up simultaneously with the analysis. For one, it can be easier to recall what was done when simultaneously writing the research report. On the other hand, writing up while analysing can lead to the trap of writing the conclusions before completing the analysis, and this is not good for research.

While every researcher will develop their preferences for writing up, it is usually useful to start with a clear outline of how the findings will be presented. For case study research, there are many ways to do this. Some researchers opt for 'thick description', a method recommended by Geertz (1973), which involves the use of many quotes from interviewees or field notes to allow the study to 'speak for itself'. This approach is more narrative in style, and may read like a story. Other researchers, particularly those who have used quantitative or less descriptive methods in their case study, may prefer to present the findings in tabular or statistical form, with more detail about how the findings can be interpreted. Hammersley and Atkinson (1983) suggest several different ideas for organizing case studies, based on time, topic, and theory. However, there is no one best way to write up research, the findings just need to be clear and concise.

Another consideration in writing up case study research is how to incorporate theory. Creswell (1998) observes that case studies may or may not use theories, using Stake's (1995) description of his experiences in a school as an example of a narrative and non-theoretical example of case study. For cases that do use theoretical models, these can come before or after the analysis, with the case alternately being informed by theory or informing theory development. In the following window into case study research, Dr Martin Müller tells about his own struggles with reconciling preconceived ideas about the unit of his case study of how Russians perceived the position and role of their country in international politics, and the complexities of writing up the findings of this research study.

---

**BOX 9.2**

### Window into case study research

'They'll send you to Siberia!' This was probably the most frequent comment I received when I talked to friends about my research project. I had just secured access to the Moscow State Institute of International Relations, a university with a reputation of educating the Russian elite, and I wanted to use it as a case study for how Russians perceived the position and role of their country in international politics. Working from a constructivist perspective, I planned to collect material through participant observation

*(Continued)*

---

*(Continued)*

of lectures and everyday life, as well as through semi-structured interviews with students and professors.

Even if I, as a researcher, aimed to enter the field without preconceptions, it was impossible to avoid them in my social environment. The cliché of Russia as a country run by the secret service that sends insubordinate citizens to Siberia is a remnant from Soviet times, and it proved difficult to dislodge. It turned out that my own initial understanding of the case was also a cliché: I had expected to find an inculcation of official ideologies, but was instead confronted with a complex mixture of consumerism, careerism and nationalism, which forced me to revise my original research question.

Writing up the research came with its own set of unexpected twists and turns. For one thing, it was not easy to maintain a critical stance towards the material without compromising those who had shared their thoughts as research. Writing a case study is not investigative journalism, after all. For another, when publishing the research, some critical voices pointed out that I had a highly specialized case, which applied to only a small fraction of the Russian population. I thus had to argue that I was not aiming at generalizability, but at presenting insights into the education of a small but crucial group of potential future decision makers in Russia.

# Quality and rigour

Case study research has often been unfairly categorized as lacking rigour. Part of the explanation for this reputation is in the lack of discipline which some of the numerous researchers conducting case study research have applied in approaching their research systematically (Yin, 2003). As with any other methodology, the case study is not in itself an inherently flawed approach. Rather, it is only when the methodology used is either inappropriate to answer the research question, or when it is not conducted with sufficient foresight and planning, satisfactory attention to the detail of gathering the data, or adequate analysis of the findings, that it leads to a poorly-conducted case study. Case study research requires a significant amount of effort to execute properly. It is therefore important to consider whether the case study methodology is an appropriate fit for the research prior to engaging in it.

Maylor and Blackmon (2005) suggest answering the following questions when judging the quality of your case study:

1. Have you conducted your research in a systematic way?
2. Does the story that you tell make sense?
3. Does your evidence support your story?
4. Is there any other story that could equally well be told with the data?
5. Have you shown something new?

# Presentation and dissemination of findings

Case studies can be one of the more difficult methodologies to present, because they do not have clear requirements for how they should be written up. The method of presentation depends largely on the research question and the methods chosen for data collection and analysis. Therefore, there is no 'best way' to present a case study (Maylor and Blackmon, 2005). However, there are clear precedents depending on the methods used in determining how to present your findings. For example, if primarily ethnographic or observational methods are used, the most common form of presentation is narrative methods with many quotes; if more quantitative data is used, it is more common to use graphics to display the findings.

Dissemination is equally diverse in case study research, and is similarly determined by the methods chosen. The best approach is to look at studies that have used similar methods, and to consider which journals they have published in. While there are many journals focused on qualitative research, some journals are more or less open to certain methodological approaches. Check, before submitting a paper to a journal, that they have a history of accepting articles using case study.

# Conclusion

Case study is one of the most widely used approaches in qualitative research, and may encompass a multitude of different methods, such as those outlined in the other chapters. Case study provides a flexible approach to examining one or more units of study, for the purpose of answering 'how' and 'why' questions about complex phenomena.

Many different fields, particularly in the social sciences and humanities, have used case study to great effect, however the origins of the case study approach are still debatable. While the strong association of the method with the field of anthropology in the early half of the twentieth century led to a number of well-founded criticisms, researchers have fought back in its defense with the result that case study is now a well-established approach. Indeed, most qualitative research could be characterized, to some extent, as a case study.

Due to the variety of methods that can be employed in a case study, the researcher's philosophical position can be used to guide the choice of methods. Regardless of the methods selected, case study research must be planned in advance, negotiated carefully, and executed in a manner that is respectful of the research participants. Data collection and analysis should be undertaken systematically to avoid common criticisms including the lack of rigour of the case study method.

Researchers seeking to use case study will find that it presents challenges in its development, but that it can be a rewarding and insightful strategy with which to investigate a research problem. There are many examples demonstrating that with proper consideration, preparation, and execution, case study can be an exceedingly valuable approach to qualitative research.

## CRITICAL THINKING QUESTIONS

1. Compare and contrast the philosophical foundations of case study research with those of ethnography. What are the points of convergence and divergence?
2. From your reading of this chapter, how does case study differ from other methodologies with which you are familiar in terms of:

   a. Complexity of the methodology
   b. Relationship of the researcher to the study
   c. Processes used in data collection and analysis

3. Case study may be more difficult to present for dissemination. What creative strategies might be employed in the presentation of case study findings?

## Suggested further reading

Yin, R. (2013) *Case Study Research*. Thousand Oaks: SAGE Publications.

'Providing a complete portal to the world of case study research, the Fifth Edition of Robert K. Yin's bestselling text offers comprehensive coverage of the design and use of the case study method as a valid research tool. The book offers a clear definition of the case study method as well as discussion of design and analysis techniques. The Fifth Edition has been updated with nine new case studies, three new appendices, seven tutorials presented at the end of relevant chapters, increased coverage of values and ethics, expanded discussion on logic models, a brief glossary, and completely updated citations. This book includes exemplary case studies drawn from a wide variety of academic fields' (SAGE Publications, 2013).

## References

Burrell, G. and Morgan, G. (1989) *Sociological Paradigms and Organisational Analysis: Elements of the Sociology of Corporate Life*. London: Heinemann Educational Books Ltd.

Creswell, J.W. (1998) *Qualitative Inquiry and Research Design: Choosing Among Five Traditions*. London: SAGE Publications.

Eisenhardt, K. (1989) 'Building theories from case study research', *The Academy of Management Review*, 14: 532–550.

Evans-Pritchard, E.E. (1940) *The Nuer: A Description of the Modes of Livelihood and Political Institutions of a Nilotic People*. Oxford: Clarendon Press.

Flyvbjerg, B. (1998) *Rationality and Power: Democracy in Practice*. Chicago: University of Chicago Press.

Flyvbjerg, B. (2006) 'Five misunderstandings about case-study research', *Qualitative Inquiry*, 12: 219–245.

Flyvbjerg, B. (2011) 'Case study', in N.K. Denzin and Y.S. Lincoln (eds), *Handbook of Qualitative Research*. 4th edn. Thousand Oaks: SAGE.

Fox, R. and Swazey, J. (1974) *The Courage to Fail: A Social View of Organ Transplants and Dialysis*. Chicago: University of Chicago Press.

Garfinkel, H. (1967) *Studies in Ethnomethodology*. Englewood Cliffs, NJ: Prentice-Hall.

Geertz, C. (1973) *The Interpretation of Cultures*. New York: Basic Books.

Gillespie, R. (1991) *Manufacturing Knowledge: A History of the Hawthorne Experiments*. Cambridge: Cambridge University Press.

Hammersley, M. and Atkinson, P. (1983) *Ethnography: Principles in Practice*. London: Tavistock.

Krathwohl, D.R. (2004) *Methods of Educational and Social Science Research: An Integrated Approach*. London: Waveland Press Inc.

Latour, B. and Woolgar, S. (1986) *Laboratory Life: The Construction of Scientific Facts*. Princeton, NJ: Princeton University Press.

Malinowski, B. (1913) *The Family Among the Australian Aborigines: A Sociological Study*. London: University of London Press.

Maylor, H. and Blackmon, K. (2005) *Researching Business and Management*. New York: Palgrave MacMillan.

McLean, B. and Elkind, P. (2003) *The Smartest Guys in the Room: The Amazing Rise and Scandalous Fall of Enron*. New York: Penguin Group.

Merriam, S.B. (1988) *Case Study Research in Education: A Qualitative Approach*. San Francisco: Jossey-Bass.

Miles, M.B. and Huberman, A.M. (1994) *Qualitative Data Analysis: An Expanded Sourcebook*. London: SAGE Publications.

Platt, J. (1992) '"Case Study" in American methodological thought', *Current Sociology*, 40: 17–48.

SAGE Publications (2013) *Case Study Research*. Available at: http://www.sagepub.com/books/Book237921?siteId=sage-us&prodTypes=Books&q=stake+case+study&fs=1.

Smith, L.M. (1978) 'An evolving logic of participant observation, educational ethnography, and other case studies', *Review of Research in Education*, 6: 316–377.

Smith, L.M. (1994) 'Biographical method', in N.K. Denzin and Y.S. Lincoln (eds), *Handbook of Qualitative Research*. Thousand Oaks: SAGE, pp. 286–305.

Stake, R.E. (1995) *The Art of Case Study Research*. London: SAGE Publications.

Uzzi, B. and Lancaster, R. (2003) 'Relational embeddedness and learning: the case of bank loan managers and their clients', *Management Science*, 48: 383–399.

Yin, R.K. (1981) 'The case study crisis: some answers', *Administrative Science Quarterly*, 26: 58–65.

Yin, R.K. (2003) *Case Study Research: Design and Methods*. London: SAGE Publications.

# 10
# Narrative Research

Patrick John Lewis and Robin Adeney

---

**Learning objectives**

After reading this chapter, you should be able to:

- Discuss the philosophical underpinnings of narrative inquiry
- Outline the key philosophies involved in the development of narrative inquiry
- Describe the different types of narrative inquiry
- Reflect on the ethical responsibility of the positioning of the researcher undertaking narrative inquiry
- Summarize strategies for data generation and analysis in narrative inquiry
- Critique mechanisms for ensuring rigour and quality in narrative inquiry

---

## Introduction

The first question when thinking about narrative research is: What is narrative? The term comes draped in many meanings and is used in myriad ways across disciplines. There is no clear and easy definition that satisfies all utilizations. Broadly speaking, narrative is the everyday practice of storytelling, the teller/speaker uses the basic story structure to organize events and/or experience to bring forward what is perceived as important and significant for the teller and the audience. Narrative research, then, is the exploration of the stories humans tell to make sense of lived experience. This chapter will examine the historical and philosophical foundations of narrative inquiry and explore concepts related to using this approach to qualitative research.

## History of the methodology

Narrative research has grown dramatically, if not exponentially since appearing on the qualitative research horizon more than 20 years ago. Narrative work can be traced back to the 1920s and the Chicago School of Anthropology, the 1960s and 1970s feminist work and the sociolinguistic work of the 1970s and early 1980s.

From Polkinghorne (1988), to Bruner (1990), Riessman (1993), Denzin (1997), Connelly and Clandinin (1988; 2000) and a plethora of others, the field has been well-cultivated and yielded fine crops of good work. Multiple and diverse disciplines have embraced narrative inquiry including community studies, history, nursing, medicine, social work, and education, to name just a few. The narrative turn was fed by diverse shifts in Western thought, epistemology, technology and social practices that began in the 1960s (Riessman, 2008).

Why are researchers turning to narrative? It may be as Bruner (2002) describes that, 'story is our medium for coming to terms with the surprises and oddities of the human condition' (p. 90). But more importantly, it may be that story is our primary mode of making meaning and understanding of lived experience, our own and others. We have a belief in, or trust of, the value of story. As humans we live storied lives and through story we experience the world and make sense of it.

Narrative is a broad term in social science research. Narrative work can involve a number of different methods such as autobiography, auto-ethnography, narrative performance and narrative inquiry. The importance of story is the common thread running through all of these approaches. This chapter will take up primarily narrative inquiry influenced by Jean Clandinin and Michael Connelly (2000), however, it will also draw on the good works of the aforementioned narrative approaches. Chase (2005) describes narrative inquiry as 'an amalgam of interdisciplinary analytic lenses, diverse disciplinary approaches and both traditional and innovative methods – all revolving around an interest in biographical particulars as narrated by the one who lives them' (p. 651).

What is narrative inquiry as a methodology? To begin it is important to understand that narrative inquiry as a research genre can be used successfully in multiple disciplines and that no two narrative studies will look alike. There is no one cookbook recipe and it seems particularly well-suited to social science questions and human inquiries. Connelly and Clandinin describe two approaches: narrative research that begins with the researcher interviewing participants who tell; or, a researcher who engages in participatory studies and enters the unfolding of a life or lives. The interview continues to be the primary working method of narrative but the field is certainly not confined to this one approach. Murray-Orr and Olsen (2007) remind us that we need not focus exclusively on the term 'narrative' and skip over the inquiry aspect of the methodology but remember that it is the inquiry into the stories that may create an educative experience as individuals find new and more expansive ways to interpret their own and others' experiences.

Often writers will use the term narrative inquiry almost synonymously with narrative analysis, however the two should not be conflated. Narrative analysis originated prior to narrative inquiry in the postpositivist movement of the 1960s. Narrative analysis pursued a renewed notion of objective reality by positioning the researcher/analyst as the sole interpreter of the narratives with a fixed meaning to the text created. It ignored the meanings that readers/listeners bring to text, the multiple interpretations of texts and the fluidity of stories. 'These methods fail to address language's radical indeterminacy, the slipperiness of signs and signifiers, and the fact that language [stories] creates rather than mirrors reality. ... These methods fail to examine the text as a meaningful whole' (Denzin, 1997: 244). Narrative analysis circumvents the inherent recursiveness and messiness of story while narrative inquiry lives through those complexities and tensions trying to hold the story space.

Paramount in any narrative work is the necessity to 'think narratively' as narrative inquirers structure a self-narrative through living, telling, re-telling and reliving (Connelly and Clandinin, 2006). The researcher is immersed in the complexity of the multiple layers of stories we live day to day. 'Humans are always already tangled up in a second hand world of meanings and have no direct access to reality. Reality as it is known is lodged in these interpretive, narrative texts ...' (Denzin, 1997: 246). Narrative research is complicated, complicating and never easy. Narratives are not fixed temporally, though a story may seem to move in a linear fashion the research work never does. 'Only narrative form can contain the tensions, the surprises, the disappointments and reversals and achievements of actual, temporal experience' (Crites, 1971: 306). There is an inherent reflexivity to narrative research that demands the attention of the researcher and her collaborators as the story emerges and changes through multiple iterations.

## Philosophical underpinnings

Narrative inquiry philosophically aims to create a space where the inquirer immerses herself in a particular world, observes, reflects and is part of. Within this space the researcher learns a deeper noticing of the world (Bateson, 1994). Narrative as a qualitative research method incorporates a range of philosophical perspectives. The approach has been influenced by ethnography, phenomenology, phenomenological hermeneutics, narrative psychology, and literary studies. The method is a social sciences and education practice with roots in the humanities under the broad heading of narratology. Narrative inquiry espouses the belief that subject matter, both human and nonhuman, are best studied in their natural settings and that authentic understanding is gained from the meanings people bring to phenomena. As a research choice this design provides both opportunities and dilemmas for the researcher. While it opens a research space for creativity and innovation, as a subjective and interpretive form of enquiry, it can also be a frustrating and inconclusive endeavour. Narrative inquiry is described as crossing many boundaries including disciplinary and international (Riessman, 2008), which can result in the researcher frequently confronting doubt that arises from a multiplicity of interpretations of methodology and methods. Researchers who choose narrative as a research approach accept a change from viewing the universal and general to the specific and local. That is, the stories of individuals often disrupt or run counter to the larger 'taken for granted' dominant narratives. Narrative researchers are open to a view that there are alternative epistemologies or ways of knowing (Clandinin, 2007).

Clandinin and Rosiek (2007) use the metaphor of a map and borderlands to locate narrative inquiry, describing how narrative has crept into what was traditionally a positivist research paradigm. These authors claim, 'in our view narratives are the form of representation that describes human experience as it unfolds through time' (p. 40). Narrative inquiry plays a vital role in its gentle push against positivist research approaches as it allows for the subtle nuances of human experience to rise to the surface and to reveal themselves, further questioning the truth claims of positivist research. The borderlands of narrative inquiry include post-structural, critical theory, and postpositivist positionings; theoretical movements sharing the notion of multiple realities and that narrative research is best suited to that task. Those in the borderlands of narrative research share the embrace of the story world, but possess 'real differences of opinion on the epistemological, ideological, and ontological commitments' (p. 37)

What makes narrative inquiry distinct from other qualitative research methodologies? Chase (2005) highlights a number of unique characteristics: primarily, narrative researchers:

> ... treat narrative, both oral or written, as a distinct form of discourse ... Unlike a chronology, which also reports events over time, a narrative communicates the narrator's point of view, including why the narrative is worth telling in the first place. In addition to describing what happened, narratives pay attention to emotions, thoughts and interpretations. (p. 656)

Each researcher will bring their own epistemological and ontological views and approaches to their particular study. Like co-researchers, our stories are fluid, constantly reworked, recreated, in motion, and never quite finished.

## Position of the researcher

In any narrative work, one of the fundamental questions the researcher must ask is: How am I positioned in this narrative?

This question is not easily answered because it is inextricably entwined with the overarching research question that both forms and informs how the narrative researcher is positioned and repositioned throughout the research process. The researcher lives within the research and is committed to studying phenomena in their natural settings. Not only is the researcher personally involved, they change as individuals as the research takes unexpected twists and turns and surprising insights are reached through working alongside participants. Narrative work entails intimate engagement of the researcher and the co-researcher(s) in the story of the relationship. You write yourself into the work (Connelly and Clandinin, 2006). Researcher participant relationships may be intense and personal, and sometimes conflicting. As we position ourselves within our research and are privy to conversations and other information involving participants we must hold closely an ethic of care and respect. Lugones (1987) speaks of narrative inquirers as needing to be playful, open and not try to conquer or 'change' the world(s) they encounter. There is a risk that the narrative inquirer may perceive arrogantly unless deliberate efforts are made to not do so. Herein lies the demand for reflexivity and an authentic self-reflection throughout the research process that may be uncomfortable and disruptive to one's self-story; coming face to face with deeply held biases, prejudices and beliefs.

Why narrative? Marmon (1996) describes how justice is gained through the power of stories and narrative. Narratives are possessed with a capacity for social justice, which allows historically marginalized and silenced peoples to tell their stories and for others to listen and respond. We make meaning through our stories, we are our narratives and our stories are who we are.

How a researcher is positioned within the research study is critical, but it is more important to keep in mind that interlaced with the positioning of the researcher is the positioning of participants. Sociocultural positioning of the researcher influences the research in a fundamental and basic way: What are the relational dynamics as you enter into the research relationship with participants? How will the hierarchy of power in the research environment be negotiated, balanced, flattened, disrupted or exacerbated? What are the social capital implications within the research? Relationality is at the heart of all narrative research work and to think and live narratively requires one to be centred in the notion of relationship through story. Such a centring realizes the sacredness of stories and the need to hold and honour the space for the storyteller.

## Aligning philosophy and methodology with purpose

There are several questions that the researcher will have to ask in this area. The first will be 'what is my research question?'. This may seem extremely simple and straightforward, but it is not. A choice of research method should not be predetermined. Rather, you should choose a method that is appropriate to what you are trying to find out. Consequently, 'does a narrative research method fit with the research question I am asking?' is a fundamental question. Narrative inquiry is all about 'voice', understanding the phenomenon, experience of people in the relationship: does this lend itself to the question being asked and how will the researcher enact an ethical relationship with the storytellers? For example, a researcher with a question around the experience of homelessness might choose to live among and interview homeless people to understand more deeply their experiences through their stories and consequently, how authentic solutions and assistance can be rendered. As Connelly and Clandinin (1990) articulated years ago, narrative inquiry is the awareness and practice that 'narrative is both phenomenon and method' (p. 2) and in that midst the narrative inquirer may begin with a well delineated research question that then changes through the storying process.

Narrative inquirers are interested in inclusion in research to enable authentic stories and observations, often those of marginalized populations, to be revealed by participants themselves – the telling of their own stories. It is about 'trusting the stories and the storyteller' (Hendry, 2007: 494). Narrative work can make a difference in terms of directly impacting the lives of individuals and communities. Often a unifying thread in narrative work is a concern with broad issues of social justice in education, within a framework of multicultural education (Phillion and Wang, 2011). However, the same is true in community work, health care and social welfare work. Narrative inquiry often concerns itself with notions of social change; the work is possessed with the potential to raise awareness and questions around practices, both institutional and everyday, that are taken for granted; studying what is unremarkable, routine and ordinary.

---

| Activity 10.1 | Using narrative inquiry |

Consider a study that you may be planning to undertake. Is narrative inquiry, using stories to gain meaning from participants, a useful methodology for addressing your research question? Could this methodology open up new and different ways of thinking about your research question?

---

## Data generation and collection

One of the important characteristics of narrative inquiry is that there is a move from the use of number to the use of words as data (Clandinin, 2007). So, the question to ask is, how will the data be generated and collected? There is not only a diversity in research topics but each inquiry will utilize a diverse range of data and this information will be represented ultimately to an audience in varying ways. Data collection might include a combination of participant stories, conversation, field notes, poetry, imagined dialogue or artwork. One approach to managing data (Adeney, 2011) is to review and analyse the data concurrently with data collection, reading and re-reading field notes and examining artwork, photographs and other data sources on a recursive and regular basis. This reflexive process allows for new insights, questions and connections to emerge.

Recruiting participants may require some preliminary relationship-building at your planned inquiry site. In Adeney's (2011) study on child's play, the researcher volunteered for several months at the school prior to commencing the study and built relationships with the teachers, families and children. The following year, when recruiting research participants, she was successful, as she had already built trusting relationships within the school. The number of participants you choose for your study will depend on the inquiry question itself and can range from a focus on the narratives of one individual or to a larger number. There is no required 'sample size', as might be required in a quantitative research approach. Recruitment of participants is varied and can be by telephone, letter, email, poster or word-of-mouth.

How best to collect your data becomes the next question? Many narrative researchers use a personal journal or notebook for reflection alongside other data collection tools such as digital audio or video recorders, digital cameras, observation notebooks, artwork or other research artifacts. Think broadly and creatively when you consider what defines data – artwork, photographs, poetry, playlets, imagined dialogue, digital media and other ways of visual representations can convey meaning narratively.

Data gathering can be overwhelming to the researcher and there is a tendency to try to see and hear it all. This is impossible. It is better to see small and to understand a piece of the puzzle and then later fit the puzzle piece into a larger picture. As you grapple with questions of too much or too little data, realize that you likely have what you need. As you gather data keep in mind that narrative work requires a certain type of wakefulness and is a process of false starts, dead-ends and unresolved tensions (Clandinin, Pushor and Orr, 2007). Narrative inquiry is essentially about relationships between the researcher and participants. It is useful, therefore to give some thought to how your own data collection (writing notes, photos, tape recorder) may interrupt establishing and sustaining authentic and trusting relationships with participants. How can you be in the moment of experience, rather than in the notebook and/or data collection? It is imperative to move data generation into the background and place story sharing squarely in the foreground.

## Analysis of data

The analysis of stories presents a dilemma for the narrative inquirer. Coles (1997) asks the question of how we write about 'other'? The narrative researcher is tasked with the difficult challenge of somehow not othering participants through the process of re-storying the stories that have been entrusted to them. Chase (2005) describes how the researcher 'develops their own voice(s) as they construct others' voices and realities; they narrate "results" in ways that are both enabled and constrained by the social resources and circumstances embedded in their disciplines, cultures and historical moments' (p. 657). Clandinin and Connelly (2006) write that the underpinnings of temporality, sociality, and place undergird all narrative studies and that these are checkpoints for novice researchers to attend to (Box 10.1).

---

**BOX 10.1**

### Considerations in narrative inquiry research

- **Temporality:** Events under study are in transition. Events, persons and objects are described as having a past, a present and future.
- **Sociality:** Social and personal conditions are important. What is the relationship between the researcher and participants? Inquirers bracket themselves into studies.
- **Place:** In narrative inquiry the specificity of place is crucial. Place may be a sequence of locations or one location. (Connelly and Clandinin, 2006)

---

By temporality these authors mean that objects, events and persons described have a past, a present and a future. Sociality refers to the relationship that researchers have with participants as they bracket themselves within the study. Finally, all studies occur in a particular place and time. Consider what is in your data but also what is not there, which does not mean that you may have missed something, rather the story and/or the storyteller(s) have been shaped and reshaped through the telling over time, place, and relationships. As you dwell in the stories (data) you have to discipline yourself to attend to the small seemingly routine or ordinary occurrences while still watching the larger big picture. Read and re-read field notes, look for commonalities, connections and patterns as well as unique moments that stand out. Be prepared for surprises. Ask yourself what these observations might mean? As you sift through the diverse research pieces it is a time to be open to 'self-discovery, which is an important part of a narrative inquirer's journey' (Murray-Orr, 2005: 277). Ely (2007) uses the term 'lift' to describe how reading and re-reading data eventually leads to moments of emancipation and understanding. The stories come to life through the narrative that emerges in and through the process of turning and returning to the stories that have been generated and the story of the research.

## Quality and rigour

Outside and inside narrative research work there often emerges a simple, but critical question about the work; 'that's a good story, but is it really research' (Ceglowski, 1997: 195). Some of this questioning has been prompted by political shifts calling into question the legitimacy not only of narrative research, but most qualitative research (see Barone (2007); Denzin and Lincoln (2005), and 'the eighth moment'). In response to or in anticipation of such questioning some researchers have carefully developed and delineated a set of design elements and commonplaces to guide and inform narrative research (Clandinin et al., 2007). Others have confronted critics directly, extolling 'narrative virtues' (Bochner, 2001) while quite possibly 'offer[ing] nothing more than the collegial comforts of a common intellectual meeting place' (Barone, 2007, p. 466). Then others have suggested the need to develop 'an ethic' that embodies 'methodological rigour' (Bagley, 2009: 298); or a new way of imagining legitimacy that is congruent with narrative research that travels outside positivist and postpositivist notions of validity and rigour.

Quality narrative research is time consuming and requires flexibility, patience and a willingness to change direction if needs be, to accommodate participants and your research committee. Researchers are often challenged on the authenticity of their narrative inquiries and may even question themselves about the reliability and trustworthiness of what they have written. Be reassured that while appearing fragmented and disjointed, the tapestry you create will have a strong and authentic voice. Ely (2007) articulates this well when he states, '[i]n the final say, it is not the fragments that move us but a wholeness that speaks to the mind and heart and taken as a whole, the piece meshes into a tapestry that signifies the unique spirit and ethic of (the participants)' (p. 596). Moustakas (1994) observes that human science approaches are concerned with finding meanings and essences rather than measurements, they rely on rich first person accounts in conversations and interviews, and that the researcher is personally involved. Importantly, as you begin to compose and consider textual form there is a need for evidence, interpretive plausibility, logical constructions and disciplined thought (Connelly and Clandinin, 2006).

A key question to ask is, 'what does good narrative inquiry research look like?'. Clandinin and Connelly describe 'good narrative as having authenticity, as having adequacy and plausibility' (2000: 185). Most people can agree that there are bad stories, good stories and even in between stories. So, what *is* a good story? In aesthetic terms we are all over the place, which on one hand is probably good, in that many stories are being told, but I am not sure how many of them are being heard. On the other hand, recall Maxine Greene's caution that, 'we have to become more critical now, I believe, of the stories that have taken the place of reports. … It is a matter of craft; it is also a matter of political insight' (Ayers, 1995: 327). Although this is about quality, or as Tom Barone (2007) called it, 'the tension between the need for quality controls and the democratic impulse of story sharing' (p. 457), in the process it will wander into the validity story. Is it enough to tell the story, all stories? And how can the story be most effectively told to ensure that it is useful (beyond a cathartic or libratory experience for the storyteller) possessed with transformative power? Clandinin and Connelly (2004) note that, 'self-knowledge is, in the end, not important' (p. 575), however, they say that as a means to revealing knowledge about the educational landscape, it is all important.

The authors contend that our work does not purport some bold TRUTH, but rather provides some *truths* about being human and human being. Others talk about transcending the language of the positivist and postpositivist research paradigm so we have notions of verisimilitude, plausibility, believability, legitimacy, trustworthiness, credibility, persuasiveness or authenticity. In the past 25 years, recall Riessman (1993), Mishler (1990), Polkinghorne (1988), Connelly and Clandinin (1990) and many others who have called for among other things, 'a radical reconceptualization of validity or 'criteria other than validity, reliability, and generalizability' (Connelly and Clandinin, 1990: 7). Or Stivers' (1993) 'believability not certitude for enlargement of understanding' (p. 424), Barone's (1992) 'accessibility, compellingness and moral persuasiveness' (p. 21), and finally, Valerie Polakow (1985) who said:

> the criteria for evaluating good research of this genre approach aesthetic ones – criteria that emphasize the power of one's narrative, the rhetorical skills of the teller and writer, and the evocation of a landscape of experience that resonates with one's audience. (Polakow, 1985, pp. 830–831)

Believability and/or authenticity are at the nexus of validity in narrative research work. Are the story and the storyteller believable? Do they engage the human imagination in the sharing of their story? Does it resonate with the broader human experience? Scholes and Kellogg (1966) remind us that story springs from myth and that:

> Mythic narrative is the expression in story form of deep-seated human concerns, fears and aspirations, the plots of mythic tales are a storehouse of narrative correlatives – keys to the human psyche in story form – guaranteed to reach an audience and move them deeply. Though rationalistic attacks on myth as falsehood tend to invalidate it historically, they are powerless against its psychological potency (p. 220).

Validity tends to be equated with authority and a concomitant notion of value that is attached to anything we create. 'Producing "things" [Laurel Richardson tells us] always involves value – what to produce, what to name the productions, and what the relationship between the producers and the named things will be. Writing "things" is no exception' (1994: 518). Consequently, 'to try and escape the value judgements that accompany storytelling is to miss the point … for the stories we tell, like the questions we ask, are all finally about value' (Cronon, 1992: 1376). Authority, then, is found in the 'social consensus that the writer appeals to' (Frye, 1982: 21), and validity becomes 'the researcher's mask of authority' (Lather, 1993: 674). We then arrive at the question: What is of value?

Mark Turner (1997) noted that,

> We devalue it [story/narrative imagining] as we devalue any plentiful resource. Since it is universal instead of scarce, the calculus of supply and demand must fix its price at zero. But it is actually worth whatever it is worth to be a human being because if you do not have this capacity, you do not have a human mind (p. 13).

If we look at the etymological meaning of plausibility (acceptable/agreeable – having the appearance of truth) or verisimilitude (likeness to truth) neither works well enough for narrative research. Yet, believability means to (hold dear, love; to like, desire) and authenticity means (original, principal, and genuine). Narrative research orbits trustworthiness because in its simplest form a story and the storyteller inherently ask for trust:

Could this happen?
How close is this to reality?
What does it tell us about life?

The nexus of validity in narrative research work is with believability, authenticity, quality, power, and authority. Trinh Minh-ha (1991) said '[a]uthorized voices authorize themselves to be heard' (p. 188), Paul Ricoeur (1984) reminds us that we 'tell stories because in the last analysis human lives need and merit being narrated' (p. 75), and Michael Toolan (1988) points out that when we tell a story we are in fact making a bid for power. In that bid for power the story aims for engagement and resonance; the story is judged upon whether it evokes in the listener the feeling that the experience shared in the story is possessed of authenticity and believability.

```
trust = believed, faithful
worthy = having merit, value
trust + worthy = of believed value
```

Simply put, a story must be of believed value. Petra Munro Hendry (2007) has suggested a need to shift narrative researchers' sense of trust from that of method to relationship, pointing out that, 'We invest our trust in our methods not in our relationships' (p. 493). But, story *is* relationship; it is that which binds us together. Hendry asserts that by situating narrative within the metaphor of research it is doomed to methodology, narrative is reduced to methods, verification, and validity all ways of legitimizing it as a means of research thereby betraying the sacredness of stories. However, Paul Ricoeur (1975) in the *Rule of Metaphor* shows that metaphor is a semantic innovation that takes two or more ideas and recontextualizes them to create new meaning. Metaphors function both epistemologically and creatively so that metaphors are in fact a form of argument. Therein lies the power of narrative. It is the power inherent in narrative and the imbalance of power among competing narratives. The artifice of the storyteller is invoked in any kind of research writing. Stories are political, some have more currency than others because the narrative landscape is uneven and at times dangerous. Narrative is the methodology, Storytelling is the method; and the stories of human experience are the body of research literature. Stories and storytelling are the original or rather *the authentic* form of research, what we used to call *wisdom*.

## Ethical Concerns and Relational Responsibility

The relationality of narrative inquiry both informs and forms the ethical process of the work. Paramount to all narrative work is the centrality of relationship in the research process and recognizing the sacredness of the stories participants share and entrust to you within the research environment. Researchers must respect the offering of these story gifts and this must take precedence in the research process. Petra Munro Hendry (2007) exhorts that our concern as narrative researchers should be

> ... with staying true to our informants' stories and not imposing our narratives on them. I would maintain that to increase our rigor we need to be more faithful to our relationships and not impose more methods. ... What I would like to suggest then is that research is not ultimately about interpretation but about faith. Trusting in the stories and the storyteller. (pp. 493–494)

To engage in narrative research work is often tantamount to a leap of faith, to trust in the stories that are shared in the research environment and beyond. 'As a narrative inquirer, I must strive to put away attitudes of judgement, and allow openness to others to guide the work' (Ross, 2003: 584). To be a narrative researcher one must always endeavour to be alongside those who are sharing their stories with us 'in a respectful and special manner, in a circular way' (Young, 2005: 144). Responsible relationality begins before the inquiry, grows and develops during the inquiry, and continues long after the inquiry, all the while forming, informing and reforming the text because 'what is told, as well as the meaning of what is told, is shaped by the relationship' (Clandinin and Connelly, 2000: 94–95). Furthermore, narrative work demands that we represent stories so that they do no harm (Sarbin, 2004). When working with participants' stories ensure that you are listening, really listening the storyteller's narrative into being. The following window into narrative inquiry illustrates Mary Isabelle Young's (2012) and Janice Huber's (2010) belief that '[r]elationship is key to what it is that narrative inquirers do' (Clandinin and Connelly, 2000, p. 189), particularly in relational narrative inquiry.

---

## BOX 10.2

### Window into narrative inquiry

This understanding of the deeply relational nature of narrative inquiry has infused and carried us. When in 2000 we, Mary and Janice, met as graduate students, we did not know that as our lives continued to unfold we would remain connected. Looking back now, over this 12-year passage of time, we see the indelible place of relationship. Our initial coming to know one another took shape in a special place, a place of storying and restorying our experiences at the Research Issues table at the Centre for Research for Teacher Education and Development, University of Alberta. At that time, Mary, as *Anishinabe kwe*[1], had worked alongside post-secondary students of Aboriginal[2] ancestry for many years; Janice, as a classroom teacher and researcher of mixed European ancestry, had worked alongside diverse children, youth, and families in rural, international, and city centre schools. In the weekly gathering that is Research Issues we each, often, storied our hope, and, too, complexities and tensions of working alongside adult students, children, youth, and families in a spirit of encouraging and supporting the dreams they hold for their lives.

Seven and a half years ago we began a national narrative inquiry alongside six Aboriginal teachers and two Elders attentive to the experiences of the teachers as they navigated post-secondary places on their journeys of becoming teachers. As we began this narrative inquiry we, Mary and Janice, shared with the teachers and Elders stories of our relationship, of our gradual coming to know and to trust one another in and through our sustained storying and restorying of our experiences. This storying of our relationship gradually grew into relationships with each of the teachers and Elders, relationships that ground our long-term relational narrative inquiry; relationships now also shaped in and through our storying and restorying of our experiences (Young, Chester, Flett et al., 2010; Young, Joe and Lamoureux et al., 2012). It is this commitment to experience, to understanding that who we each are and who we are each becoming is always in the midst, always shaped and reshaped across time, place, and situations that has been key in sustaining our *living* of relationship as key to what it is that narrative inquirers do. As noted by Clandinin and Connelly (2000), 'As we tell our stories as inquirers, it is experience ... that is the driving impulse. ... Our guiding principle in an inquiry is to focus on experience and to follow where it leads' (p. 188). In living our relationships as key in our relational narrative inquiry we have followed where our experiences have led us ... with laughter and tears.

[1] Following our work in *Warrior Women* (Young, et al., 2012) we are grateful for Linda Tuhiwai Smith (1999) and her teaching us to italicize the *Anishinabe* language and the names and languages of each nation as a way to honour Aboriginal people.

[2] We use the term Aboriginal to include First Nations, *Métis*, and *Inuit*.

---

| Activity 10.2 | Commitment in narrative inquiry |

Think again about a study you may be planning to undertake. Are you prepared to give the time commitment and ethical integrity required to engage in the relational minefield that can be narrative inquiry? You may wish to write a short reflective piece that identifies the issues you are likely to encounter and potential strategies for addressing these.

## Presentation and dissemination of findings

The final text you create will be a blending of stories composed and recomposed all within the midst of life. Think about who the audience is for your work. Who could benefit from, and who needs to hear, your research narratives. Policymakers? The public at large? Students we teach? Other researchers within our discipline? How can your research incite collective action? (Chase, 2005).

Narrative inquiry invites the researcher to present in novel and creative ways. This might include the use of poetry, theatre, imagined dialogue, film and video, creating a website or a children's book. The following window into narrative inquiry written by Robin Adeney uses quotes from child participants to create a poem that enhances our understanding of children's play.

---

**BOX 10.3**

**Play Poem**

My brain wants to play! (Luke)
When can we play? (Kate)
You have to work before you play. (Nina)
But then can we play? (Taylor)

*(Continued)*

(Continued)

> Me playin' tea party now. (Kate)
> I'm playing with my shadow. (Declan)
> Let's play bad queen. (Reila)
> Let's play power rangers. (Adam)
> You have to work before you play! (Luke)
> And then can we play? (Kate)

'The researcher is within the stories researched' (Gergen, 2003: 280), as they enter into a relationship with the storytellers a new narrative is being created and woven through the shared stories. Not only is there the story itself, there is also the meta story 'the story of the story's telling'. Story 'is not clear, hard, linear and defined but is rather, fragmented, even wordless expressions of experience and emotion' (Neumann, 1997: 109), which causes the researcher to draw upon the artifice of the storyteller and listen it all into being.

How we finally express what we have learned from participants is a delicate dance of researcher care and ethical integrity. Coles (1989) writes 'their story, yours, mine, it's what we all carry with us on this trip we take, and we owe it to each other to respect our stories and learn from them' (p. 30). Josselson (1996) writes about the dread, guilt and shame as she struggled with imposing her own meaning making on participants stories. She said 'we do narrative work in anguish' and 'to be uncomfortable with this work, protects us from going too far' (p. 70).

Marmon (1996) points to the personal dilemma of the researcher to create an authentic text that does no harm to participants. Ely (2007) goes even further suggesting that the act of writing is wrenchingly difficult, lonely and upsetting. A particular challenge is determining a writing genre that is fair and authentic. What is essential is that an ethic of care be used when conveying information garnered from others. This may include rewriting and rethinking texts, negotiating research texts with participants and using pseudonyms for participant's names. In narrative research work we collect 'raw data of human experience' (Josselson, Lieblich and McAdams, 2003: 8) and while we are cautioned as researchers to stick to traditional formats it is here in the messiness of the raw data that using an 'I' voice is encouraged.

Unlike other forms of research a narrative approach does not lend itself to one definitive finding, rather, as Clandinin and Connelly (2000) claim, 'narrative inquiry carries more of a sense of a search, a "re-search", a search again' (p. 124). Schwab (1962) claims in a similar vein that 'narrative inquiry cannot be predicted or defined in the ways that stable forms of inquiry can' (p. 64). As you begin to organize and gather your stories the task can be formidable. It is useful to accept that the job will be 'messy and emergent' and 'like a collage rather than the construction of a building' (Eisner in Clandinin and Murphy, 2007: 20). Be patient with yourself. Narrative inquiry does not lead to conclusions and certainty. Rather, 'narrative work holds the reader in a space of inconclusivity' (Pinnagar, 2006: 179). Uncertainty and tension will guide the work, you cannot predict or anticipate the outcome, narrative inquiry does not seek a conclusive finding or findings; rather, it looks for understanding and meaning.

# Conclusion

Life is often mixed with ambiguity and uncertainty, doing narrative research work is no exception. However, one must remember that it is in and through narrative meaning making that humans gain insight and understanding of lived experience; we are stories and stories are us. Narrative has both epistemological and ontological implications in being human and human being; it is who we are.

---

## KEY POINTS

- Narrative research has grown dramatically, if not exponentially since appearing on the qualitative research horizon more than 20 years ago
- Often the term narrative inquiry is used synonymously with narrative analysis, yet the two should not be conflated
- The purpose of narrative inquiry is to examine the meaning of participants' experiences as expressed through their story
- Temporality, sociality and place undergird all narrative studies
- Narrative inquiry philosophically aims to create a space where the inquirer immerses themself in a particular world
- The position of the researcher within the research is critical and is interlaced with the positioning of participants
- The researcher lives within the research and is committed to studying phenomena in their natural settings
- The relationality of narrative inquiry both informs and forms the ethical process of the work
- There is no one-size-fits-all or cookbook recipe that one can follow to be a narrative researcher
- Narrative work can involve a number of different methods such as autobiography, auto-ethnography, narrative performance and narrative inquiry
- Believability and/or authenticity are at the nexus of validity in narrative research work
- Narrative inquiry invites the researcher to present in novel and creative ways
- Narrative work can make a difference in terms of directly impacting the lives of individuals and communities

- Consider your existing conception of qualitative research. How does narrative inquiry fit with that conception? Do you consider stories to be research? Can they be trusted?
- Narrative inquiry demands that the researcher is a strong writer, an empathetic listener, is creative, works closely with people in intensive and close relationships, and is able to be flexible, patient and accommodating. Are these characteristics largely personal attributes or can they be learned?
- Explore your own institution. Is there a supervisor and/or a community of narrative inquiry researchers that could support a study using this methodology?

## Suggested further reading

Clandinin, J. (2007) *Handbook of Narrative Inquiry: Mapping a Methodology*. 1st edn. Thousand Oaks: SAGE Publications.

'Composed by international researchers, the *Handbook of Narrative Inquiry: Mapping a Methodology* is the first comprehensive and interdisciplinary overview of the developing methodology of narrative inquiry. The Handbook outlines the historical development and philosophical underpinnings of narrative inquiry as well as describes different forms of narrative inquiry. This one-of-a-kind volume offers an emerging map of the field and encourages further dialogue, discussion, and experimentation as the field continues to develop' (SAGE Publications, 2013).

## References

Adeney, R. (2011) *Tales from the Dollhouse: Children Composing Identities Through Play, Language and Story*. Regina, Saskatchewan: University of Regina.

Ayers, W. (1995) 'Social imagination: a conversation with Maxine Greene', *Qualitative Studies in Education*, 8: 319–328.

Bagley, C. (2009) 'The ethnographer as impresario-joker in the (re)presentation of educational research as performance art: towards a performance ethic', *Ethnography and Education*, 4: 283–300.

Barone, T. (1992) 'A narrative of enhanced professionalism: educational researchers and popular storybooks about school people', *Educational Researcher*, 21: 15–24.

Barone, T. (2007) 'A return to the gold standard? Questioning the future of narrative construction as educational research', *Qualitative Inquiry*, 13: 454–470.

Bateson, M.C. (1994) *Attending a World. In Peripheral Visions: Learning Along the Way*. New York: Harper Collins Publishers, pp. 95–110.

Bochner, A. (2001) 'Narrative's virtues', *Qualitative Inquiry*, 7: 131–157.

Bruner, J. (1990) *Acts of Meaning*. Cambridge, MA: Harvard University Press.

Bruner, J. (2002) 'So why narrative?' In *Making Stories: Law, literature, life*. Cambridge, MA: Harvard University Press, pp. 89–107.

Ceglowski, D. (1997) 'That's a good story, but is it really research?', *Qualitative Inquiry*, 3: 188–201.

Chase, S.E. (2005) 'Narrative inquiry: multiple lenses, approaches, voices', in N.K. Denzin and Y.S. Lincoln (eds), *Handbook of Qualitative Research*. Thousand Oaks: SAGE, pp. 651–679.

Clandinin, D.J. (2007) *Handbook of Narrative Inquiry: Mapping a Methodology*. Thousand Oaks: SAGE.

Clandinin, D.J. and Connelly, M. (2000) *Narrative Inquiry: Experience and Story in Qualitative Research*. San Francisco: Jossey-Bass.

Clandinin, D.J. and Connelly, M. (2004) 'Knowledge, narrative and self-study', In J. Loughran, M. Hamilton, V. LaBoskey, et al. (eds), *International Handbook of Self-Study of Teaching and Teacher Education Practices*. Dordrecht: Springer, pp. 575–600.

Clandinin, D.J. and Murphy, S. (2007) 'Looking ahead. Conversations with Elliot Mishler, Don Polkinghorne and Amia Lieblich', in D.J. Clandinin (ed.), *Handbook of Narrative Inquiry: Mapping a Methodology*. Thousand Oaks: SAGE, pp. 632–650.

Clandinin, D.J. and Rosiek, J. (2007) 'Mapping a landscape of narrative inquiry: borderland spaces and tensions', in D.J. Clandinin (ed.), *Handbook of Narrative Inquiry: Mapping a Methodology*. Thousand Oaks: SAGE, pp. 35–75.

Clandinin, D.J., Pushor, D. and Orr, A. (2007) 'Navigating sites for narrative inquiry', *Journal of Teacher Education*, 58: 21–35.

Coles, R. (1989) *The Call of Stories: Teaching and the Moral Imagination*. Boston, MA: Houghton Mifflin.

Coles, R. (1997) *Doing Documentary Work*. New York: Oxford University Press.

Connelly, F.M. and Clandinin, D.J. (1988) *Teachers as Curriculum Planners: Narratives of Experience*. New York: Teachers College Press.

Connelly, F.M. and Clandinin, D.J. (1990) 'Stories of experience and narrative inquiry', *Educational Researcher*, 19: 2–14.

Connelly, F.M. and Clandinin, D.J. (2006) 'Narrative inquiry', in J. Green, G. Camilli and P. Elmore (eds), *Handbook of Complementary Methods in Education Research*. Mahwah, NJ: Lawrence Erlbaum, pp. 375–385.

Crites, S. (1971) 'The narrative quality of experience', *Journal of the American Academy of Religion*, 39: 291–311.

Cronon, W. (1992) 'A place for stories: nature, history, and narrative', *The Journal of American History*, 1347–1376.

Denzin, N.K. (1997) *Interpretive Ethnography: Ethnographic Practices for the 21st Century*. Thousand Oaks: SAGE.

Denzin, N.K. and Lincoln, Y.S. (2005) *The Sage Handbook of Qualitative Research*. Thousand Oaks, CA: SAGE.

Ely, M. (2007) 'In-forming representations', in D.J. Clandinin (ed.), *Handbook of Narrative Inquiry: Mapping a Methodology*. Thousand Oaks: SAGE, pp. 567–598.

Frye, N. (1982) *The Great Code. The Bible and Literature*. Toronto: Academic Press Canada.

Gergen, M. (2003) 'Once upon a time: a narratologist's tale', in C. Daiute and C. Lightfoot (eds), *Narrative Analysis: Studying the Development of Individuals in Society*. Thousand Oaks: SAGE, pp. 267–285.

Hendry, P.M. (2007) 'The future of narrative', *Qualitative Inquiry*, 13: 487–498.

Josselson, R. (1996) 'On writing other people's lives. Self-analytic reflections of a narrative researcher', in R. Josselson (ed.), *Ethics and Process in the Narrative Study of Lives*. Thousand Oaks: SAGE, pp. 60–71.

Josselson, R., Lieblich, A. and McAdams, D. (2003) *Up Close and Personal: The Teaching and Learning of Narrative Research*. Washington, DC: The American Psychological Association.

Lather, P. (1993) 'Fertile obsession: validity after poststructuralism', *Sociological Quarterly*, 34: 673–694.

Lugones, M. (1987) 'Playfulness, "world travelling", and loving perception', *Hypatica*, 2: 3–19.

Marmon, S.L. (1996) 'Introduction', in *Yellow Woman and a Beauty of the Spirit*. New York: Simon and Schuster, pp. 13–21.

Minh-ha, T.T. (1991) *When the Moon Waxes Red: Representation, Gender and Cultural Politics*. New York: Routledge.

Mishler, E.G. (1990) 'Validation in inquiry-guided research: the role of exemplars in narrative studies' , 60: 415–440.

Moustakas, C. (1994) *Phenomenological Research Methods*. London: SAGE Publications.

Murray-Orr, A. (2005) *Stories to Live By: Book Conversations as Spaces For Attending to Children's Lives in School*. University of Alberta: Edmonton.

Murray-Orr, A. and Olsen, M. (2007) 'Transforming narrative encounters', *Canadian Journal of Education*, 30: 819–838.

Neumann, A. (1997) 'Ways without words: learning from silence and story in post-Holocaust lives', in A. Neumann and P.L. Peterson (eds), *Learning From Our Lives: Women, Research and Autobiography in Education*. New York: Teachers College Press, pp. 91–120.

Phillion, J. and Wang, X. (2011) 'Multicultural and cross-cultural narrative inquiry: conversations between adviser and advisee', in S. Trahar (ed.), *Learning and Teaching Narrative Inquiry*. Amsterdam, NL: John Benjamin, pp. 85–106.

Pinnagar, S. (2006) 'Afterword: re-narrating and indwelling', in D.J. Clandinin, J. Huber, M. Huber, et al. (eds), *Composing Diverse Identities: Narrative Inquiries Into the Interwoven Lives of Children and Teachers*. New York: Routledge, pp. 176–181.

Polakow, V. (1985) 'Whose stories should we tell? A call to action', *Language Arts*, 62: 826–835.

Polkinghorne, D.E. (1988) *Narrative Knowing and the Human Sciences*. New York: State University of New York Press.

Richardson, L. (1994) 'Writing: a method of inquiry', in N.K. Denzin and Y.S. Lincoln (eds), *The Handbook of Qualitative Research*. 1st edn. Thousand Oaks, CA: SAGE Publications, pp. 516–529.

Ricoeur, P. (1975) *The Rule of Metaphor: Multi-Disciplinary Studies in the Creation of Meaning in Language*, Toronto: University of Toronto Press.

Ricoeur, P. (1984) *Time and Narrative Vol. 1. (K. McLaughlin and D. Pellauer, Trans.)*. Chicago: The University of Chicago (Original work published 1983).

Riessman, C.K. (1993) *Narrative Analysis*. Boston, MA: Boston University.

Riessman, C.K. (2008) *Narrative Methods for the Human Sciences*. Los Angeles, CA: SAGE Publications.

Ross, V. (2003) 'Walking around the curriculum tree: an analysis of a third/fourth-grade mathematics lesson', *Journal of Curriculum Studies*, 35: 567–584.

SAGE Publications (2013) *Handbook of Narrative Inquiry*. Available at: http://www.sagepub.com/books/Book227281?siteId=sage-us&prodTypes=Books&q=clandinin&fs=1 - tabview=title.

Sarbin, T.R. (2004) 'The role of imagination in narrative construction', in C. Daiute and C. Lightfoot (eds), *Narrative Analysis: Studying the Development of Individuals in Society*. Thousand Oaks, CA: SAGE, pp. 5–20.

Scholes, R. and Kellogg, R. (1966) *The Nature of Narrative*, London: Oxford University Press.

Schwab, J.J. (1962) *The Teaching of Science: Teaching of Science as Inquiry*. Cambridge, MA: Simon and Schuster.

Stivers, C. (1993) 'Reflections on the role of personal narrative in social science', *Journal of Women in Culture and Society*, 18: 408–425.

Toolan, M.J. (1988) *Narrative: A Critical Linguistic Introduction*. New York: Routledge.

Turner, M. (1997) *The Literary Mind: The Origins of Thought and Language*. London: Oxford University Press.

Young, M. (2005) *Pimatisiwin: Walking in a Good Way: A Narrative Inquiry Into Language as Identity*. Winnipeg, MB: Pemmican.

Young, M., Chester, J.L., Flett, B.M., et al. (2010) 'Becoming "real" aboriginal teachers: attending to intergenerational narrative reverberations and responsibilities', *Theory and Practice*, 16: 285–305.

Young, M., Joe, L., Lamoureux, J., et al. (2012) *Warrior Women: Remaking Post-secondary Places Through Relational Narrative Inquiry*. London: Emerald Publishing.

# 11
# Phenomenology

## Kim Usher and Debra Jackson

---

**Learning objectives**

After reading this chapter, you will be able to:

- Outline the philosophical underpinnings of phenomenology
- Identify the key philosophers involved in its development
- Describe the different types of phenomenology
- Discuss the role of the researcher undertaking a phenomenological study
- Describe the strategies for data generation and analysis
- Outline some of the ways that phenomenological research findings can be presented

---

## Introduction

Phenomenology is the careful and systematic reflective study of the *lived experience*. While there are a number of differing iterations of phenomenology, all proponents share an interest in understanding the notion of what it is *like* to be human and what constitutes our *lived world* (Smith, Flowers and Larkin, 2009a). Phenomenology's influence in the health sciences is such that it has been described as the 'dominant means in the pursuit of knowledge development in nursing' (Dowling, 2006: 131). As a research design, phenomenology is particularly suited to disciplines that place high value on understanding the patient/client experience (Miller, 2002). Yet, despite the impact phenomenology has had, Dowling (2006) notes that though the term is used often in the literature, there is some confusion surrounding it. This confusion can be attributed in part at least to the fact that there are multiple phenomenological perspectives, which continue to develop making a single definition of the term 'phenomenology' impossible (Miller, 2002).

Phenomenology is considered to be both a philosophy and methodology/ method with early phenomenological work being philosophical in intent rather than research motivated. Husserl, Heidegger, Gadamer and Merleau-Ponty were the main philosophers who developed phenomenology as a way of thinking about the world (Earles, 2010). While the term lived experience is often used in relation to research, it has special significance for phenomenology. Van Manen and Adams (2010) explain that the term *lived experience* derives from the German *Erlebnis*, or experience as we live it, which recognizes it as a particular type of experience. It is this notion of *lived experience* in phenomenology that makes it distinct from other types of qualitative research that also focus on the human experience. In contrast to the other qualitative research designs, phenomenology is the:

> … [S]ober reflection on the *lived experience* of human existence – sober, in the sense that it must be thoughtful, and as much as possible, free from theoretical, prejudicial and suppositional intoxications. But, phenomenology is also a project that is driven by fascination: being swept up in a spell of wonder, a fascination with meaning. (van Manen, 2007: 11)

In other words, phenomenologists are committed to understanding what our experiences in the world are like; experience should be examined as it actually occurs and on its own terms (Smith et al., 2009a).

Phenomenology therefore does not aim to develop a theory that might help us to control or explain the world; rather, it aims to bring deeper insight to help us be in greater contact with the world (van Manen, 1990; Smith et al., 2009a). More recently, phenomenology has been developed as a human science for the study of lived or *experiential* meaning using a variety of techniques to describe and interpret meanings (Adams and van Manen, 2008; Smith et al., 2009a; van Manen, 2011). This chapter describes the emergence of the phenomenological traditions, outlines the key philosophical underpinnings and methods used in phenomenology, and provides an overview of some of the associated issues such as rigour and quality, and the position of the researcher.

## History of the methodology

The philosophy of phenomenology evolved from the late nineteenth century and throughout the twentieth century in an attempt to counteract the objectification of the world (positivistic scientific thought) that arose from the reliance on empir-ical scientific enquiry. In other words, great thinkers were concerned about an over- reliance on positivistic notions of the world and so proposed the view that to understand human experience required a different approach to that used in the natural sciences (Schwandt, 2003). Phenomenology is said to have originated in Germany and later spread across Europe, eventually reaching Asia, North America and other continents (van Manen and Adams, 2010; Earles, 2010), with early work undertaken by Franz Brentano (1838–1917) and Carl Stumpf (1848–1936). The notion of *intentionality*, is the main focus of the early philosophers in the movement, meaning that consciousness is always conscious of something. The object of our perception is out in the world, in time and in space – and our perception of the object is in our consciousness. Within phenomenological thinking, the intentional structure of consciousness infers a reaching out of one's consciousness to interact with objects and concepts as a means of relating to the world (Crotty, 1996). Moustakas (1994) describes intentionality using a broader descriptor that includes subscribing a questioning and/or theorizing nature to the world, so that actors become more a part of the world under observation.

## Philosophical underpinnings

Husserl (1857–1938) is often considered the originator of the phenomenological movement. Using and modifying the thinking of others before him, Husserl developed what came to be known as transcendental phenomenology. *Transcendence* refers to the idea that we can never see a thing from all of its different perspectives at once (Moustakas, 1994; van Manen and Adams, 2010). Husserl believes that a person's subjective perception of reality should be important to scientists because this perception is what motivates people to act (Lopez and Willis, 2004). For Husserl, phenomenology is the way knowledge comes into being in the consciousness, helping to clarify the assumptions underlying all human understandings of the everyday world (Adams and van Manen, 2008). For Husserl, intentionality is the key to understanding human experience. For him, experience should be examined in the way it occurs, as he is interested in understanding how individuals come to know their *own* experience of a phenomenon, which allows them to identify the *essential* qualities of that experience. Husserl believes that if such understanding could be achieved, the essential features of an experience would *transcend* the circumstances of their appearance, illuminating the experience for others (Smith, Mitton and Peacock, 2009b). Thus, *intentionality* remained important for Husserl throughout his career, with him using the term to imply the process that occurs in the consciousness and the object of that attention. As Crotty (1998) explains, 'consciousness is always consciousness *of* something' (p. 79). Hence, our everyday life is consumed with the usual activities of the world and that experience of the world is taken for granted. For us to take on a phenomenological stance, we need to turn to the activity and attend to the taken-for-granted experience. For example, we hear a noise outside, we attend to the noise, wonder why the person is making the noise and performing the activity, perhaps even wish we could be outside performing that activity as well; once we stop and reflect on this hearing, seeing, wondering, wishing, we are being phenomenological.

Husserlian phenomenology is thus understood as *eidetic* description, or determining the essential nature and acts of consciousness. To achieve the required level of reflection necessitates the process of *eidetic reduction*, or bracketing; also known as the *epoche* (Moustakas, 1994; van Manen and Adams, 2010). Here, the researcher puts aside the taken-for-granted world to instead focus on the perception of the world (Smith et al., 2009a). In other words, Husserl suggests we should shut out all that we know about a phenomenon so that we can come to a deeper understanding of that phenomenon, free from any preconceived taken-for-granted notions of the phenomenon. The notion of bracketing is considered as one of the key elements that distinguish Husserlian phenomenology from the other types.

Martin Heidegger (1889–1976), Husserl's pupil, moved phenomenology from a descriptive to an interpretive endeavour. Known as *existential* phenomenology, Jean-Paul Sartre (1905–1980), Maurice Merleau-Ponty (1908–1961) and Simone de Beauvoir (1908–1986) were also associated with the movement. Heidegger moved phenomenology beyond a philosophy of how things are constituted in consciousness to one that recognizes how the being of beings reveals itself. In other words, he moved away from the Husserlian notions of *eidetic, consciousness and intentionality*, to focus instead on the *hermeneutic* perspective which recognizes that human existence is always embedded in a world of meanings. In this way, phenomenology

> … is the study of what shows itself in the unique manner that it shows itself to us. Every mode of being … is always simultaneously a way of understanding the world. These modes of being in the world need to be interpreted. (van Manen and Adams, 2010: 451)

Therefore, phenomenology becomes hermeneutical when its method becomes interpretive rather than purely descriptive, as is the case in transcendental phenomenology. However, van Manen and Adams (2010) argue that the distinction between transcendental and interpretive phenomenology is not as clear cut as this statement may appear to indicate as Heidegger points out that all description is in fact already an interpretation. The notion of *dasein*, or the phenomenology of being-there, of being in the world, is central to Heidegger's hermeneutic phenomenology. This concept refers to the fact that there is an aspect of human-ness which is capable of wondering about its own existence and inquiring into its own being (Heidegger, 1927/1962). It was from this position that Heidegger rejected Husserl's notion of bracketing, believing instead that in order to understand a phenomenon, the person must first of all have his or her own knowledge and experience of the phenomenon.

While earlier forms of hermeneutics were preoccupied with the interpretation of texts (Geanellos, 1998), Heidegger's hermeneutics is a phenomenological return to being; the notion of Being itself. In this case interpretation becomes an attempt to develop more complete or deeper understanding and to bring that which is hidden to the forefront (Geanellos, 1998). Heidegger describes his hermeneutical phenomenology as a circular process where in our quest to understand Being, we begin with and form a pre-understanding. In our attempt to understand this being, we come to know the 'existentials' or the structures that make human existence possible – the very nature of Being itself then returns to enrich our existence in the world (Crotty, 1998). Contrary to common opinion, Heidegger did not describe the term *hermeneutic circle*; its origin remains unknown (Koch, 1995); the *hermeneutic circle* is concerned with the relationship between the part and the whole on a number of levels. Basically, it is the process of analysis that moves from a naïve reading of the text, to a more structured analysis where the reader begins to look for patterns of connection, to the final stage where the interpretation of the whole incorporates the first two phases (Streubert Speziale and Rinaldi Carpenter, 2003). In this way, there is no true starting point from where understanding can be developed, as understanding the whole involves understanding the parts, even where the understanding is preliminary (Geanellos, 1998).

Merleau-Ponty shares Husserl's and Heidegger's commitment to understanding the notion of being-in-the-world but he focuses much of his work on the embodied nature of our relationship to the world. In other words, our body can no longer be understood as an object of the world but rather as a means of communicating with the world, and a way of seeing 'others', which develops from our own embodied perspective. Ultimately, assuming this perspective means while we may feel empathy for another, we can never truly share their experiences, because their experiences are part of their unique embodied experience in the world (Smith et al., 2009b). Although Merleau-Ponty loosely aligned his work with Husserl's thinking, he rejected transcendental philosophy in favour of existential philosophy. While Merleau-Ponty's phenomenology is descriptive rather than interpretive, which is in line with Husserl's thinking, he rejects the idealized notion of bracketing as suggested by Husserl, describing instead the need to return to the perceptual preconceptual experience of the child (Earles, 2010). Heidegger believes interpretation occurs within a background of preconceptions or presuppositions from which the interpreter can never be free. Hence, the need to demonstrate awareness of pre-understandings in terms of the phenomenon being investigated is critical (Geanellos, 1998).

Along with Heidegger, Ricoeur and Gadamer were also pivotal to the development of hermeneutic phenomenology. In recent years others have added to the work in this area; for example, Moustakas, Georgi and van Manen (van Manen and Adams, 2010; Earles, 2010). There are a number of key concepts in phenomenology that require attention prior to progressing to the planning and implementation of a study using this qualitative methodology.

## Being in the world

Heidegger set about revealing the assumptions and stripping away centuries of thinking about being. He wrote of humans as questioning Beings, which differentiates them from other animals. This need to question is more important than other forms of interacting and reveals the 'purely human mode of "being-in-the-world" as a kind of projective caring and involvement in the world' (Moran, 2000: 198). Van Manen (1997) defines being-in-the-world as the 'way human beings exist, act or are involved in the world' and exemplifies this with '… as parent, as teacher, as man, as woman, or as child' (p. 175).

## Embodiment

Embodiment is the bodily knowledge of the world – that all of our understanding of the world is based on our perceptions and thus our initial awareness of the object. Our senses offer a consciousness of the world that each individual experiences according to 'history, knowledge of the world and openness to the world' (Merleau-Ponty, 1962: 24).

## Lifeworld

The lifeworld is life as we experience it rather than as we conceptualize it. It is what Husserl termed the 'natural attitude' or the 'world of immediate experience' (Adams and van Manen, 2008). The authors go on to explain that we inhabit different lifeworlds at different times of the day, for example the lifeworld of work or school or home; these lifeworlds may also intersect.

## Reduction

Reduction describes the phenomenological process that permits us to discover an experiential understanding of the lifeworld as we experience it rather than as we conceptualize or theorize it to be (van Manen and Adams, 2010).

## Lived experience

As discussed earlier, *Erlebnis* means experience as we live and recognize it (Adams and van Manen, 2008). In other words, the term lived experience indicates a phenomenologist's interest with the pre-reflective understandings of the world as we experience it, prior to putting language to it.

## Bracketing

Crotty (1996) explains reduction as a purification process that resulted from Husserl's attempts to purify consciousness (i.e., remove the overlying understandings, the natural attitude) by suspending 'belief in the actual existence of the objects of experience' (p. 59). The goal of reduction is to isolate the central core meanings or features of the phenomenon; to accomplish this task, the thinker must strip away all prior understandings of the phenomenon and approach it with a fresh and new attitude. This neutral stance (without either believing or disbelieving in the existence of the phenomenon, or anything about it) is called bracketing (Streubert Speziale and Rinaldi Carpenter, 2003). The concept of bracketing is the subject of some debate in the literature (Miller, 2002). As you have read previously in this chapter, bracketing is a Husserlian concept; not all phenomenologists support the notion.

## Verstehen

Phenomenologist's argue that the discovery of understanding (*Verstehen*) cannot occur through the empirical–analytical sciences alone; it occurs through sharing common meaning, culture and language as it is lived together (Van der Zalm and Bergum, 2000).

## The phenomenological nod

The *phenomenological nod* occurs as a form of validation when a person reads a phenomenological description and thinks 'that is an experience I could have' (Van der Zalm and Bergum, 2000).

# Position of the researcher

Researchers undertaking qualitative research become the instrument of the research (Janesick, 2000). In phenomenology, the researcher takes on the special responsibility of transforming information provided by participants as researcher partners as they explore and elucidate a particular phenomenon. For the researcher, it also means taking a reflective stance, in order to understand the nuances of your own experience/s of a phenomenon and then to appreciate the subtleties of being a person experiencing the phenomenon in a specific context (O'Brien, 2003). Developing the thoughtful, phenomenologically-oriented question (van Manen, 1990) is an essential first step in conducting a phenomenological study. The question arises from who the researcher is both professionally and personally; with a concomitant set of experiences and contexts that informs their thinking, together with their ego (the self-interested nature of the question). All of these aspects inform the position of the researcher; phenomenology requires us to 'interrogate [as] something from the heart of our existence' (van Manen, 1990: 43), as the phenomenological researcher is extremely important to the research process. It is their ability to communicate and put the participants at ease (Streubert Speziale and Rinaldi Carpenter, 2003) that will help to ensure the collection of deep and meaningful data. It is therefore necessary for the researcher to be extremely self aware and perceptive, to be able to recognize when a participant is not at ease and to change the data collection process accordingly.

In phenomenological research, the researcher is a writer, as the craft of writing is central to this design. Writing is inextricably linked to analysis as the researcher attempts to capture the essential characteristics of the phenomenon – the essences – in a written document. Hermeneutic phenomenological writing is the heart of human science research, and the creation of a phenomenological text is the desired outcome of each project. The researcher must therefore position themselves as a writer whose performance as such will be eventually judged by the presence (or not) of the 'phenomenological nod' (Van der Zalm and Bergum, 2000) when the text is read by the participants.

# Aligning philosophy and methodology with purpose

It is important to achieve coherence between the philosophical ideas informing the research, the methods chosen to gather and manage data, and the purpose of the project. In other words, the choice to undertake phenomenology should be driven by the nature of the research question. It must be acknowledged, however, that there are various approaches to phenomenology (Miller, 2002) and these approaches will inform the methods of a particular study. However, despite the phenomenological approach selected, phenomenology is the study of the lived experience and that aspect should be prominent in the research question. A typical phenomenological research question might be 'What is the lived experience of or what is the meaning of [phenomenon under investigation]?' Often these are written as problem or research statements rather than questions, and so may be presented in a statement such as 'This study will provide insights into the lived experience of [phenomenon under investigation]'.

## Data generation and collection

The aim of phenomenology is to generate understanding into the essential nature of a particular phenomenon under investigation. The way of coming to know the experience is through those people who have had the lived experience – who have first-hand lived experience of the phenomenon of interest (Miller, 2002; Finlay, 2011). Prior to the commencement of interviewing participants, particularly in descriptive phenomenology or where bracketing is essential, the researcher needs to reflect on their previous experience and identify anything that may hinder their ability to listen and hear the participant's experiences authentically or might trigger an emotional response in the researcher (Liamputtong, 2010). More contemporary phenomenologists suggest instead that the researcher critically engages with their own subjectivity (Finlay, 2011) during this process.

Depending on the phenomenon under investigation, recruitment can be quite time consuming and it is important to allow adequate time for this process when developing the timeline for the project. Recruitment normally continues until data saturation is achieved; that is, that no new data is being revealed. The term 'data saturation' is well accepted although researchers have various practices when this happens and it is not uncommon to see statements such as 'data saturation plus two', which means that once data saturation was established, two additional participants were recruited, just to ensure that no further insights emerged.

The most common form of data collection is audio-taped phenomenological interviews with persons who have lived through the experience under investigation (Priest, 2002), though other forms of data such as diaries can also be used as phenomenological data. Phenomenological interviews are in-depth interviews (Miller, 2002; Liamputtong, 2010), most often semi-structured in nature, and featuring open-ended questions carefully chosen to elicit the desired information. It is important to create questions that will generate relevant information, but avoid being leading or causing the participant to give answers they think the researcher wants to hear. Steps need to be put in place to avoid eliciting this type of response. Prompts and probing questions can be used to clarify information or to elicit a fuller response. For example, a researcher might begin an interview by asking: 'can you tell me your first recollections of experiencing weight gain associated with your medications?' An interview guide with suggested probing questions as well as primary questions is usually helpful. Interviews may also be framed as focused conversations, rather than interviews, and this is a strategy that can assist in making the participant feel more relaxed, and so enhance rapport and therefore optimize data quality. Phenomenological interviews can be intense and potentially tiring for participants, and can be quite lengthy. A scan of published papers based on data derived from phenomenological interviews indicates that they can range from 45–90 minutes. Audio-taped interviews are transcribed into text, and this text becomes the data for analysis.

The authors have been using phenomenological ideas for a number of years now in their research. One issue we would raise in applying phenomenological approaches is the issue of culture. Because of the focus on lived experience, it is very important to understand the role that culture can play in: first, experiencing a phenomenon; secondly, making meaning of that phenomenon; and thirdly, telling the story or recounting the experience of the phenomenon. Understanding that in order to disclose experiences, participants need to have the language skills to articulate their experience is vital to effective data generation. Furthermore, and depending on the focus of the study, participants sharing their lived experience can be very revealing for them, meaning that they can be left feeling vulnerable and exposed. This is so for all participants in phenomenological studies, but where there are also particular cultural mores around sharing of personal information or discussing very personal matters this is more apparent. In addition, some language around very personal or emotional feelings can be difficult to adequately express. This experience is so for all people, but may be even more for people for whom English is a second language. In working with phenomenology within the context of a multicultural environment, it is very important to focus on the micro skills of effective communication, such as: being respectful; active listening; use of questioning in various forms, including funnelling and clarifying questioning; clarity in speaking; allowing enough time for participants to make their responses as full as desired; being comfortable with silence (this is necessary to allow participants to reflect and gather their thoughts); and, reflective communication.

## Analysis of data

Data analysis is a crucial step in the research process, and for the phenomenological researcher, represents the stage in the research process in which the essential nature – the essence – of the phenomenon of interest may be understood and represented (Priest, 2002). Despite the centrality of the analytical process to phenomenology, in some ways, the analytical processes may seem to be taken for granted and poorly explicated because many published phenomenological papers only deal very briefly with analysis, and do not describe these methods fully. Priest (2002) suggests that some phenomenologists, because of their particular ideological stances, may prefer not to focus on specific analytical steps. Regardless of under-reporting in research papers, phenomenological data analysis has been the subject of considerable attention by methodologists and there are a number of detailed systematic approaches to phenomenological data analysis (Miller, 2002; Dowling, 2006) that have been published.

Regardless of the particular phenomenological approach taken, phenomenological data analysis begins with a process of close and repeated engagement with the data (Miller, 2002; Liamputtong, 2010). Text is organized into units, noteworthy phrases are identified and units are transformed into meanings, represented as phenomenological concepts or themes, which are then linked to form a detailed deep description of the experience (Miller, 2002; Priest, 2002) that is sometimes referred to as a thematic analysis (Borbasi and Jackson, 2012). During analysis, phenomenological reduction is practised, which involves bracketing, eidetic reduction and epoche (Priest, 2002). In engaging with the data, questioning (of the data) can be used to investigate all conceivable meanings of the data. This process is known as imaginative variation or intuiting, and it continues until a common understanding of the phenomenon of interest has been generated across the data (Priest, 2002).

The first step of the data analysis process is usually the process of reading and re-reading. In this way the experiences of the participant become the focus for the researcher. Following the reading process the researcher begins an initial note-taking process; a detailed and time consuming task where the researcher notes everything of interest while maintaining an open mind. The next process involves isolation of meaning units that are then selected as emergent themes that are considered central to the experience. Here the researcher simultaneously attempts to reduce the detail while maintaining the complexity in terms of relationships, connections, patterns and notes. Finally, the researcher identifies the explicative themes and sub-themes, or those that appear to have referential characteristics while bracketing their own thoughts and biases about the topic. Following the reductive and intuiting processes comes the phase of description – of identifying the essential structure of the experience. The complexities and intricacies of the phenomenon need to be captured and reported in ways with which others can understand and engage (Grbich, 2007; Liamputtong, 2010).

Van Manen (1990) provides six guidelines to approaching phenomenology (Box 11.1). It is important to realize that van Manen did not intend for these guidelines to be a prescriptive, linear procedure for conducting phenomenological research but rather a way to provide researchers with some structure. The intent was that these guidelines would serve to 'animate inventiveness and stimulate insight' (van Manen, 1990: 30).

---

**BOX 11.1**

### Van Manen's guidelines for phenomenological analysis

1. Turning to a phenomenon of interest;
2. Investigating the experience as we live it rather than as we conceptualize it;

3. Reflecting on the essential themes which characterize the phenomenon;
4. Describing the phenomenon through the art of writing and re-writing;
5. Maintaining a strong and oriented relation to the phenomenon;
6. Balancing the research context by considering the parts and the whole.

(van Manen, 1990, p. 30–31)

Michael van Manen outlines how he used these guidelines to analyse data he collected on the parental experience of transfer of a newborn baby to a neonatal intensive care unit (van Manen and Adams, 2010). To begin he undertook line-by-line readings of the transcripts using reflection to explore the fundamental lifeworld themes of the parental transfer experience: lived space (spatiality), lived body (corporeality), lived time (temporality), and lived human relation (relationality). Anecdotes taken from the interviews were used to assist the researcher to access the experience of transfer from the perspective of the parents. To achieve this goal, he deleted extraneous material and identified material to strengthen stories that moved in the direction of the phenomenon and its themes. The process of writing was important and he describes how he sent drafts of the text for review by a diverse group of health care professionals and parents of children who had been cared for in a neonatal intensive care unit to ensure the phenomenological descriptions and anecdotes resonated with their lived experience (van Manen, 2011).

Another process for data analysis is proposed by Moustakas (1994). To begin, the researcher highlights significant statements, sentences or quotes that provide insight into the phenomenon of interest (called horizonalization). Clusters of meaning are then developed from those significant statements from which textual descriptions are developed. Creswell (2007) uses a modified version of Moustakas' analytic process, outlines the process as including a number of steps: (i) describe personal experiences with the phenomenon under study – this helps to set aside personal experiences; (ii) develop a list of significant statements from the interviews, treat all statements equally, and develop a list of non-overlapping statements; (iii) group these statements into larger units – meaning units; (iv) write a description of 'what' the participants experienced with the phenomenon – the textual description; (v) write a description of the 'how' experienced by the participants – structural description; and (vi) write a composite description of the phenomenon incorporating both the textual and structural description – the 'essence' of the experience (p. 159).

| Activity 11.2 | Approaches to data analysis in phenomenology |

Consider the preceding discussion on phenomenological data analysis. How do the data analysis processes for phenomenology differ from other qualitative approaches? Construct a list of the differences between the van Manen (1990), Moustakas (1994) and Creswell (2007) approaches to phenomenological analysis.

# Quality and rigour

Quality and rigour are two issues that have caused much concern among qualitative researchers, and some considerable debate in scholarly circles. Like other qualitative methods, phenomenology is considered by some to be 'soft science' because it does not draw on numerical data. Furthermore, phenomenologists do not practice measures such as randomization, which is seen as an indicator of quality in positivist research. In order to try to establish research quality and rigour, qualitative researchers have sought to establish quality criteria appropriate for their methods. This has been attempted in various ways, including appropriating some of the language of positivism. However, as Rolfe (2006) has argued, this has proven to be rather problematic, partly because of the iterative nature of phenomenology, a characteristic it has in common with other qualitative approaches (Onwuegbuzie and Leech, 2007).

As a result of the difficulties associated with adopting the language of positivism, qualitative researchers developed their own set of criteria, which includes strategies such as: stating presuppositions, member-checking, achieving representativeness, and dependability, establishing an audit trail and transferability (Priest, 2002; Rolfe, 2006; Onwuegbuzie and Leech, 2007; Borbasi and Jackson, 2012). However, these criteria are also not without debates, problems and challenges. The concept of member-checking is an example of the debates around quality and rigour. Member-checking has been proposed as a strategy for establishing credibility (Guba and Lincoln, 1989) and is widely accepted as such. This process involves going back to participants or drawing on a peer panel following data analysis to ensure that analysis is valid and is a legitimate representation of the phenomenon that is the focus of the study (Rolfe, 2006). However, member-checking has generated debate in the literature, with Sandelowski (1993) challenging the practice based on notions of participant's multiple realities. Additional concerns associated with member-checking exist around potential breaches in confidentiality that could occur as a result of contacting participants again subsequent to participation, and the potential for distress associated with the potential for trauma in participants when reading accounts of their experience. Both of these difficulties can be overcome with careful attention to the research design. Others have argued that attempts at member-checking, which they claim are stemmed by positivist notions, are unnecessary. Rather, it is important to let the text manifest itself instead of trying to control researcher bias, and to remember that interpretation varies between interpreters (Geanellos, 1998).

In a critical appraisal of the literature, de Witt and Ploeg (2006) developed a 'framework of expressions' (p. 227) for establishing rigour in relation to interpretive phenomenology. These are balanced integration, openness, concreteness, resonance, and actualization. In developing some language for rigour that is specific to interpretive phenomenology, these authors hope to stimulate further debate and developmental work in this area. What is also evident is that as a methodological approach, phenomenology is continuing to develop, which reflects the dynamic and contemporary nature of this qualitative methodology.

When designing projects it is vitally important that close attention be paid to ensuring strategies are in place to enhance research quality and rigour. However, many current approaches are contested, and each has particular strengths and weaknesses. Indeed, Rolfe (2006) calls for attempts to create a standard structure for evaluating the quality of qualitative research to be discontinued, in preference for individual decisions for individual studies. Furthermore, as we have stated earlier, phenomenology is a philosophy as well as a methodology and because of this, it is an area that attracts continued scholarly discourse. This ongoing scholarly attention ensures that phenomenology as method continues to develop, and that strategies for researchers to ensure rigour and research quality will continue to be refined and enriched.

---

**Activity 11.3** — **The phenomenological research process**

Return to the paper you obtained for Activity 11.1. Consider the selection criteria employed. How were participants chosen to be in the study? Are methods appropriate to the aim of the study? How did the author/s address the issue of quality and rigour? Did they describe their strategies? Do you think they were adequate?

---

## Presentation and dissemination of findings

There are various ways phenomenology can be presented. Commonly, findings are presented as a series of themes or motifs that capture the essential aspects of the phenomenon of focus. Excerpts of participants' narratives support themes. Generally, phenomenology is highly engaging to an audience/reader, because of its focus on the human experience. However, care needs to be taken about how much of the philosophical aspects of the method should be included in research reports. Obviously there needs to be enough so that the reader/audience member can understand why certain decisions were made, but not enough so that the actual findings of the study being presented are obscured in any way. In the following window into phenomenology Karen Yates provides an example of how findings are reported in this type of qualitative design. Yates, Usher and Kelly's (2011) study of rural midwives resulted in three themes that describe the lived experience of participants located in rural areas of far north Queensland, Australia.

---

**BOX 11.2**

**Window into phenomenology**

I undertook a phenomenological study of midwives' experiences of working in a dual role as nurse and midwife in rural areas of far north Queensland, Australia. The methodology was informed by Heidegger's interpretive phenomenological philosophy and data analysis was guided by van Manen's analytical approach. Data was generated by unstructured, conversational

*(Continued)*

---

*(Continued)*

interviews with eight midwives. The interviews were recorded and transcribed verbatim, then analysed and interpreted using a hermeneutic phenomenological approach. Three themes were identified that helped to explain what it is like to work in a dual role as nurse and midwife in rural far north Queensland. These were: Making choices between professional role and lifestyle: 'Because I choose to live here'; Integration of maternity and general nursing: 'All in together this fine weather' and, Shaped by location: 'That's part of working in a small place'. Findings reveal that the midwives see their employment options as limited by their rural location, however these limitations were largely accepted as being part of living in a rural area. A number expressed concern that they were deployed back and forth between midwifery and nursing areas, sometimes more than once during the same shift. There was philosophical conflict identified between the biomedical, illness-based model of nursing and the partnership, wellness model of midwifery, and concern about the lack of support for midwifery services. While the midwives expressed a preference to work as midwives only, they did acknowledge that the variety offered by the dual role had some benefits in terms of maintaining nursing knowledge and skills. While the participants recognized that in rural areas it is important to be a multi-skilled generalist, they were concerned that midwifery skills could be eroded or even lost with the diminishing amounts of midwifery work available.

# Conclusion

In this chapter we have presented a brief overview of phenomenology as philosophy, methodology and research method. From a research perspective, phenomenology is most appropriate when the aims of a study are to gain insight into the lived experience of a particular phenomenon. Phenomenology has been identified as having real benefits in a wide range of disciplines, because it provides a means through which authentic understanding of human experiences can be ascertained.

## KEY POINTS

- The aim of phenomenology is to generate a representation of a phenomenon of everyday experience, so as to understand its essential nature and characteristics
- There are various published and well-cited approaches to phenomenological data analyses, and the choice of approach will depend on how the study is framed. However all approaches to phenomenological analysis feature close and repeated engagement with data, and a process of writing and rewriting to assist in distillation and refinement of the essential nature of the phenomenon of interest
- Rigour and quality have long held the interest of researchers and scholars. Various strategies are presented in the literature and each has particular strengths and weaknesses. The nature of phenomenology – as both philosophy and method – means ways of establishing rigour and quality will continue to captivate scholars for years to come, and thus strategies will continue to develop and be refined

- Review the philosophical underpinnings of phenomenology discussed in this chapter. From your readings of other methodologies in this text, what do you consider to be the key points of difference?
- Reflect on the different types of phenomenology. How does the role and position of the researcher differ across these types?
- Locate a selection of published articles that have employed phenomenology. How are the findings presented? In what ways is this presentation different from the way in which other forms of qualitative research is presented?

## Suggested further reading

### Journal article

O'Reilly, R., Peters, K., Beale, D. and Jackson, D. (2009) 'Women's experiences of recovery from childbirth: focus on pelvis problems that extend beyond the puerperium', *Journal of Clinical Nursing*, 18: 2013–2019.

### Book

Smith, J., Flowers, P. and Larkin, M. (2009) *Interpretive Phenomenological Analysis*. London: SAGE Publications.

'This book presents a comprehensive guide to interpretative phenomenological analysis (IPA) which is an increasingly popular approach to qualitative inquiry taught to undergraduate and postgraduate students today. The first chapter outlines the theoretical foundations for IPA. It discusses phenomenology, hermeneutics, and idiography and how they have been taken up by IPA. The next four chapters provide detailed, step by step guidelines to conducting IPA research: study design, data collection and interviewing, data analysis, and writing up. In the next section, the authors give extended worked examples from their own studies in health, sexuality, psychological distress, and identity to illustrate the breadth and depth of IPA research. Each of these chapters also offers a guide to other good exemplars of IPA research in the designated area. The final section of the book considers how IPA connects with other contemporary qualitative approaches like discourse and narrative analysis and how it addresses issues to do with validity. The book is written in an accessible style and will be extremely useful to students and researchers in psychology and related disciplines in the health and social sciences' (SAGE Publications, 2013).

## References

Adams, C. and van Manen, M. (2008) 'Phenomenology', in L. Given (ed.), *The SAGE Encyclopedia of Qualitative Research Methods*. Thousand Oaks: SAGE, pp. 614–619.

Borbasi, S. and Jackson, D. (2012) *Navigating the Maze of Nursing Research: An Interactive Learning Adventure*. Marrickville, NSW: Mosby/Elsevier.

Creswell, J.W. (2007) *Qualitative Inquiry and Research Design. Choosing Among Five Approaches*. Thousand Oaks, CA: SAGE Publications.

Crotty, M. (1996) *Phenomenology and Nursing Research*. Melbourne: Livingstone.

Crotty, M. (1998) *The Foundations of Social Research: Meaning and Perspective in the Research Process*. Crows Nest: Allen & Unwin.

De Witt, L. and Ploeg, J. (2006) 'Critical appraisal of rigor in interpretive phenomenological nursing research', *Journal of Advanced Nursing*, 55: 215–229.

Dowling, M. (2006) 'From Husserl to van Manen. A review of different phenomenological approaches', *International Journal of Nursing Studies*, 44: 131–142.

Earles, V. (2010) 'Phenomenology as research method or substantive metaphysics? An overview of phenomenology's uses in nursing', *Nursing Philosophy*, 11: 286–296.

Finlay, L. (2011) *Phenomenology for Therapists. Researching the Lived World*. West Sussex: Wiley-Blackwell.

Geanellos, R. (1998) 'Hermeneutic philosophy. Part II: a nursing research example of the hermeneutic imperative to address forestructures/pre-understandings', *Nursing Inquiry*, 5: 238–247.

Grbich, C. (2007) *Qualitative Data Analysis: An Introduction*. Los Angeles: SAGE Publications.

Guba, E.G. and Lincoln, Y.S. (1989) *Fourth Generation Evaluation*. Newbury Park: SAGE.

Heidegger, M. (1927/1962) *Being and Time*. Oxford: Blackwell.

Janesick, V.J. (2000) 'The choreography of qualitative research design', in N.K. Denzin and Y.S. Lincoln (eds), *Handbook of Qualitative Research*. Thousand Oaks: SAGE, pp. 379–399.

Koch, T. (1995) 'Interpretive approaches in nursing research: the influence of Husserl and Heidegger', *Journal of Advanced Nursing*, 21: 827–836.

Liamputtong, P. (2010) *Research Methods in Health: Foundations for Evidence-Based Practice*. Melbourne: Oxford University Press.

Lopez, K. and Willis, D. (2004) 'Descriptive versus interpretive phenomenology: their contributions to nursing knowledge', *Qualitative Health Research*, 14: 726–735.

Merleau-Ponty, M. (1962) *Phenomenology of Perception*. London: Routledge.

Miller, S. (2002) 'Analysis of phenomenological data generated with children as research participants', *Nurse Researcher*, 10: 68–82.

Moran, D. (2000) *Introduction to Phenomenology*. London: Routledge.

Moustakas, C. (1994) *Phenomenological Research Methods*. London: SAGE Publications.

O'Brien, L. (2003) 'Phenomenology', in D.E.Z. Schneider, G. LoBiondo-Wood and J. Haber (eds), *Nursing Research: Methods, Critical Appraisal and Utilisation*. 2nd edn. Sydney, Australia: Mosby, pp. 193–204.

Onwuegbuzie, A.J. and Leech, N.L. (2007) 'Validity and qualitative research: an oxymoron?', *Quality & Quantity*, 41: 233–249.

Priest, H. (2002) 'An approach to the phenomenological analysis of data', *Nurse Researcher*, 10: 50–63.

Rolfe, G. (2006) 'Validity, trustworthiness and rigour: quality and the idea of qualitative research', *Journal of Advanced Nursing*, 53: 304–310.

SAGE Publications (2013) *Interpretive Phenomenological Analysis*. Available at: http://www.sagepub.com/books/Book227528?siteId=sage-us&prodTypes=any&q=flowers&fs=1.

Sandelowski, M. (1993) 'Rigor or rigor mortis: the problem of rigor in qualitative research revisited', *Advances in Nursing Science*, 16: 1–8.

Schwandt, T.A. (2003) 'Three epistemological stances for qualitative inquiry', in N.K. Denzin and Y.S. Lincoln (eds), *The Landscape of Qualitative Research: Theories and Issues*. Thousand Oaks, CA: SAGE Publications, pp. 292–331.

Smith, J.A., Flowers, P. and Larkin, M. (2009a) *Interpretative Phenomenological Analysis: Theory, Method and Research*. London: SAGE.

Smith, N., Mitton, C. and Peacock, S. (2009b) 'Qualitative methodologies in health-care priority setting research', *Health Economics*, 18: 1163–1175.

Streubert Speziale, H.J. and Rinaldi Carpenter, D. (2003) *Qualitative Research in Nursing: Advancing the Humanistic Imperative*. Philadelphia: Lippincott Williams & Wilkins.

Van der Zalm, J.E. and Bergum, V. (2000) 'Hermeneutic-phenomenology: providing living knowledge for nursing practice', *Journal of Advanced Nursing*, 31: 211–218.

van Manen, M. (1990) *Researching Lived Experience: Human Science for an Action Sensitive Pedagogy*. Michigan, USA: The Althouse Press.

van Manen, M. (1997) *Researching Lived Experience: Human Science for an Action Sensitive Pedagogy*. London: The Althouse Press.

van Manen, M. (2007) 'Phenomenology of practice', *Phenomenology & Practice*, 1: 11–30.

van Manen, M. (2011) 'Carrying: parental experience of the hospital transfer of their baby', *Qualitative Health Research*, 22: 199–211.

van Manen, M. and Adams, C.A. (2010) 'Phenomenology', in P. Peterson, E. Baker and B. McGraw (eds), *International Encyclopedia of Education*. Oxford: Elsevier, pp. 449–455.

Yates, K., Usher, K. and Kelly, J. (2011) 'The dual roles of rural midwives: the potential for role conflict and impact on retention', *Collegian: Journal of the Royal College of Nursing Australia*, 18: 107–113.

# PART III

# 12
# Proposing Your Research

Jane Mills and Melanie Birks

---

**Learning objectives**

After reading this chapter, you should be able to:

- Identify characteristics of a strong qualitative research proposal
- List the three main types of qualitative research proposals
- Outline key considerations in writing a qualitative research proposal
- Discuss how to successfully defend your qualitative research proposal

---

## Introduction

The process of writing your research proposal is an opportunity to clarify and solidify aspirational thinking into a realistic plan of action. Usually we approach a potential qualitative research study with only a loose idea of what we would like to investigate. For those considering a graduate research program, there is often lots of rather romantic talk among your peers, and sometimes your lecturers and supervisors, about the importance of having a 'passion' for your topic that will sustain you through the three plus years that you will engage in this work. We take a much more pragmatic, project management approach to the conceptualization and execution of a qualitative research study that will become apparent as you read through this chapter. Completing a graduate research qualification means engaging a program of research training where you acquire knowledge and skills, which if successfully applied, will result in your becoming an independent researcher. Undertaking graduate research studies does not need to equate to climbing Mt Everest; however, key to keeping your project under control and in perspective is a well thought out and achievable research proposal. Of course not all research proposals are written for entry to a graduate research program; we also write proposals for research ethics approval, and importantly to secure competitive grants. A number of authors suggest important strategies for success when writing a qualitative research proposal (Sandelowski and Barroso, 2003; Penrod, 2003; Padgett and Henwood, 2009) each of whom use one of their successful applications to illustrate specific points. In this chapter, we have summarized these strategies in check boxes to provide easy reference points when writing sections of a typical research proposal, which are as follows.

1. Front material
2. Background
3. Research plan (methods and techniques)
4. Outcomes and significance
5. Budget and timeline

Figure 12.1 provides further detail of the content of each of these sections that require attention when constructing a qualitative research proposal.

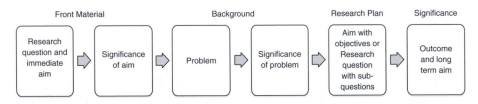

**Figure 12.1**   Constructing a qualitative research proposal

As general principles apply in the production of a qualitative research proposal, the first section in this chapter will discuss a generic approach to producing a comprehensive submission. The chapter will then focus on particular information that should be considered when preparing a proposal for a specific purpose. Here we focus on the three main types of qualitative research proposals, being those produced for: admission to a graduate research program, submission for ethics approval and application for competitive grants. To conclude the chapter we will discuss important points to consider in the defense of your qualitative research proposal.

## Qualitative research proposals

Before you begin to put together a research proposal for any purpose, the first task is to print the application guidelines and have them to hand as you write your proposal. Refer to the guidelines often, and mark off when you have completed each one of the steps required for your application. Reviewers will be attuned to the required format and you don't want to disorientate them by straying from this prescription. Following on in this theme, as a rule, the use of plain English in a qualitative research proposal works well. Plummer (2009) shares his thoughts about why the researcher as author is sometimes tempted to dazzle the reader by the use of overly intricate language.

> Maybe it is the complexity of the ideas which require more complex narratives. Maybe it is the translations from some difficult work of the past. Maybe. More often I think it is more to do with the puffed up pretense – to

make our understandings appear more scientific, deep, serious, truly profound – that we dress it all up in a language that obfuscates and obdurately masks what we see and say. (para. 5)

When writing your qualitative research proposal the one thing you don't want to do is unintentionally mask your intent with impenetrable terminology. Remember a number of different reviewers will read your proposal and not all of them will be as au fait with the subject matter and methodology as you are. As LaRossa (2005) explains,

much the same as a newspaper report or novel will have a slant to it, so also research narratives will have a slant. And that slant may make the difference in whether an article or book is read – and, if read, remembered. (p. 851)

Just like in the case of an article or a book, if reviewers remember the aim of your proposed qualitative research study for the right reasons and understand the difference the findings might make, your chance of success will increase dramatically. If an unfamiliar reviewer can easily read and understand your research plan they will feel more confident in recommending that it go forward.

---

**Activity 12.1** ┤ **Conceptualizing a qualitative research proposal**

Think about your own purposes for reading this chapter. Are you planning to produce a qualitative research proposal for a specific purpose? Obtain a copy of the guidelines and, as you read through the following discussion, make notes on the guidelines to assist you when you come to prepare your own proposal.

---

## Front material

Front material of your qualitative research proposal includes the title, key words, research question, the immediate aim of your study and an abstract. Penrod (2003) argues it is '...critical that these sections concisely describe the need, significance, research question, and potential for the study to fill a critical gap in current understanding of a phenomenon' (p. 830).

Creating a 'snappy' title for your proposal that is useful, clear and memorable tends to be a work in progress from conception to completion. What do we mean by a useful title? In the past decade, the way people search for information, including research findings, has become reliant on the World Wide Web. Planning ahead to successfully disseminate your findings with the aim of creating impact means a title and abstract including phrases that others would likely be interested in (SAGE Publications, 2013a). Restrain any urge to write a title that is quirky; instead chose a title in plain English that encapsulates the intent of your proposal. Writing succinctly is an art in itself, and the composition of an abstract challenges the author to balance key messages and detail in a very constrained number of words or characters. You need to tie together your title and abstract by including the key words selected in each of these elements. For those researching in health sciences it is vital to use keywords listed in the US National Library of Medicine's list of medical subject headings. These keywords are often referred to as 'MeSH' terms and are easily located by using the library's web-based database (US National Library of Medicine, 2012). For other disciplines, there are web-based generators (The University of Texas Libraries, 2013) that will analyse your research topic and provide you with a list of possible keywords to choose from.

In Chapter 1 we argue for a well-constructed research question to guide the selection of an appropriate methodology and subsequent research design. Tied to this research question is the immediate aim of a research proposal, which creates an anchor point for the entire body of work. Sandelowski and Barroso (2003) argue that the aim and significance of the study need to be threaded through the proposal in a specific manner that results in the reviewer understanding the links between each section and the importance of the study overall.

These authors include justifying the significance of the study in the front material and background sections even though there is usually an additional section later on in the proposal that specifically addresses this point. Reminding the reviewer of the potential consequence of the study throughout the proposal is important in getting them to remember your work when it comes to making a decision regarding it going forward or not. In saying this, don't be repetitive in your writing and be careful not to duplicate sentences in different sections, otherwise you risk boring your reviewer or raising doubt in their mind as to your ability as an author.

The immediate aim of a qualitative research proposal 'reveals your intentions to the readers of your study and tells them what you wish to achieve' (Holloway and Brown, 2012: 32). Holloway and Brown (2012) caution against writing an aim that only includes a solution to the problem that has led to the proposed study. Qualitative research may be exploratory, descriptive and explanatory by nature and one of these elements should be included in the aim of the study in combination with a possible outcome that could be realized at the end of the study, or in later work. For example, a recent action research study we conducted had the following aim: '…to identify, describe, implement and evaluate contextually relevant support strategies for student learning in the Bachelor of Nursing Science at the Torres Strait Islands campus of James Cook University'.

Once the title, research question, immediate aim and keywords of the study are written you need to compile a draft abstract of your study proposal. The abstract provides a brief summary of how you will answer your research question and again justifies the need for the proposed study. Possible uses of the abstract include focusing the researcher's thinking, communicating with other possible members of the future research team, forming the body of an expression of interest to garner an invitation to submit a full proposal for funding, or seeking an advisor prior to applying for admission to a graduate research program of study (Locke, Spirduso and Silverman, 2007). The abstract of a research proposal requires constant revision to ensure that it remains aligned to sections of the proposal that will be written and rewritten in the iterative process of developing a final submission. The summative nature of an abstract means that you have few words to use in getting across your key messages. Format wise, the abstract of a research proposal generally covers the same ground as the larger document, however there may be specific guidelines for what is required so check to make sure you have included all necessary information. Knowing your audience's priorities for action is an important factor to consider when writing the abstract of a research proposal. Understanding the reviewers' motivations and addressing these at the outset will improve your rate of success.

---

**BOX 12.1**

**Checklist for writing the front material section**

Ensure that your front matter includes:

- ☐ A useful title
- ☐ Key words
- ☐ A well constructed research question
- ☐ A statement of the immediate aim of the study
- ☐ An abstract that includes all of the above

---

## Background

The background to your research proposal includes a clear and focused discussion of what is known and what is not known about your substantive area of inquiry. How will the proposed research study address a gap in the evidence base? It may be that you have already conducted a small study that has produced preliminary findings that you now plan to build on. If this is the case you need to cite publications reporting these findings to demonstrate your developing expertise in the area, while explicating the need for further research to meet the aim of the proposal already stated in the front matter. As Penrod (2003) states, your goal when writing the background section of a research proposal is '... the development of an argument backed by adequate evidence to create and support a clear purpose statement that compels reviewers to consider ... the project' (p. 822). Importantly for qualitative research proposals you need to account for previous research designs used as well as their key findings. The mantra that the research design must fit the question is important to deliberate on when arguing for further investigation of a substantive area of enquiry already examined using an alternative research design. It may be that an additional study using a qualitative methodology will more fully dimensionalize, describe or explain the issue at hand – but you may need to argue this case.

Many recipients of proposals expect the background section to include a conceptual or theoretical framework, which '... helps reviewers to understand how the researcher is approaching the research analytically' (Penrod, 2003: 822). Including extant theory at this point in the development of a research design can be antithetical for many qualitative researchers posing questions best answered by methods of data collection and analysis that are largely inductive in nature, with the aim of developing their own theory regarding the substantive area of enquiry. As with many things in life however, this is a moment where a prudent compromise can be required of the researcher in order to progress their study. Penrod (2003) suggests a useful approach to meeting the requirement of providing extant theory in a qualitative research proposal is to choose a theoretical or conceptual framework that is abstract, yet able to provide the researcher with a way to organize their thinking and guide their actions. Examples of this type of theoretical or conceptual frame are broad paradigms of feminism, critical theory, post positivism, postmodernism or post structuralism.

In both the background and research plan (methods and techniques) sections practice strategic disarmament by anticipating controversial areas and pre-empting them with an answer (Sandelowski and Barroso, 2003). Be collegial and respectful in your discussion of previous research in the area. Do not say that others have failed, rather, make reference to areas where the need for further work was identified, and report their findings accurately and in context.

---

### BOX 12.2

**Checklist for writing the background section**

When writing your background section:

☐ Don't assume the reviewer is familiar with the area of enquiry, start by detailing the problem introduced earlier in the aims section while re-emphasizing the significance of your proposal

☐ Ensure your literature review **focuses** on making a case for the proposed study by identifying a 'gap' in research conducted to date

☐ Include the findings of preliminary research studies you have conducted that led to the current proposal

☐ Emphasize the proposed investigators' previous work in the substantive area by citing their publications in the background to the study

☐ Use the **device of contrasts** to highlight the differences between your proposal and previous studies

☐ Use the **device of 'yet'** to communicate to the reader that you acknowledge differences between your opinions and those of others who have published in the area

---

## Research plan (methods and techniques)

Locke et al. (2007) provide some sensible advice to the novice researcher, which is to begin the research plan section of your proposal with a one paragraph description of the overall study design. As these authors point out, the reviewer needs to know if this is a qualitative, quantitative or mixed methods study from the outset. By not clearly identifying your research design as a qualitative study, you can leave a less experienced reviewer grasping at the means to identify what you are planning to do. As well, they suggest you include the parameters of the study in this opening paragraph to orientate the reviewer to the scope of the proposed research study. Revisiting the action research study referred to earlier, the following window into writing a research proposal provides an example of how this can be achieved.

---

**BOX 12.3**

### Window into the qualitative research proposal

This qualitative study aims to identify, describe, implement and evaluate contextually relevant support strategies for student learning in the Bachelor of Nursing Science program delivered at the Torres Strait Islands campus of James Cook University. Using an action research design underpinned by theories of decolonization, students currently enrolled in the BNSc at this campus (n=12) will be invited to participate in a mentoring circle. The mentoring circle will be facilitated by experienced Indigenous student support officers and will not include lecturers employed to teach and assess the students. Meeting fortnightly during semesters one and two, data will be generated by mentoring circle participants in the form of artifacts including: minutes of meetings, group activity sheets, photographs, and other creative outputs. As well, an Indigenous research assistant will conduct a series of participant interviews at the end of semester two. Throughout the study, participants will determine, implement and evaluate their actions, with facilitators working alongside the group to assist in this process. The research team including experienced Indigenous and non-Indigenous researchers, Indigenous student support officers and the Indigenous research assistant will conduct group data analysis at the end of semester two, to identify cycles of action and evaluation in the process of developing student determined strategies to support individual and group learning at this remote site.

---

The introductory paragraph in the section describing the research plan sets the scene for the reviewer, providing a broad-brush description of the proposed qualitative research study. In writing the introductory paragraph you also have an opportunity to practice strategic disarmament. You will notice how in the 'window into' example, we were very clear about the different roles members of the action research team would play in supporting student participants, the large majority of whom identify as Indigenous people. As non-Indigenous researchers we led this study from behind, supporting and working with Indigenous people who facilitated the group, generated the data with participants, and then analysed the final data set with us, using a collaborative group approach. By outlining this process in the introductory paragraph we practiced a form of strategic disarmament through explicitly applying a decolonizing approach to this qualitative research study.

Typically the introductory paragraph in the research plan section is followed by a number of sub-headings, the first of which concerns the sample for the proposed study. A common pressure point for reviewers less familiar with qualitative methodologies is the small size of the sample required for many research plans. Even more confusing for many reviewers are qualitative methodologies such as grounded theory where it is very difficult to predict both the final size and constitution of the study sample (Birks and Mills, 2011). One way of communicating the scope of data that can be generated by a relatively small sample is to use estimated numbers of, for example, pages of transcribed text, hours of interview time, pages of documentation generated by participants such as diaries or blog entries, hours of time related to artifacts such as films, television and documentaries, or digital stories created by participants. This added quantification of the sample is another example of strategic disarmament in the writing of your qualitative research proposal. In this section you will also need to address ethical issues, including potential risks to participants and an explanation of how you will ensure informed and voluntary participation in your study. These issues will be discussed in more detail later in this chapter.

Following on from a description of the sample is a detailed explanation of the process of data collection/generation and analysis. As experienced reviewers of research proposals, mainly for competitive grant schemes, we concur with the advice of many that it is valuable to break up the text of this section with the judicious use of diagrams, flow charts and tables. There are a number of reasons for using different forms to present this information, the most compelling one being the need to economize on text, followed by you being able to demonstrate a clarity of thought through elegant and parsimonious expression. The notion that a picture speaks a thousand words can either play out extremely well in this context, or backfire badly depending on how clearly you are able to encapsulate elements of your research plan pictorially. In deciding if your message is clear, or not, you need to rely on a panel of critical friends who are able to provide you with fearless advice on the quality of your research proposal from the beginning of writing this document. Peer review is commonly recognized as a useful strategy to clarify a research proposal prior to submission, however we would advise you to seek this type of feedback from early on and not risk an unpleasant surprise close to the end. In particular, illustrations of any sort require the scrutiny of a number of people to ensure that they all understand what you are trying to say.

Many qualitative researchers choose to frame up the specifics of their research plan using research sub-questions, as opposed to objectives (see Chapter 1). A clearly articulated overall research question can lend itself to examination either way. Both objectives and sub-questions provide the reader with more concrete detail about how the researcher plans to answer the research question and achieve the immediate aim. When writing objectives and sub-questions, the researcher needs to make them '... specific (precise), clearly defined (identifiable) and tangible ...' (Denicolo and Becker, 2012: 54). Using our previous worked example, the objectives of this action research study were for students to:

1. Describe and define success in the context of higher degree study in the Torres Strait Islands
2. Collaboratively design a suite of student driven and evaluated support strategies specific to the Torres Strait Islands
3. Identify and describe contextual enablers for student success
4. Identify and describe contextual barriers to student success

You can see how these objectives could have just as easily been framed up as a series of sub-questions to the overall research question: 'What are contextually relevant support strategies for student learning in the Bachelor of Nursing Science program delivered at the Torres Strait Islands campus of James Cook University?'

1. How do students describe and define success in the context of higher degree study in the Torres Strait Islands?
2. What do students consider to be useful support strategies in relation to their BNSc studies in the Torres Strait Islands?
3. What are contextual enablers for student success?
4. What are contextual barriers to student success?

Whether you choose to use a research question and immediate aim followed by either objectives or sub-questions is influenced by the chosen qualitative methodology, your preference and the preference of your advisers or research team members – not to mention the application guidelines provided by the body receiving your application. Regardless, the objectives/sub-research questions can be used to create a structure for your explanation of the research methods to be used. We would suggest that you consider emphasizing the objectives/sub-research questions in bold or italics at the beginning of a paragraph that describes how you will collect or generate data to address this element of the proposed research study.

Sometimes the temporal flow of the research study means that different phases may meet a number of objectives/sub-research questions. If this is the case, then consider presenting the research plan using phases or stages as an organizing framework. Again consider if a flowchart will capture the planned phases, allowing the reviewer a 'bird's eye view' of the proposed study. Most word processing programs have templates that will assist you to produce a high quality flowchart or diagram, try and use these where possible to reduce the chances of your pictorial representation losing its integrity when printed elsewhere.

In research proposals more generally, there is usually a divide between the methods of data collection or generation and the methods of analysis. Of course in a qualitative research plan this can be a false separation given the preponderance of concurrent data collection and analysis that occurs. However, for the purposes of your qualitative research proposal it may be that you need to write up these methods in a sequential manner. In saying this, you do need to demonstrate to the informed reader your understanding of the often-iterative process of qualitative data collection or generation and analysis as appropriate to your adopted methodology. When writing up each of these components, don't assume that the reviewer understands what you mean by a particular method or technique. Provide a brief explanation of each of these including how you will operationalize this process in the context of your research plan. As well, provide relevant citations to assure the reviewer of your knowledge of the field (Locke et al., 2007). When defining methods of analysis, relate these to the objectives/sub-research questions asked and explain how the products of this analysis will integrate in order to address the research aims through articulation of the findings. Techniques such as the use of computer software to aid analysis need to be described and justified, as does the management and translation of data more generally (National Institutes of Health, 2001).

For many qualitative researchers the concept of validation is antithetical to their epistemological position, however be aware not all reviewers are of the same view. Experienced researchers such as Sandelowski and Barroso (2003) argue that '… the concern to ensure valid findings is foundational to every design choice. Accordingly, we embed these techniques throughout the design [plan] section' (p. 799). A position endorsed by a number of other authors (Denicolo and Becker, 2012; Holloway and Brown, 2012; Padgett and Henwood, 2009) all of whom argue for the explication of strategies to ensure the trustworthiness of findings (see Chapter 13 for an extended discussion of quality in qualitative research). To interrogate the quality of their qualitative research proposal the researcher can begin by considering the following three questions.

1. How will you ensure that descriptions of participants and context are accurate and complete?
2. Are your personal biases a threat? If not, why not, and if so, what do you plan to do about them?
3. In what ways and to what degree will participant reactions to you (and to the procedures used in the study) impede acquisition of valid data, and what are your plans for dealing with that problem? (Locke et al., 2007: 104)

We agree with Sandelowski and Barroso's (2003) approach of threading methods of quality assurance in respect of data collection, generation and analysis throughout the section addressing the research plan. Using an applied approach is much more powerful than a 'catch all' paragraph at the end stating you will maintain an audit trail, document decision making etcetera. Consider the possibility of an expert panel to advise the research team and as a method of checking and balancing each phase of the study.

---

**BOX 12.4**

## Checklist for writing the research plan (methods and techniques) section

Ensure that your research plan section:

☐ Includes an introductory paragraph that summarizes your overall plan and sets the stage for the more detailed explanation to come
☐ Expands on the aim of the proposal by identifying specific objectives/sub-questions
☐ Lays out your research plan in a temporal order – consider using phases or stages to describe the proposed study
☐ Links each phase of the study to one of the objectives/sub-questions
☐ States explicitly what you are **not** going to do if you anticipate the reviewers may consider the scope of the study too extensive for either the funding or timeline
☐ Uses devices such as section headings and visual displays to break up the text

## Outcomes and significance

The projected outcomes of your study need to be linked to the immediate aim of the study and should answer the question – 'How will you know if you have succeeded?' When discussing the projected outcomes, formulate them in terms of products and discuss the likely impact of these products on the field. In our preparation to write this chapter we have noted differences between countries in relation to a specific section in the research proposal where the overall significance of the proposed qualitative study is argued. It may be that there is not a specific requirement to summarize the significance of the study at the end of the proposal, however, similar to previous sections we would advise that you weave this message into the description of the projected outcomes and their likely impact (see Chapter 14).

---

**BOX 12.5**

### Checklist for writing the outcomes and significance section

When writing the outcomes and significance section:

☐ Prepare the section addressing the significance of your research proposal as an executive summary

☐ Refer to international, national and institutional priorities when arguing the significance of your proposal

☐ Identify methods of disseminating the products of your research to target a range of audiences including policymakers and consumers

---

## Budget and timeline

Developing a carefully costed and logically planned-out budget and timeline for your qualitative research proposal is a very important step in both planning for the success of your eventual study, and convincing the reviewers of your ability to manage a feasible project. Part of costing a study is justifying the need for expenditure and this component of a proposal needs to be both detailed and accurate. Initially you need to acquaint yourself with your institution's requirements for costing a research proposal. There are a number of factors for you to account for including salary on-costs (supplementary allowances), institutional overheads and the processes for requesting waivers for these costs if appropriate, and the daily rate for compensating members of the research team who might be required to travel for fieldwork. As an example, Table 12.1 outlines the budget prepared for the action research study conducted in the Torres Strait Islands. This study was funded by a small internal university grant so it was not necessary to account for an institutional overhead charge, however salaries were calculated to include on-costs and overheads in the hourly rate. You will also note that there is no salary backfill for the majority of the research team, as this was not a requirement of this particular granting scheme, however it would be normal to calculate the cost of a percentage of the chief investigator's time and include this figure as an in-kind contribution. In addition, you would also include an amount for administrative costs such as telephone, power and printing in an outside grant application but as a rule this cost does not apply to internal grants or graduate research proposals unless specific to participant recruitment or data collection.

**Table 12.1**  Example budget

| BUDGET | Justification | Cost |
|---|---|---|
| **Staffing** | | |
| Indigenous Student Support Officer (HEWL 6/Step 10) (Staff Relief) x 14 days $40.84/hr − casual including on-costs and overheads $296.09/ day (7.25hr day) | The ISSO will travel to Thursday Island seven times over the duration of the study for two days at a time. In SP1, the ISSO will lead the facilitation of the mentoring circle activities, while at the same time capacity building the local AO to be able to continue on with this role in SP2 and into the future. Additional time spent by the ISSO on the study will be incorporated into their duties in the Indigenous Health Unit. | $4,145.26 |
| Thursday Island Campus Administrative Officer (HEWL 4/ Step 10) (Additional Employment) x 24 days = 1 day/ week SP1 and SP2 $32.69/hr − casual including on-costs and overheads $237.00/ day (7.25hr day) | The local AO employed at the Torres Strait Islands Campus will work with the ISSO in SP1 to facilitate the mentoring circles. As well, this person will act as a liaison between the students, local stakeholders and the broader research team based at the Townsville and Cairns campuses. In SP2 the AO will lead the mentoring circle meetings with reduced onsite support from the ISSO who will visit twice during this time period and provide phone support at other times. | $5,688.00 |
| Research Assistants (ACA-B/Step 10) x 21 days $51.08/hr − casual including on-costs and overheads $370.33/ day (7.25hr day) | A casual RA will be employed periodically throughout the study to complete the ethics application, conduct a literature review; assist the ISSO and the AO with logging data generated and maintaining an audit trail for the study. In addition, a casual RA will be employed in the Torres Strait Islands to conduct participant interviews. | $7,776.93 |
| **Travel** | | |
| Return Airfare Townsville − Horn Island x 7 (SP1: Wks 3, 5,7,9 &11) (SP2: Wks 1 & 5) @$776 (return flight) 7 days notice | ISSO travel from Townsville to Horn Island, Torres Strait Islands on seven occasions. | $5,432.00 |
| Ferry Horn Island to Thursday Island to Horn Island x 7 @$30 return | | $210.00 |

| BUDGET | Justification | Cost |
|---|---|---|
| JCU Policy Meals ($105/day) x 14 days | Meals allowance for the ISSO during trips to the Torres Strait Islands. | $1470.00 |
| Accommodation @ $250/ night | Seven nights accommodation for the ISSO in the Torres Strait Islands. | $1750.00 |
| **Catering** | | |
| Lunch Mentoring Circles 10 occasions x $11 head x 15 people | Light lunch provided for the mentoring circle participants and facilitators. | $1,650.00 |
| Student and Family BBQs 2 occasions x $15 head x 30 people | Potential strategy to develop links with supportive people outside of the immediate university community. | $900.00 |
| **Administrative Costs** | | |
| Interview Transcriptions x 20 @ $100 | Recording of participant interviews and professional transcription of these digital recordings for the purpose of analysis. | $2,000.00 |
| Total Budget | | $31,022.19 |

There are a number of ways of formatting a timeline for inclusion in your qualitative research proposal. As you can see from Table 12.2, we used a very straightforward approach and followed the steps of the research process to indicate how our action research study was planned for implementation.

Another technique for presenting a timeline is to develop one that is output based. This approach is particularly useful for contract research or consultancies where funders expect particular outputs at milestones in the study. Using an output based timeline is also very useful for post graduate research candidates when planning their qualitative research proposal as creating a self-imposed deadline for drafts of components of your thesis can keep you on track and writing throughout. When

**Table 12.2**  Example timeline

**Timeline**

| | Jan 2012 | Feb 2012 | March 2012 | April 2012 | May 2012 | June 2012 | July 2012 | Aug 2012 | Sept 2012 | Oct 2012 | Nov 2012 | Dec 2012 |
|---|---|---|---|---|---|---|---|---|---|---|---|---|
| **Planning Phase** | ▓ | | | | | | | | | | | |
| **Literature Review** | ▓ | ▓ | ▓ | ▓ | | | | | | | | |
| **Ethics App** | ▓ | | | | | | | | | | | |
| **Data Collection** | | ▓ | ▓ | ▓ | ▓ | | ▓ | ▓ | ▓ | ▓ | | |
| **Data Analysis** | | | | | ▓ | ▓ | | | | ▓ | ▓ | ▓ |
| **Final Report** | | | | | | | | | | | | ▓ |

you are creating a pictorial representation of your timeline try not to make it too complicated, do use colours that are meaningful and consider using either a word processing or spreadsheet template to provide a professional finish. There are a number of very useful resources on the World Wide Web that can assist you in using spreadsheets, in particular, to create a Gantt chart that maps tasks/outputs and time.

---

**BOX 12.6**

### Checklist for writing the budget and timeline section

When writing your budget and timeline section:

☐ Familiarize yourself with your institution's requirements prior to preparing your budget
☐ Seek assistance from your institution's research office in the development of your budget
☐ Ensure your budget is accurately costed and well justified
☐ Identify in-kind contributions and cost these appropriately
☐ Consider framing your timeline against the predicted outcomes from the study

---

## Proposals that form part of an application for further graduate research study

Qualitative research proposals that form part of an application for enrolment into a graduate research program are much shorter in length than those produced as applications for a competitive grant scheme. A prospective candidate needs to complete the outline of their research proposal including identifying a title, the substantive area of enquiry, the research question, an overview of relevant literature, the proposed methodology and methods, a timeline and budget in order to be considered for admission to the degree program. All of this information needs to be provided in 600 to 1500 words, depending on the institution concerned. Writing a qualitative research proposal for admission to a graduate research program can therefore be a very difficult task, and one that if possible should be undertaken in consultation with a prospective adviser or supervisor.

We would suggest that your first task when thinking about enrolling in a graduate research program of study is to identify your area of interest, and then look around various universities to see who is researching in this area and most importantly, who is publishing in this area. Choose your advisers based on their knowledge of both your substantive area of inquiry and/or their methodological expertise. Getting your advisory team right is fundamental to having a positive experience as a graduate research candidate. Of course your draft research proposal may be very influential in attracting the attention of potential advisers and as such, it is important that you invest time in each aspect of the document prior to circulation to make sure that it demonstrates your potential. The qualitative research proposal you submit in the process of applying for admission to a graduate research program is unlikely to be the same proposal you present for other purposes later in your candidature. Nevertheless, craft this document as carefully as you can and seek feedback from critical friends whenever possible.

# Ethics proposals

Proposals produced to satisfy the requirements of an ethics committee or Institutional Review Board (IRB) serve a very specific purpose. These committees have a very important function – to protect research participants from potential risk that may result from their involvement in research. Ethics committees may also often concern themselves with the qualifications and experience of the researcher, as the integrity of the study reflects on the institution and has implications for the wellbeing of the participants. Any research study involving human participants, including material featuring or drawn from human participants, requires clearance from an ethics committee. In Box 12.7, Simon Burgess provides a window into the reasons why ethical issues require consideration when designing a research study.

---

**BOX 12.7**

### Window into the qualitative research proposal

As you may have gathered, ethical considerations are taken very seriously by today's universities and research institutes. If you propose to conduct research involving human participants or animal experimentation, for example, you will need to complete a detailed application process that explains the purpose and methodology of your investigation. This will be closely scrutinized by an ethics committee and you will have no choice but to accept the requirements that the committee imposes. Some researchers initially find this process a little frustrating. Rather than indulge in deep self-pity, however, it may be worth reflecting upon some of the activities undertaken by the infamous Nazi doctor, Joseph Mengele. The Tuskegee syphilis experiments could also be borne in mind. Ethics committees were established to help ensure that such 'research' is never again permitted.

Over time, most researchers actually come to find that the process of gaining ethics approval can be used to their advantage. The application process generally serves as a fairly efficient way of prompting us to think through various ethical and methodological details that we were always going to have to deal with at some stage. When a research proposal involves human participants, some of the common ethical issues to be addressed concern matters of participant risk, vulnerability, and consent; confidentiality; data security; data disposal; conflicts of interest; and differences in power between the researchers and the research participants. Measures that help to prevent sampling errors can also be important. In many cases such measures are required simply to correct an innocent kind

*(Continued)*

---

(Continued)

of methodological flaw. In some other cases, however, the ethics committee will recognize that a proposed sampling method appears to be motivated by a preference for a certain kind of result, and in such cases it can be reflective of a subtle kind of ethical failing.

Some scholars in the humanities (e.g., in history, literature and philosophy) rely largely upon comparative analysis and other non-experimental methods, and rarely need to engage with human research participants in any direct way. As a result, some of them never need to formally gain ethics approval for the work they undertake. Yet in all academic fields there is an obligation to demonstrate a scholarly acquaintance with the relevant existing literature. And we all need to understand and accurately represent the views of our opponents, regardless of how profoundly mistaken we may believe them to be. It is perhaps also worth remembering that although vanity and pride are merely human, such vices can easily prompt us to write in defence of our own pet theories, even after the critics have conclusively refuted them. Researchers are seldom celebrities. Our first duty is to advance the world of scholarship through honest, informed and productive debate, it is not merely to gain publication, attract attention or perpetuate discussion.

Each institution will have its own guidelines and forms that require completion in order to secure ethical approval to conduct the research. The processes involved in securing ethics clearance will vary from institution to institution and will also increase in complexity when dealing with particularly vulnerable participant groups such as children and the elderly. You should therefore ensure that adequate time is included for obtaining ethics clearance when planning your qualitative research study. Even if you are preparing a research proposal for purposes other than securing ethics clearance, you will need to include reference to potential ethical issues. Reviewers of applications for initial enrolment in a research program of study, or for funding, will expect to see that you have considered such issues as they potentially impact on the viability of your project.

## Competitive grant proposals

There are few explicit guidelines for qualitative researchers seeking to apply for competitive grants. A search of the government research council sites for Australia, New Zealand, the United Kingdom and Europe failed to return any specific instructions for qualitative research proposals. There is however an archived discussion paper published by the National Institutes of Health in the United States (2001), which provides guidance that is still relevant today for those wishing to strengthen competitive grant proposals that use qualitative methodologies. A key recommendation from this report is the need for a focused background section organized in relation to the area that you wish to investigate as opposed to covering too broad a range of information, some of which may be irrelevant to your argument. Another important point when writing qualitative research proposals for competitive grants is to demonstrate the research team's track record of previous research and publication in the area, both individually and collectively. Researchers who can demonstrate shared outputs, including peer-reviewed publications and measures of research impact from previous studies will have an advantage over those who cannot. Chief investigators' findings from previously published preliminary studies that provide evidence for further research will also immeasurably strengthen a larger competitive grant application by demonstrating the feasibility of research in the area using qualitative methodologies. Be consistent in how you define and use various concepts and integrate the research question and immediate aim throughout the research plan. As discussed previously, consideration of participant burden and strategies to mitigate such a burden need to be built into the research plan, as do other methods of ensuring the ethical integrity of the study (National Institutes of Health, 2001).

---

**Activity 12.2** —— **Evaluating a qualitative research proposal**

Institutions that review research proposals for various purposes often make available de-identified examples of successful submissions to guide you in the development of your own proposal. Obtain a copy of a sample submission that has relevance to your own purposes. Using the checklists provided in this chapter, and taking into account the specific requirements applicable to proposals produced for different purposes discussed previously, review the proposal to identify to what extent the author(s) of that document successfully address the various elements of each section of their proposal. What strengths and weaknesses have you noted that may influence the preparation of your own proposal?

---

## Defending your qualitative research proposal

There are two types of defense that an investigator is called upon to provide in relation to their qualitative research proposal: a written rejoinder or an oral defense. Written rejoinders are often required in the process of applying for a competitive grant. Once reviewers have provided initial feedback on applications, researchers are invited to respond to their comments in defense of their proposal, and to clarify particular points. Sandelowski and Barroso (2003) provide a strategic treatise on their experience of defending a qualitative research proposal which describes how they identified commonalities and differences in the reviewers' responses and then worked with these to their advantage. They began by emphasizing the positives in the reviewers' commentaries, and then followed by playing off reviewers against each other where there were inconsistencies in their responses. After summarizing the overall themes in the reviewers' comments, the authors then addressed individual's issues – sometimes providing a counter-argument, and sometimes responding with an amendment to the proposal. If amendments were made to the original research proposal, the page number was provided to make this easier for the reviewers to track.

In addition to written rejoinders, it is becoming more common for grant review panels to request an oral presentation from short-listed applicants prior to them making a final decision about the allocation of funds. The oral defense of a qualitative research proposal therefore can be part of the process of applying for a competitive grant, but more commonly novice researchers will be required to provide an oral defense of their research proposal in order to meet the requirements of confirming or progressing their graduate research candidature. There is an excellent chapter on the oral presentation of a research proposal (Locke et al., 2007) that we would recommend graduate research candidates in particular read prior to preparing for this event. However in summary, there are a number of points to consider in both the preparation and implementation of an oral defense of a qualitative research proposal.

---

### BOX 12.8

**Checklist for the oral defense of a qualitative research proposal**

When presenting an oral defense of your qualitative research proposal:

- Realize that the time allocation for an oral defense is much shorter than would be required for a reader to appraise your written research proposal
- Balance the content of your presentation so that the audience are able to clearly discern the research question, immediate aim, background and research plan
- Be discerning with regard to how much of the background you present – don't overload your audience with endless references to the literature
- Ensure the audience knows what your research plan entails – focus on the methods of data collection or generation and analysis
- Identify the expected outcomes from the study, link these to the immediate aim and argue for the significance of these
- Don't read a script if you can avoid it – practice your delivery with your peers in advance
- If you are using presentation software, ensure your audience has a copy of the slides in handout format – this is particularly important if some attendees have English as their second language
- When fielding questions, make sure you understand what is being asked – use rephrasing techniques if need be to clarify the point being made

---

# Conclusion

The novice researcher will often find the need to produce a written proposal of the research a daunting task. It can nonetheless be a particularly satisfying experience as they see the conceptualization of their study unfold in a concrete form. The qualitative research proposal provides the opportunity for the researcher to articulate the purpose and processes of their study and enables identification of potential gaps in planning and thinking that can be overcome in the early stages of its development. Regardless of the purpose for which you produce this outline of your proposed study, you should be aware that in preparing your research proposal, you provide the reader with an important first – and often only – impression of your research study and its potential impact. In the following chapter, we explore how the quality of your proposal can be carried through into implementation and ultimately the outcomes of your study.

---

### KEY POINTS

- The qualitative research proposal provides an opportunity to convert aspirational thinking about a study into a realistic plan of action
- Generally, the research proposal requires inclusion of front material, background, the research plan, outcomes and significance of the study and a budget and timeline
- Each section of the proposal should provide a comprehensive overview, and checklists provided throughout this chapter aid in ensuring that all salient aspects are addressed
- Proposals produced for specific purposes, such as to secure admission to a graduate research program, ethics approval to conduct the study or funding for a competitive grant, will need to be tailored to address specific requirements of the reviewing body
- A copy of the application guidelines for the relevant institution should be kept to hand when preparing a qualitative research proposal to ensure that all requirements are addressed
- Researchers producing a qualitative research proposal may be required to defend the proposal either via a written response or oral presentation
- Knowledge of specific requirements of approving bodies and an approach of strategic disarmament contribute to likely successful outcomes for qualitative research proposals submitted for review

---

### CRITICAL THINKING QUESTIONS

1. Reflect on the discussion of the generic attributes of a quality qualitative research proposal. Which elements do you think carry the most weight? How might this vary depending on the purpose and perspective of the reviewer?

Refer back to the guidelines obtained for the purpose of Activity 12.1. Based on your knowledge of the different methodologies discussed in Section 2 of this text, consider how the different philosophical positions of different researchers might find greater ease or difficulty in addressing the various sections of the application. Do the guidelines favour a particular methodological approach?

## Suggested further reading

Locke, L., Spirduso, W. and Silverman, S. (2013) *Proposals that Work: A Guide for Planning Dissertations and Grant Proposals*. Thousand Oaks: SAGE Publications.

'Covering all aspects of the proposal process, from the most basic questions about form and style to the task of seeking funding, *Proposals That Work* offers clear advice backed up with excellent examples. In the fifth edition, the authors have included a discussion of the effects of new technologies and the internet on the proposal process, with URLs listed where appropriate. In addition, there are new sections covering alternative forms of proposals and dissertations and the role of academic rigor in research. As always, the authors have included a number of specimen proposals, two that are completely new to this edition, to help shed light on the important issues surrounding the writing of proposals. Clear, straightforward and reader friendly, *Proposals That Work* is a must-own for anyone considering writing a proposal for a thesis, a dissertation, or a grant' (SAGE Publications, 2013b).

# References

Birks, M. and Mills, J. (2011) *Grounded Theory: A practical guide*. London: SAGE Publications.

Denicolo, P. and Becker, L. (2012) *Developing Research Proposals*. London: SAGE Publications.

Holloway, I. and Brown, L. (2012) *Essentials of a Qualitative Doctorate*. Walnut Creek: Left Coast Press, Inc.

LaRossa, R. (2005) 'Grounded theory methods and qualitative family research', *Journal of Marriage and Family*, 67: 837–857.

Locke, L., Spirduso, W. and Silverman, S. (2007) *Proposals That Work: A Guide for Planning Dissertations and Grant Proposals*. Thousand Oaks: SAGE Publications.

National Institutes of Health (2001) *Qualitative Methods in Health Research: Opportunities and Considerations in Application and Review*. Bethesda, MD: Office of Behavioral and Social Sciences Research.

Padgett, D.K. and Henwood, B.F. (2009) 'Obtaining large-scale funding for empowerment-oriented qualitative research: a report from personal experience', *Qualitative Health Research*, 19: 868–874.

Penrod, J. (2003) 'Getting funded: writing a successful qualitative small-project proposal', *Qualitative Health Research*, 13: 821–832.

Plummer, K. (2009) *On Pragmatism and Poetics*. Available at: http://www.dur.ac.uk/writingacrossboundaries/writingonwriting/kenplummer/.

SAGE Publications (2013a) *Help Readers Find Your Article*. Available at: http://www.uk.sagepub.com/journalgateway/findArticle.htm.

SAGE Publications (2013b) *Proposals That Work: A Guide for Planning Dissertations and Grant Proposals*. Available at: http://www.sagepub.com/books/Book227683.

Sandelowski, M. and Barroso, J. (2003) 'Writing the proposal for a qualitative research methodology project', *Qualitative Health Research*, 13: 781–820.

The University of Texas Libraries (2013) *How to Generate Keywords*. Available at: http://lib.utexas.edu/keywords/.

US National Library of Medicine. (2012) *Medical Subject Headings*. Available at: http://www.nlm.nih.gov/mesh/MBrowser.html.

# *13*
# Quality In Qualitative Research

Melanie Birks

| **Learning objectives** |
| --- |

After reading this chapter, you should be able to:

- Define the concept of quality in relation to qualitative research
- Outline current debates in respect of what constitutes quality in research
- Identify factors that influence quality in the conduct of your own study
- Conduct an evaluation of a qualitative research study

## Introduction

In undertaking a research study the intent is usually to produce findings that will make a contribution to knowledge and ultimately make a difference to the relevant disciplinary area. Such an outcome requires the research to have credibility with the potential end user. Thus quality must be evident in both the products and processes of the research. In this chapter we explore concepts relevant to evaluation of qualitative research and revisit ongoing debates about what constitutes quality. We then explore mechanisms to ensure quality processes in the conduct of qualitative research and examine criteria for evaluation of completed studies. This chapter will be of value for both ensuring quality in your own research and evaluating quality in the work of others.

## Quality in qualitative research

Lincoln and Guba (Lincoln and Guba, 1985) originally argued for the importance of *trustworthiness* in qualitative research as a means for reassuring the reader that a study was of significance and value. While making judgements about the quality of a research study is usually reserved for the assessment of the finished product, Tracy

(2010) argues that processes and outcomes of research cannot be separated. Similarly, we have since argued (Birks and Mills, 2011) that procedural quality in research 'must not only be done, but also be seen to be done' (p. 39). In discussing how procedural quality can be achieved in the following section, we draw upon and expand our earlier work.

## Defining quality

What do we mean when we talk about quality in relation to research? The concept of quality receives a good deal of attention in the literature, including considerable debate surrounding how quality can and should be evaluated with respect to research undertaken within various paradigmatic frameworks. Regardless of the philosophical and methodological approach used to guide a study, the credibility of outcomes is dependent on the researcher employing measures to ensure quality throughout the entire research process. In other words, you must be able to demonstrate rigour in the conduct of your research.

In the context of research, the concept of quality is synonymous with rigour. Often perceptions of rigour involve images of severe or difficult situations. The weather may be described as rigorous, as may military training or academic assessment. In such circumstances there is a high degree of control and limited room for error. Conceptualizing rigour in this way is appropriate when considering quality as it applies to the conduct of your research. This is not to suggest that you should stifle creativity. Rather, you must be sufficiently in control of the processes that you employ in order to accommodate or explain all factors that can impact on, and thereby potentially erode, the value of your research outcomes.

In Part II of this text you explored a number of qualitative research methodologies and will have seen from your reading that there is potential for employing the strategies that accompany each methodology in various ways. In conducting your research, regardless of how flexible, ethereal or intangible you consider your philosophical position, research topic or methodological interpretation to be, you must be rigorous in conducting your study if you wish to produce a credible piece of research.

## Current debates

In most instances, the only opportunity to evaluate a research study is on the basis of what is presented in published articles and summary reports. Many generic textbooks provide guidelines for the critique of published research studies, with most of these focusing on whether methodological strategies and techniques were correctly applied by the researcher when conducting the research. This is particularly the case in studies using quantitative data. The prescriptive objectivity required of the traditional scientific method provides a similarly structured framework for the evaluation of studies in which numerical data is the unit of analysis. The perceived value of objectivity by those who subscribe to a positivist paradigm has resulted in a devaluing of research that employs qualitative data sources. The debate over how research with a qualitative component can and should be evaluated has raged for decades. It is not our intention to rehash the substance of these debates, but it is worthwhile briefly reviewing current arguments surrounding the evaluation of research.

The main premise of the positivist position is that research outcomes can only be deemed accurate if they are produced in situations and through methods and processes that are rigidly controlled. Measures to ensure that the results are valid (that is, they reflect the study variables accurately) and reliable (in that they are likely to be consistently accurate) are central to the issue of control. How rigidly various control measures are implemented will determine the extent to which we can rely on the research results. Often these concepts are reflected in levels of evidence tables that present guidelines for interpreting evidence within a hierarchical structure (Nagy, Mills, Waters and Birks, 2010). Levels of evidence tables are commonly used in disciplines where perceived reliability of research is critical. Evidence-based medicine and health care, for example, use levels of evidence tables to determine the value of research-derived interventions in practice. Invariably, systematic reviews and randomized controlled trials sit at the top of the hierarchy (Joanna Briggs Institute, 2012; NHMRC, 2009; Oxford Centre for Evidence Based Medicine Levels of Evidence Working Group, 2011; Silverman, 2010). Positionality of evidence within these tables is arbitrary, however, as it is the research question, rather than the methodology, that ultimately determines what value is placed on research outcomes within such frameworks (Nagy et al., 2010; Sandelowski, 2008).

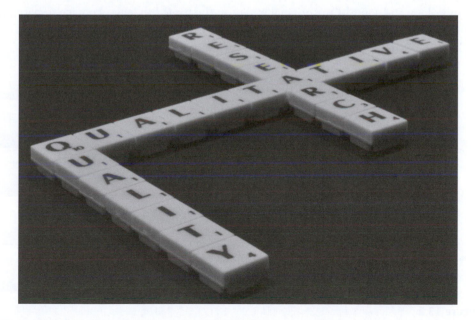

**Figure 13.1** (Photograph courtesy of Benjamin Birks)

The suggestion that quantitative methods are superior because of greater attention to issues of validity and reliability implies that the treatment of qualitative data lacks rigour. The tendency for commonly espoused criteria for evaluating qualitative research to appear simplistic and unsystematic results in poor application (Ryan-Nicholls and Will, 2009) and the perception that qualitative research is not rigorous. As a result, there is a tendency for research using qualitative data to be judged on the basis of a one-way comparison with quantitative data, with researchers subsequently apologizing for any perceived shortcomings that are in fact simply differences between the two paradigms (Sandelowski, 2008).

## Factors influencing quality

Various factors have the potential to impact on the quality of a qualitative research study. We have previously devised a model for discussing these determinants (Birks and Mills, 2011) categorized as *researcher expertise, methodological congruence* and *procedural precision* (Figure 13.2) and re-present this discussion in the context of this chapter.

### Researcher expertise

The fact that you are reading this text suggests that you do not have extensive experience in undertaking research, or perhaps are an experienced researcher who is a newcomer to the qualitative paradigm. The complexities of qualitative research terminology and some of the original works on the topic can leave a novice researcher

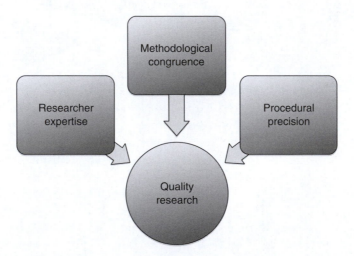

**Figure 13.2**  Factors influencing quality in the conduct of qualitative research (adapted from Birks and Mills, 2011, p. 34)

a little overwhelmed when commencing a study (and often throughout the later stages). It is important to remember that, while in many cases a researcher may have limited experience when commencing a qualitative study, most will possess experiential knowledge that will make an important contribution as they undertake their research. Even the neophyte researcher is likely to possess a number of generic skills that will contribute to their research endeavours. Skills in scholarly writing, accessing resources and the ability to manage a project are examples of such abilities.

You may draw comfort from the preceding discussion and our assurances that your generic skills will stand you in good stead as you undertake your qualitative research study. You will nonetheless need to acquire considerable knowledge about your chosen methodology from the beginning phases of conceptualization of your research through to completion. This can be achieved through a variety of means and should be consistent with your resources and preferred scholarly style. Each of the chapters in Part II make reference to sources that can assist you in learning more about your chosen research approach. Note that there is enormous variation in the style and content of the published work on the various methodologies and you should explore this work in order to establish what it is able to offer you in terms of enhancing your understanding of the various methods and processes from your own philosophical perspective. In actuality, it is the philosophical position of the author(s) of these texts that will determine their approach to the methodology in question and you should therefore keep an open mind and be willing to learn from those authors who have contributed to the literature.

In addition to extensive reading of the available literature, you should explore other options to develop your knowledge, skills and understanding of research methodologies and methods. Opportunities to participate in workshops that specialize in qualitative research and your chosen methodology should be seized; however, these are often limited. You should also seek out conferences, workshops and seminars as these provide an opportunity to discuss your research activities with other researchers who have varying levels of experience and expertise. There are a number of resources available on the internet, including articles, mailing lists and forums that will promote your engagement with the research community and provide you with a wealth of resources.

Corbin and Strauss (2008) identify a number of conditions that foster quality in research, the majority of which relate directly to personal and professional researcher characteristics. Self-awareness, clarity of purpose, commitment to hard work and internal motivation to do research are examples of these characteristics. Note that these are largely a manifestation of individual attitude. Your attitude will determine how successful you are in achieving the personal and professional goals that are tied to your research. We often hear potential researchers lament that they have yet to find a topic that they feel intensely passionate about. We emphasize with our own students that their research study should be managed as a project. You need to have an appreciation of the importance of your study, you need to feel an affinity for the topic area and you must be committed to achieving quality outcomes. These characteristics are more important than a romanticized attachment to an idea of research.

Make a list of the generic skills and personal characteristics that you possess that will be of value in your role as a researcher. Now list areas that you need to develop in order to ensure that you have the necessary expertise to undertake a study in a proposed methodological area. Locate some resources that may assist you in developing the skills and traits that will enhance your effectiveness as a researcher.

## Methodological congruence

Throughout this text we emphasize the importance of acknowledging your personal philosophy in relation to your study area. How you see the world will influence how you approach your study and the techniques that you use in achieving your research goals. Methodological congruence occurs when there is accordance between:

- Your personal philosophical position
- The stated aims of your research
- The methodological approach you employ to achieve these aims

Tracy (2010) makes reference to 'meaningful coherence' (p. 848), which includes the need to ensure alignment of research design and the conduct of the study with its foundational framework and goals. She goes further to assert that coherence can occur with attention to this alignment even when a study borrows from other paradigms. Methodological congruence is therefore the foundation of credible research, regardless of the methodological framework or philosophical dimension in which you position your study. Ensuring such congruence enables you to take risks, be creative and break new ground (Tracy, 2010).

   Invest time prior to the commencement of your research establishing methodological congruence. You need to be able to engender trust (in both yourself and the outcomes of your study) among those most likely to benefit from your research efforts. Do not make promises that you cannot keep in the course of conducting your research. Do not describe your study as existing in a philosophical and methodological framework when it does not demonstrate consistency with such an approach. Do be honest about the limitations of your research. Do acknowledge and address philosophical and methodological inconsistencies as they arise. Attention to detail from the outset will ensure that you do not drift too far off course as your study progresses.

## Procedural precision

Procedural precision refers to deliberate, planned and consistent application of methodological strategies in the conduct of research. Burns (1989), when writing about qualitative research generally, discusses a similar concept of 'procedural rigour' (p. 49). In this work she focuses almost exclusively on processes related to the generation and collection of data. This perspective is limited for our purposes in that it does not address the fact that qualitative investigation involves complex processes that precede and surpass the gathering of data.

In order to ensure procedural precision in your research, you must pay due attention to:

- Maintaining an audit trail
- Managing data and resources
- Demonstrating procedural logic

Maintenance of an audit trail is essential in any research project. The decisions that you make in relation to your research should be recorded as you carry out your research activities. Maintaining a record of research activities, changes in research direction and a rationale for choices made can protect you from loss of confidence and prevent you from 'second guessing' decisions made. Securing confidence in your own actions is a prerequisite for securing the confidence of those who may judge the products of your research. How you choose to record events and decisions throughout your study is a personal decision. You may retain a logbook, diary or electronic file for this purpose. Incorporating this process into memos is a practical approach and one that we recommend.

Cutcliffe and McKenna (2004) have argued that audit trails do nothing to establish credibility of research findings in studies using qualitative data, particularly when the researcher is an 'expert'. We, on the other hand, contend that a requirement for transparent accountability, whether in professional or scholarly activities, is incontrovertible. One cannot argue that experience negates the need for demonstrating procedural precision in research work. Certainly, research with an interpretive component may result in the generation of concepts through more ethereal means. This does not mean that the tangible processes that foster and engender such intuitive renderings cannot be articulated. Conversely, Burns (1989) argues that audit trails in qualitative research should be so detailed as to result in other authors being able to replicate your processes and reach the same conclusions. As we have discussed throughout this text, however, each qualitative researcher will have an individual perspective on a piece of research and a unique relationship with data, particularly that which was gathered by someone else. The outcome of a second researcher's experience with the data is therefore unlikely to mirror that of the first.

When planning your study you should make decisions about how you intend to manage the data that you collect. Qualitative data is often obtained from a relatively small number of sources, yet the amount of data generated from even a single interview can be extensive. You need to establish mechanisms to record, store, retrieve, analyse and review data and other resources that you will generate and collect while undertaking your research. Various software programs are available that will help you to organize and manage your data. These range from simple word processing and spreadsheet applications (for an example of how one such program can be used to manage qualitative data, see Meyer and Avery, 2009), through common quantitative data analysis systems, to powerful qualitative data management programs that can store digital voice recordings, interview transcripts, images and memos. Whatever system you decide to use, remember that these are tools to assist you in the conduct of your research. It is not what approach you use, but rather how you use it that will determine how effective your data management procedures will be.

Regardless of how you choose to manage your data, your system should be logical and secure, and your files should be backed up frequently. An awful lot of analytical products can be produced in a single day of intense activity, products that can be wiped away in seconds as a result of a virus or system failure. The way you store your data, the duration for which you retain it, and whether it may be used for secondary analysis in a future study will be governed by prescriptive policies of institutional bodies (such as review boards and ethics committees) and you should therefore be familiar with these.

In this chapter we emphasize the relationship between rigorous use of qualitative research methods and a quality end product. Analytical progress in qualitative research is often dependent on conceptual leaps, many of which may occur at unexpected times, such as when you are asleep (Burns, 1989). Our own experience is that analytical breakthroughs are most likely to occur when pen and computer keyboard are inaccessible, such as in the shower or while driving! In spite of the disregard your subconscious self may have for due process, you must be careful to preserve procedural logic by returning to your original data to ensure that conceptual leaps can be supported by your analysis, thus avoiding bringing into question the quality of your research.

Keeping track of the processes used in your research and establishing structured mechanisms for managing your data, as discussed above, are investments in your credibility. In so doing you are positioning yourself well to respond to questions relating to how you came to the end point of your analysis, such as may be required, for example, when presenting an oral defence of your dissertation or when publishing your results. While publication constraints in scholarly journals may limit your ability to articulate fully the measures that you employed to preserve quality, you should nevertheless endeavour to make reference to these, where possible, in the discussion of your methods.

## Evaluation of qualitative research

Reference to the possibility that qualitative research could be evaluated using criteria designed for evaluating quantitative studies continues to rear its head (Denzin and Lincoln, 2011; Pratt, 2009; Ryan-Nicholls and Will, 2009). In reality such practice forces the subject of evaluation into a mould that is not fit-for-purpose. Conversely, the development of guidelines that attempt to address the specifics of each qualitative methodology and its various potential iterations is impractical. In this text we have discussed quality and rigour in the context of each of the methodologies described in Part II. Each methodology is embedded in a different philosophical foundation and this foundation can be interpreted from different traditions and in the context of the individual researcher's philosophical position.

It would therefore be easy to assert that the numerous paradigms that inform qualitative research and the consequential selection of methods and strategies to achieve research outcomes mean that a single set of evaluation criteria would not be effective. Tracy (2010) argues that the development of criteria that has broad application in the evaluation of qualitative research facilitates dialogue and a united voice with the effect of enhancing the spoils of qualitative inquiry. We support this assertion and in the following section propose the use of a single generic framework for the evaluation of qualitative research.

# Criteria for evaluation

In an attempt to enhance the credibility of qualitative research, frameworks for evaluation have been developed over time. Many of these are built on criteria for establishing trustworthiness proposed by Lincoln and Guba (1985). Others represent more original perspectives (see for example Birks and Mills, 2011; Pratt, 2009; Tracy, 2010). The following section of this text examines traditional and contemporary evaluation criteria.

## Traditional criteria

In response to suggestions that qualitative research may lack discipline and rigour, Lincoln and Guba (1985) propose four criteria for establishing that a study demonstrates *trustworthiness*. These criteria are *truth value, applicability, consistency* and *neutrality*, which they operationalize as *credibility, transferability, dependability* and *confirmability*. In keeping with the covert tendency of the qualitative researcher community of that time (and arguably to this day) to feel the need to

**Table 13.1**   Comparison of evaluation criteria terminology (adapted from Murphy and Yielder, 2010)

| Qualitative criteria | Quantitative criteria |
| --- | --- |
| Credibility | Internal validity |
| Transferability | External validity |
| Dependability | Reliability |
| Confirmability | Objectivity |

justify equality with quantitative inquiry, these criteria align with established concepts for evaluation of positivist research as depicted in Table 13.1 (Murphy and Yielder, 2010).

## Contemporary criteria

In spite of considerable progress in the status and acceptability of qualitative research in recent decades, the need to demonstrate valuable outcomes from research (as further discussed in Chapter 14) has seen the establishment of fairly prescriptive criteria for the evaluation of qualitative research. Thomas and Magilvy (2011) argue that attention to such rigour is antithetical to qualitative research because it imposes boundaries on what is intended to be an open process of discovery. This assertion is reinforced by Newton, Rothlingova, Gutteridge, LeMarchand and Raphael (2012), who suggest that evaluation tools, like qualitative research itself, are contextually and temporally bound and thus no single set of criteria can be broadly applied. Unfortunately, rigid criteria are often used by funding, ethical and publication review panels where negotiation is usually not an option. We suggest that the application of a single generic framework in the evaluation of qualitative research can be effective, as long as the review is undertaken from the philosophical position of the methodology employed (Murphy and Yielder, 2010). We refer you to chapters in this text relevant to each methodology to review the philosophical underpinnings and researcher positionality that will inform effective evaluation.

While a number of evaluation criteria tools exist for qualitative research, we will focus in this section on that developed by the United Kingdom-based Critical Appraisal Skills Program (CASP, 2010). Newton et al. (2012), in reviewing a selection of qualitative research evaluation tools, found that CASP was a happy medium between those examined and was particularly user-friendly for novices. The CASP tool is gaining wider acceptance for use by bodies that oversee conduct and dissemination of research. Similarities exist between the various tools available for the evaluation of qualitative research and thus the CASP tool provides an exemplar upon which discussion of the process can be based.

## The CASP tool

The CASP tool contains ten items (Box 13.1), each designed to assess the validity, content and applicability of the research being evaluated (CASP, 2010). The tool is presented as a checklist comprised of initial screening and subsequent detailed questions to guide the evaluation of qualitative research. In most cases, evaluation can only be undertaken on the basis of the information presented in the published work, which does not always fully reflect the quality of that work (Newton et al., 2012). This limitation should be kept in mind when reviewing research that is often at the mercy of publication constraints.

**CASP Qualitative research checklist items**

**Screening questions**

1. Was there a clear statement of the aims of the research?
2. Is a qualitative methodology appropriate?

**Detailed questions**

1. Was the research design appropriate to address the aims of the research?
2. Was the recruitment strategy appropriate to the aims of the research?
3. Were the data collected in a way that addressed the research issue?
4. Has the relationship between researcher and participants been adequately considered?
5. Have ethical issues been taken into consideration?
6. Was the data analysis sufficiently rigorous?
7. Is there a clear statement of findings?
8. How valuable is the research?

## Screening questions

Initial screening questions posed by the CASP tool enable important prima facie evaluation of the study. How the evaluation process proceeds is largely based on your reason for conducting the review and prima facie evaluation allows you to make decisions about how and whether to proceed (Birks and Mills, 2011). The first question is intended to establish whether there is a *clear statement of the research aim*. This inclusion enables the reviewer to make a judgement as to the *appropriateness of a qualitative design* to meet the stated aim. There should therefore be a clear statement of the goal, significance and relevance of the research (CASP, 2010).

Qualitative research is useful for addressing questions that focus on 'how' rather than 'how many' (Pratt, 2009). During the screening phase, evaluation should establish whether the intent of the research was to interpret or bring to light experience of phenomena from the perspective of research participants (CASP, 2010). You will recall that qualitative research does not aim to test theory and thus will usually address areas of study about which little is already known. We have discussed these concepts in detail throughout this text and you will no doubt recognize the importance of understanding the principles underpinning qualitative research generally and methodological persuasions specifically as the foundation for effective evaluation of qualitative research studies.

## Detailed questions

Detailed questions contained in the CASP tool focus on issues related to the relevance of the methodology, ethical considerations, validity of processes and significance of the research. The study must employ a *research design appropriate to address the aims of the research* in order to instil confidence in the reader that the findings will be credible. To this end the researcher should justify the methodological approach and application (CASP, 2010). Once again it is necessary to have a fundamental understanding of the various qualitative methodologies in order to be able to make judgements as to whether the justification provided is valid.

As part of this more comprehensive stage of evaluation, the CASP tool questions whether the recruitment strategy was appropriate to the aims of the research and whether data were collected in a way that addressed the research issue. These questions largely seek to establish whether the methods and strategies employed in data collection have been articulated in the research. Once the reviewer is required to make assumptions, there is potential for misinterpretation and thus a clear indication of how characteristic methods were employed in the research aids in the evaluation process.

Questions surrounding whether the relationship between the researcher and participants had been adequately considered and whether ethical considerations had been taken into account require clear articulation. Researchers have a responsibility to maintain focus on ethical issues in their research. Most qualitative research relies on interview data (Perakyla and Ruusuvuori, 2011) and there is therefore potential for the rights of participants to be infringed. The researcher should clearly state how ethical issues were addressed, including how their own potential personal bias may have influenced the research, as well as articulating the nature of approval by the relevant ethics committee (CASP, 2010). Ethical considerations are the least negotiable aspect of research and the reviewer should feel assured that any and all such issues were adequately identified and managed in the conduct of the study.

Final questions in the CASP checklist relate to the analysis of data, presentation of findings and significance of the research. Evaluation of the study requires consideration of whether the data analysis was significantly rigorous. Once again an understanding of the overarching methodology is necessary to evaluate whether the specific methods used and their application in the research were appropriate. In Part II of this text you will see that different methodologies use the same methods for data collection and analysis, yet their application will be different as a result of the overarching philosophy and intent of the approach. Interviewing for example, is a different process in phenomenology than it is in grounded theory (Wimpenny and Gass, 2000). Evaluation of qualitative research should be undertaken with such variations in mind.

The question of whether the researcher has provided a clear statement of findings goes beyond simply stating the outcomes of the research. This question also has an expectation that the researchers will include a critical discussion of the findings in the context of the original research question, along with some discussion of measures used to ensure credibility (CASP, 2010). This latter point can be achieved through discussing issues such as those outlined in Fig 13.1, although the capacity of the researcher to report on these elements of the research process may once again be limited by publication requirements and other reporting restrictions.

We have previously argued for the need for the researcher to engage in evaluation of their own studies as a matter of promoting integrity of their work and themselves (Birks and Mills, 2011). This process may include addressing the final question in the CASP checklist: How valuable is the research? Issues such as implications for practice, policy and further study, as well as strategies for application and dissemination, should be included (CASP, 2010). A study that is well conducted and comprehensively reported should leave the reader in no doubt as to the significance of the research and its potential to make a difference.

---

**Activity 13.2** — **Evaluating qualitative research**

Select a published research study that you may have to hand. Conduct an evaluation using the criteria in Box 13.1. Was this process easy or more difficult than anticipated? Did you have to tailor the checklist to effectively evaluate this work?

---

# Conclusion

Qualitative research has the potential to make a significant contribution to our understanding of phenomena in the social world. Debates continue about the relative value of research conducted in the qualitative tradition and much of the contention surrounds the perception that qualitative inquiry is the poor relation of formal scientific method. In undertaking qualitative research that will contribute to the scholarly knowledge base, we have a responsibility to produce quality research. This obligation is not only to our professional peers and our various disciplinary arenas but also to ourselves. In so doing we increase the credibility of our own work and that of those who follow.

---

**KEY POINTS**

- Quality in qualitative research refers to rigour in the conduct of a study
- Debates about the quality of qualitative research have raged for decades and are centred around the perceived inability of such studies to match the rigour of those undertaken from a positivist perspective
- Ensuring quality in the conduct of a qualitative study requires *researcher expertise, methodological congruence* and *procedural precision*
- Qualitative research may be undertaken from various philosophical and methodological perspectives and this raises questions about the ability of a single evaluation tool to be fit-for-purpose
- Evaluation of qualitative research can be undertaken using a single framework providing that the reviewer has knowledge of qualitative philosophy and methodology and their impact on the application of methods

- Consider the concept of quality in research. How might it differ from how you conceive quality in other aspects of life (for example, manufacturing or the provision of services)?
- What do you think of the debates that continue in respect of quality in qualitative research? How might such debates help or hinder the status of non-positivist approaches as rigorous traditions?
- Think about a study you are undertaking or are planning to undertake. What consideration have you given to quality in the processes of your research?

## Suggested further reading

### Journal article

Tracy, S.J. (2010) 'Qualitative quality: eight 'big-tent' criteria for excellent qualitative research', *Qualitative inquiry*, 16: 837–851.

### Book

Flick, U. (2008) *Managing Quality in Qualitative Research*. London: SAGE Publications.

'The issue of quality in qualitative research is one that is often neglected. In Managing Quality in Qualitative Research attention is given to the fundamental question of how to define and assess the quality of research. Uwe Flick examines how to distinguish good research from bad research when it comes to teaching, planning, evaluating and publishing qualitative research' (SAGE Publications, 2008).

## References

Birks, M. and Mills, J. (2011) *Grounded Theory: A Practical Guide*. London: SAGE Publications.

Burns, N. (1989) 'Standards for qualitative research', *Nursing Science Quarterly*, 2: 44–52.

CASP (Critical Appraisal Skills Program) (2010) 10 questions to help you make sense of qualitative research. Available at: http://www.casp-uk.net/.

Corbin, J.M. and Strauss, A.L. (2008) *Basics of Qualitative Research: Techniques and Procedures for Developing Grounded Theory*. Los Angeles: SAGE Publications.

Cutcliffe, J.R. and McKenna, H.P. (2004) 'Expert qualitative researchers and the use of audit trails', *Journal of Advanced Nursing*, 45: 126–133.

Denzin, N.K. and Lincoln, Y.S. (2011) *The SAGE Handbook of Qualitative Research*. 4th edn. Thousand Oaks: SAGE Publications.

JBI (Joanna Briggs Institute) (2012) *Level of Evidence FAME*. Available at: http://www.joannabriggs.edu.au/Levels of Evidence FAME.

Lincoln, Y.S. and Guba, E.G. (1985) *Naturalistic Inquiry*. Beverly Hills, CA: SAGE.

Meyer, D.Z. and Avery, L.M. (2009) 'Excel as a qualitative data analysis tool', *Field Methods*, 21: 91–112.

Murphy, F. and Yielder, J. (2010) 'Establishing rigour in qualitative radiography research', *Radiography*, 16: 62–67.

Nagy, S., Mills, J., Waters, D., and Birks, M. (2010) *Using Research in Healthcare Practice*. Broadway, NSW: Lippincott Williams and Wilkins Pty Ltd.

Newton, B.J., Rothlingova, Z., Gutteridge, R., LeMarchand, K., and Raphael, J.H. (2012) 'No room for reflexivity? Critical reflections following a systematic review of qualitative research', *Journal of Health Psychology*, 17: 866–885.

NHMRC (National Health and Medical Research Council) (2009) NHMRC additional levels of evidence and grades for recommendations for developers of guidelines. Available at: http://www.nhmrc.gov.au/guidelines/resources-guideline-developers.

OCEMB (Oxford Centre for Evidence-Based Medicine) Levels of Evidence Working Group (2011) *The Oxford 2011 Levels of Evidence*. Available at: http://www.cebm.net/mod_product/design/files/CEBM-Levels-of-Evidence-2.1.pdf.

Perakyla, A. and Ruusuvuori, J. (2011) 'Analyzing talk and text', in N.K. Denzin and Y.S. Lincoln (eds), *The SAGE Handbook of Qualitative Research*. 4th edn. Thousand Oaks: SAGE Publications, pp. 529–543.

Pratt, M.G. (2009) 'From the editors: for the lack of a boilerplate: tips on writing up (and reviewing) qualitative research', *Academy of Management Journal*, 52: 856–862.

Ryan-Nicholls, K.D. and Will, C.I. (2009) 'Rigour in qualitative research: mechanisms for control', *Nurse researcher*, 16: 70-85.

SAGE Publications (2008) *Managing Quality in Qualitative Research*. Available at: http://www.sagepub.com/books/Book225077?siteId=sage-us&prodTypes=Books&q=quality+in+research&fs=1.

Sandelowski, M.J. (2008) 'Justifying qualitative research', *Research in Nursing & Health*, 31: 193–195.

Silverman, M.J. (2010) 'Applying levels of evidence to the psychiatric music therapy literature base', *The Arts in Psychotherapy*, 37: 1–7.

Thomas, E. and Magilvy, J.K. (2011) 'Qualitative rigor or research validity in qualitative research', *Journal for Specialists in Pediatric Nursing*, 16: 151–155.

Tracy, S.J. (2010) 'Qualitative quality: eight "big-tent" criteria for excellent qualitative research', *Qualitative Inquiry*, 16: 837–851.

Wimpenny, P. and Gass, J. (2000) 'Interviewing in phenomenology and grounded theory: is there a difference?', *Journal of Advanced Nursing*, 31: 1485–1492.

# 14

# A New Generation of Qualitative Research

Jane Mills

## Learning objectives

After reading this chapter, you should be able to:

- Identify the key debates in qualitative research from both a global and generational perspective
- Discuss the place of mixed methods in the future of qualitative research
- Outline the impact of generational difference on qualitative researchers' perceptions of key debates
- Define realist causality and its relationship to qualitative research
- Construct qualitative research findings to increase their impact

## Introduction

In this final chapter, key debates in qualitative research are discussed using generational theory as an analytical heuristic. The predominance of an ethnocentric North American generational unit on qualitative research is identified, and its focus on the politics of evidence as the most important issue facing researchers worldwide is explored. An alternative view on the key debates and issues facing qualitative research is provided, largely from the perspectives of Generation X (Gen X) and Generation Y (Gen Y). In particular, questions regarding the assessment of research impact are examined in depth. Potential strategies to employ in the planning, implementation and reporting of qualitative research findings to improve potential impact are provided. Possible impact measures are identified, and methods for elucidating evidence to support claims are considered. For Gen Y qualitative researchers, concerns about the false homogenization of their generational grouping are acknowledged. In particular, the assumption that all people of this generation are digital natives is examined and debunked.

# The politics of evidence

Current debates, largely conducted within the dominant North American qualitative research community, constitute a backlash against what is conceived as the growing dominance of positivistic science in major western countries such as the United Kingdom, the United States, Canada and Australia (Denzin, 2009; Lather, 1993; Lather, 2004; Torrance, 2011; Adams St Pierre, 2011; Denzin, 2011). What motivates this cohort of distinguished researchers to fight a losing war in the politics of evidence? As Denzin (2009), one of the global leaders of qualitative research states, the significance of the politics of evidence lies not in the notion of evidence itself, but rather in the 'question of who has the power to control the definition of evidence, who defines the kinds of materials that count as evidence, who determines what methods best produce the best forms of evidence, whose criteria and standards are used to evaluate quality evidence?' (p. 142).

While some of the elder statesmen of qualitative research rage against the 'right' of governments, bureaucrats and funders to define what constitutes valid science, others engage in a more moderate and pragmatic approach to debates about the politics of evidence, albeit uneasily. Cheek (2011) speaks of her search for 'the middle ground ... a place from which to engage the politics and practices of funding qualitative inquiry and the research marketplace on my terms, not someone else's' (p. 266), a place where academics can 'sell' research, while at the same time not selling out; while others (Morse and Niehaus, 2009; Morse, 2011) have turned to mixed methods as a way to raise an appetite for funding qualitative research. Creswell in particular is noteworthy in leading a team to develop the US Government commissioned report on *Best Practice for Mixed Methods Research in the Health Sciences* (Creswell, Klassen, Plano Clark and Clegg Smith, 2011).

There will always be critics of such guidelines for the conduct of qualitative research, or in this case the conduct of mixed methods research with a qualitative component. When Giddings (2006) wrote of concerns that mixed methods studies were 'positivism dressed in drag', she foretold of a funding scenario where qualitative research would be marginalized by this new movement, saying: '"How many?" renders the individual invisible, squashes metaphorical and emergent understandings and strips away context. The unique, the contradictory and the contestable need words not numbers to hold their place among the "many"' (p. 202). It is this sentiment that answers the question of why the North American vanguard keep fighting a good fight in the war about evidence, however in countries around the world they and their acolytes are losing many battles.

The reality of the world in which we live means that we have to make a space for compliance that balances the risk of selling out, with the demands that funders and, by default, universities are placing upon us. Lincoln (2012) provides an insightful thesis on the transformation of higher education to now operate as a new political economy. Compellingly, she argues that academic work has become a short-term commodity traded two ways both for promotion of self and the institution. Fostered by a culture of audit and a regime of rankings, the role of the academic and by association in relation to this argument, qualitative research is being contained and consciously discouraged. For Lincoln, future strategies for the survival and growth of qualitative research will have to centre on 'at least partially dismantling the Master's house with at least some of the Master's tools' (p. 1458). It is in this tentatively stated reference to the essay of Audre Loude (Academy of American Poets, n.d.) that the financial imperative towards mixed methods as a compromise position for qualitative researchers begins to shape as a viable alternative for survival.

## Gen X: The view from here is of a different landscape

When considering the idea that the politics of evidence constitutes the key issue in contemporary debates (as demonstrated in Denzin and Lincoln's (2011) *Handbook of Qualitative Research*, which is the most popular contemporary text globally), we asked ourselves, is this our 'big ticket' issue too, or are the arguments those of louder voices than ours? Reading through the often passionate, angry, complex and multi-layered dialogue about who has the power to control what is evidence, the contrast between these voices and those in the preceding chapters of this book is striking. No such emotive undertones are evident in the contributions of these authors in spite of there being opportunity to address what they thought was important for a new or novice qualitative researcher to know in relation to concepts of evidence in their field.

So where are the voices of our generation in this hotly contested debate? Largely silent, possibly because our concerns are not nearly as rarefied as our seniors, possibly because 'we take for granted what early generations fought to establish' (Denzin and Lincoln, 2011: 681), but most likely because we are so-called traditional right pole methodologists (Eisenhart and Jurow, 2011). We take the position that securing a future in the academy enables us to continue to make a difference and that this can be achieved. The loudest noise does not necessarily reflect the greatest contribution. This is not to say that we don't care about issues of social justice (Birks and Mills, 2011). Our commitment to this end is demonstrated by the authors who have contributed chapters and 'windows' in this book, however the focus of this commitment is different. The way we instigate change is through the conduct of qualitative research that is rigorous, local and careful, with the aim of discerning and demonstrating the impact this might have on individuals, communities, policy and practice. Let's think about why this might be so.

Mannheim's (1952 [1923]) essay *The Problem of Generations* is considered a seminal text on generational theory (Herrera, 2012; Pilcher, 1994), much of which resonates for us as we consider the tangled web of debates both within and outside of qualitative research.

The problem of generations is important enough to merit serious consideration. It is one of the indispensable guides to an understanding of the structure of social and intellectual movements. Its practical importance becomes clear as soon as one tries to obtain a more exact understanding of the accelerated pace of social change characteristic of our time. (p. 163)

[A]ny two generations following one another always fight different opponents, both within and without. While the older people may still be combating something in themselves or in the external world in such fashion that all their feeling and efforts and even their concepts and categories of thought are determined by that adversary, for the younger people this adversary may be simply non-existent: Their primary orientation is an entirely different one. (Mannheim 1952: 178)

Since the publication of this essay in the mid-twentieth century, the idea of generational difference has captured popular imagination as a way of explaining the actions of individuals and collectives in relation to others in society. In 1965, for example, The Who released one of the most popular songs of all time (*Rolling Stone Magazine*, 2011) *My Generation* – Pete Townshend's anthem to youth resistance, which typifies pop culture's conceptualization of push and pull between different generations who co-exist in the same time and place.

Broad classifications of current generational cohorts are represented by the following images (Unknown, 1968; Suau, 1989; Jorgensen, 1945) depicting 'historical events and cultural phenomena' (Costanza, Badger, Fraser, Severt and Gade, 2012: 377) said to have provided the context for a new generation to form. The end of the Second World War, a man landing on the moon, the fall of the Berlin Wall symbolizing the end of the Cold War, and the internet as our main method of global communication (Figure 14.1) are all significant world events that triggered social and cultural change. Other images we could have chosen include those relating to the 'rupture of 1968' such as the death of Martin Luther King, or the student riots that occurred around the world, and clearly 9/11 profoundly shook the western world.

The labels, including biological years, attached to each of the images are indicative of 'generations' both popularized in the media (Gordinier, 2008; Howe and Strauss, 1992; Coupland, 1991) and investigated by researchers mainly concerned with questions of workplace relations (Costanza et al., 2012; Lyons, Schweitzer, Ng and Kuron, 2012; Twenge, 2010), and education (Wilson and Gerber, 2008). Such classifications come with an important caveat however; generational thinking and perceptions are not limited by years and decades, but rather, 'contemporaneity is conceived … as a subjective condition of having experienced the same dominant influences' (Pilcher, 1994: 486). While we may be accused of hedging our bets on the idea of defining generations for the purpose of this chapter, this is a premise borne out by dialogue we initiated with our contributory group and colleagues in order to get a sense of how they positioned themselves with regard to generational difference. When asked in a personal communication (27/12/2012) 'what generation do you belong to?' Bob Dick (b. 1935) responded *I'm 77, but that may not be a reliable guide.*

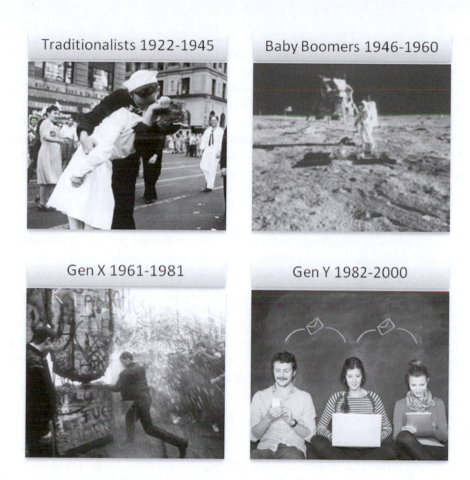

**Figure 14.1**  Images depicting triggers for generational change

| Activity 14.1 | Generational positioning |
| --- | --- |

Take a moment to think about what you know about the different generations listed. Do you know which generational grouping you could belong to? Are pop culture representations of your generation a good fit with how you perceive yourself?

While mindful of its limitations, generational difference can still provide a useful heuristic with which to theorize competing priorities in qualitative research. In summary: generations are formed by a combination of location, including time and place, and exposure to the dynamic destabilization of society and culture at a formative age when individuals are first capable of independent, critical, reflective thought (around 17 years) (Mannheim, 1952 [1923]; Pilcher, 1994). Each generation is stratified, which results in units that experience a concrete bond (Mannheim, 1952 [1923]) as they share common experiences determined by particular characteristics, for example, gender, politics, education, and nationality. It is these generational units that provide the material expression of a new generation.

Across the range of qualitative researchers world wide, traditionalist and baby boomers by far hold the most prestigious positions within universities. As baby boomers reach what has been a traditional retirement age, there are beginning trends around the world to abolish mandatory retirement ages in workplace agreements, with people staying in the workplace longer. Reasons for delaying retirement include: dedication to work, status, structured time, opportunities for social interactions and a sense of accomplishment (Frieze, Olson and Murrell, 2011). As well, the global financial crisis (2007–2008) has placed extra pressure on older academics to stay in the workforce due to the impact of this event on superannuation funds. Words used to describe baby boomers more generally include: 'optimistic', 'idealistic', 'driven', they are hard workers, work long hours, and want to have it all – career, family and material possessions (Glass, 2007; Favero and Heath, 2012).

Within the traditionalist/baby boomer elite of qualitative research is a generational unit committed to resistance, methodological revolution, epistemological commitment, and social justice. This group lived through the social and political ruptures of 1968, and situate themselves to the left – radical qualitative researchers under threat from the political, epistemological and ethical right (Denzin and Lincoln, 2011). Of course, not all of their peers are as concerned with the same issues as this generational unit, with Atkinson and Delamont (2006) stating that '[g]iven the size of the American research community with regard to the rest of the world … American ethnocentrism has a disproportionate effect on the field as a whole' (p. 750). Rejecting the notion of a crisis in qualitative research, based on the politics of evidence, these and other UK based researchers in the same broader generational groupings (Hammersley, 2008) argue for a renewed focus on reducing methodological pluralism and producing exemplary qualitative research studies thereby contributing cumulative social theory with the ability to impart impact. Reinforcing the argument against the current ethnocentrism of qualitative research and a leaning too far towards the 'art' of qualitative research as opposed to a balance between development and rigour, German researcher Flick (2009) argues for a much stronger internationalization of qualitative research and the establishment of common criteria for when particular research designs are indicated.

So who are Gen X in the qualitative research milieu? To be cynical about it (a trait often attributed to this generation), Gen X are early and mid-career academics who make traditionalist and baby boomer qualitative researchers look good. They are assistant and associate professors, senior lecturers, readers and research assistants who work on other people's research grants in the hope of establishing their own track records. They are members of supervisory panels of graduate students, co-authors who tackle online journal submissions, compile bibliographic databases and handle online grant submissions. Traversing the divide between so-called digital immigrants and digital natives (Bennett, Maton and Kervin, 2008), Gen X use technology with ease, and ease the path of their less 'tech savvy' bosses. They administer, teach, and do the minimum research and writing to ensure professional survival. Unlike the professoriate they don't have time to try and save the

**Figure 14.2**

world, instead they are busy trying to save themselves and avoid banging their heads on glass ceilings created by their traditionalist and baby boomer predecessors. Descriptors used for Gen X include: cynical, independent, emphasis on outcomes not process, work/life balance, time is more important than money, focus on self improvement (Favero and Heath, 2012; Glass, 2007).

In universities around the world, Gen X qualitative researchers are focused on securing tenure, building track and preparing for promotion, while at the same time applying for grants to conduct their own high quality research and ensuring the quality of their research students' studies. Cheek (2011) enunciates the reality of Gen X's world when she says:

> The effect of wheeling and dealing, and the translation of research funding into other forms of funding, cascades down to the level of the individual researchers. The amount of dollars received by that researcher, and where they come from, are used as indicators of individual research performance and impact. What those dollars are used for, or even if they are really needed is not the point. (p. 265)

The difference between Gen X, and the traditionalist/baby boomer professoriate is that the latter have 'made it', while Gen X is largely still on the way up. Accountability and governance aspects of research that concern government, policymakers and university administrators are not unfamiliar concepts for Gen X qualitative researchers. Graduating with undergraduate degrees in the late 1980s and early 1990s meant entering a world of employment scarcity and corporatization. As compared to the experience of traditionalists and baby boomers, opportunity was scarce on '… a playing field that has not only shifted beyond recognition but has also taken on shifting as its very business model' (Gordinier, 2008: 297). Because of their experience with widespread corporatization, rationalization and change, Gen X's response to evidence hierarchies, research performance measures, quality assurance and other points of contention in the debates around the politics of evidence is, to coin a (Gen Y) phrase, 'whatever'. In a personal communication, Wayne Babchuk (b. 1954) writes, *where battle lines were drawn in my generation, my students seem to think the whole thing is silly and advocate a more pragmatic, mixed methods agenda. They are interested in 'what works' more than making an epistemological stand.*

---

| Activity 14.2 | Working with 'what works' |

When you think about qualitative research 'what works' for you? List your most important considerations in planning, implementing and disseminating a qualitative research study.

---

## Causality and impact

The notion of 'what works' is of major importance to many Gen X qualitative researchers, including us (Mills b.1966, Birks b.1963). 'What works' needs to be considered from a number of perspectives. As qualitative researchers we need a solid fit between the questions we ask, and the methodology we choose to use. At the risk of being labelled conservative fundamentalists, we agree with our traditionalist and baby boomer forerunners who argue against the proliferation of complicated methodological pluralism for its own sake (Schwandt, 2006; Atkinson and Delamont, 2006). Instead, the continued application of well-described qualitative methodologies to substantive areas of inquiry will result in a cumulative body of knowledge, which can make a significant contribution through illuminating findings that elucidate and theorize issues of social and political concern. Implicit in this agenda is the concept of causality, which has been a point of contention in qualitative research since the publication of Lincoln and Guba's (1985) seminal text *Naturalistic Inquiry* where they reject the application of a regularity view of causation (Maxwell, 2004) to qualitative research findings. Maxwell (2012) builds on his previous work to present a realist view of causality that he argues is well placed to serve qualitative researchers. Realist causality places identifying process at the centre of analysis, makes context intrinsic to causality and links outcome to each of these elements. Saldaña (2013) provides the qualitative researcher with a comprehensive exposition of causal coding, identifying three elements of attribution, '… the cause, the outcome, and the link between the cause and the outcome' (p. 164), with the link being concerned with the process at hand.

'What works' also needs to be considered from the perspective of the public, government and policymakers. The utility of qualitative research findings is of major importance in the translation of knowledge to application in society. While there are many who would caution that the pressure of government on researchers to address national priorities constitutes a threat to qualitative research (Atkinson and Delamont, 2006), we see it as providing an opportunity to contribute to our society as a whole. It is not unreasonable for a funder to expect a positive return on investment, a principle that also applies to research dollars where there is an expected outcome of both economic growth and societal advancement (ATNU/Group of 8, 2012). As qualitative researchers, we are not above the 'grubby' issue of money and it behooves us to think beyond the immediate circumstance that has inspired a research question to the responsibility that we have as a member of the wider community, and to the institution that employs us. Prosaically, in many countries the main source of research funding is provided by democratically elected government, which means national priorities shape the assessment panels and processes that they use to determine success, so it is best to 'get with the program' if you want to succeed. In saying this, we are not advocating for research decentred from our responsibility to participants; unfounded in the ethical principles of respect for human beings, research merit and integrity, justice, and beneficence (National Health and Medical Research Council, 2009). Rather we are advocating for a reality check about where and how we can make a difference as qualitative researchers.

From the perspective of Gen X, questions about qualitative research that need to feature strongly in future debates, include:

1. How do we instigate the translation of qualitative research findings into practice?
2. How do we assess and report the impact of qualitative research findings?
3. How can we build effective impact assessment into our original qualitative research designs?
4. How do we increase the utility of qualitative research findings in a corporatized academe that has expectations of fiscal accountability and return on investment?

The last of these questions is already a debate in progress, centring on the use of mixed methods as a way of addressing the concerns of the public, funders, governments, policymakers and universities in relation to the translation and application of research findings for greater good. Morse (2011) sees the popularity of mixed methods as positive for qualitative research pulling it 'almost into the limelight' (p. 1020). Taking this further, we would argue that the integration and reporting of mixed methods findings is one way of beginning to address the first three questions posed about instigating, assessing and reporting qualitative research impact. However, mixed methods is not a 'silver bullet', and there is still a solid case for the use of qualitative research methodologies in rigorous research studies investigating questions not amenable to measurement, we just need to figure out how to demonstrate the worth of these findings.

Bloor (2011) discusses two case studies of ethnographic research resulting in assessable impact demonstrated by positive changes in models of service provision. There are two key areas for potentiating impact suggested in this book chapter. First, choosing multiple forms of local dissemination in the field that promote reflection through: contrasting practices observed with other organizations, highlighting examples of good practice, providing personal briefings to participants on findings, and providing short written reports. Second, using participant/observer fieldwork to demonstrate the potential need for new or adapted service provision.

In Australia, the publication of a recent report (ATNU/Group of 8, 2012) on the use of case study to assess research impact, based on the United Kingdom's *2014 Research Excellence Framework*, provides a number of examples of other ways researchers can assess the impact of findings. The following table contains suggested impact indicators distilled from this report that are applicable to qualitative research. We have loosely organized these indicators into general areas of concern from which different disciplines can draw.

In many ways, the table below summarizes the end product of our research aspirations – making a difference to someone or something, somewhere. Importantly though, we need to think more about how we **instigate** the translation of qualitative research findings into practice. In Chapter 7, we discuss contemporary ways to promote the dissemination of findings from a grounded theory study, which are relevant to all qualitative research methodologies. For people to want to read your findings though, they need to be clear, incisive and in 'plain English'. We have written elsewhere about the problem of the masking of qualitative findings through the use of impenetrable terminology (Birks and Mills, 2011), a point reinforced by Sandelowski and Leeman (2012) who provide useful strategies for formulating thematic sentences designed to capture segments of findings in a 'comprehensive … highly structured but also parsimonious rendering of findings' (p. 1407).

These authors also discuss the idea of 'intervention talk' as a method to increase the utility of qualitative research findings in healthcare, an idea supported by Donmoyer (2012) who states 'any researcher who hopes her or his work will be used in the policymaking process is virtually required to speak and write in the language of causes and effect' (p. 666). Reflecting on Table 14.1 it is

**Table 14.1**   Indicators for assessing the impact of qualitative research

- Policy decisions or changes to legislation regulation or guidelines have been informed by research evidence with resultant benefits realized
- Policy implementation (for example: human rights, education, health, environment, foreign affairs or agricultural policy) has been enhanced with resultant benefits realized
- Improvement in the quality, accessibility, acceptability or cost-effectiveness of a public service
- Public benefit from public service improvements
- Provision of consultancy based on previous research findings
- Expert and legal work informed by research
- Reduced cost of treatment or healthcare services as a result of evidence-based changes in practice
- Public health and wellbeing has improved

- Clinical or lifestyle interventions demonstrate a definitive outcome
- Adoption of new diagnostic or clinical technology
- Disease prevention or markers of health have been enhanced
- Disease control has been improved
- Understanding of international relationships, including historical analysis, which enhance diplomatic relationships
- Enhancements to heritage preservations, conservation and presentation
- Production of influential cultural artifacts: fine art, theatre, film, novels, poems, dance and television
- Challenges to established norms, modes of thought or practices that have shaped public or political debate
- Shaping or informing public attitudes and values towards cultural understandings of issues and phenomena
- Contributing to processes of commemoration, memorialization and reconciliation
- Development of technologies or products including software
- Development of communications technologies or protocols
- Development of technical standards which influence policy, design or protocols with resultant benefits realized
- Improved business performance measures: turnover, products, profits, employment creation
- Improved business practices: strategy, operations, management
- Creation or protection of jobs
- Mitigation of potential future business losses
- Policy introduction with positive impact on economic growth, or incentivizing productivity
- Contributing to the quality of the tourist experience
- Improvement in educational practices
- Improvement in educational outcomes
- Improved service delivery as a result of evidence-based organizational change
- Professional standards, guidelines or training are influenced by research
- Practitioners/professionals have used research findings in conducting their work
- Improved quality and efficiency of service provision
- Productivity gains as a result of evidence based changes in practice
- Environmental improvements from the introduction or improvement of processes or services
- Environmental improvements arising from: new methods, models and monitoring techniques
- Positive influence on the management or conservation of natural resources: energy, water and food
- Planning decisions have been informed by research

clear that the need for effectively communicating the findings of a study using intervention talk and implementation frameworks (Damschroder, Aron, Keith, Kirsh, Alexander and Lowery, 2009) applies to the broader church of qualitative research. The following (Box 14.1) summarizes suggestions for translating the findings of qualitative research into the language of implementing interventions (Sandelowski and Leeman, 2012). A number of these points can be linked to strategies operationalized by Bloor in the example of ethnographic case studies previously cited.

> **BOX 14.1**
>
> ### Translating qualitative research findings using the language of interventions and implementation
>
> - Consider using an implementation framework to organize and present findings
> - Write up findings in terms of the feasibility and compatibility of alternative interventions
> - Consider different types of providers in terms of how the findings of a qualitative research study could be operationalized through interventions
> - Consider using a systems approach to presenting findings as potential interventions for implementation at different levels of an organization
> - Translate findings into a guide for the development, implementation and evaluation of a particular intervention
> - Offer findings that theorize how to implement an existing intervention in a particular setting
> - Use findings to compare existing service providers with the aim of discerning best practice

Deriving impact from qualitative research is not a serendipitous process in the connected world in which we now live; 'a woven world of distant encounters and instant connections' (Yergin and Stanislaw, 1998: 9). Building potential impact assessment tools into the planning of a qualitative research study is a reasonable idea, and a useful strategy for making a difference not only to the individual participants in a study, but also to individuals who may be affected positively by your findings in other settings. The question then arises, how do you track the impact of your research findings post release? There are two strategies that we would suggest are possible in this quest.

The first strategy is commissioning the external evaluation of a program of research after a period of time in order to assess the impact of findings. For many of the indicators listed in Table 14.1 related to cost benefit, this is the most rigorous way of establishing what the outcome is. Establishing a program of qualitative and mixed methods research that investigates a substantive area of inquiry over time is an important strategy to building profile, track record and sustainable grant income. Aligning doctoral student research with this same area results in a constant flow of publications reporting findings, which complement larger aspirations in relation to future research and impact. When engaging in clearly-defined programs of research, individual university departments will see value in investing in outside evaluation to assist in securing future sustainability through demonstrated impact.

As part of a wider program of research though, it is important to establish individual impact portfolios for completed studies. While '[p]ublications are the hard currency of the track record needed for researchers to be able to compete for funding' (Cheek 2011: 259), it is insufficient to rely on standard metrics such as journal impact factors, numbers of peer reviewed publications and importantly, competitive grant income to appraise your worth as a qualitative researcher. What might an individual qualitative research project's impact portfolio contain? Box 14.2 includes some suggestions, again drawn from the recent Australian report on assessing research impact (ATNU/Group of 8, 2012) which argues that the central message of research impact is demonstrating 'what was done, why it was done, what difference it made and how the research made it happen' (p. 19).

---

**BOX 14.2**

**Qualitative research study portfolios**

- Evidence of qualitative research utilization through the implementation of findings that have *changed knowledge, behaviour and attitude* with significant, demonstrated benefit
- Evidence of qualitative research utilization through the implementation of findings that have *changed practice* with significant, demonstrated benefit
- Evidence of qualitative research utilization through the implementation of findings that have resulted in *new or improved services* with significant, demonstrated benefit
- Evidence of qualitative research utilization through the implementation of findings that have resulted in *new or amended policy* with significant, demonstrated benefit
- Evidence of the reach of qualitative findings, global, national, regional and local, in the *implementation of change* that has resulted in significant, demonstrated benefit

---

A qualitative research project's impact portfolio needs to be maintained over a long period of time, with the accumulation of various artifacts that provide significant, demonstrable evidence of impact. Using technology such as Google® and Google Scholar®, it is possible to set up alerts for the products of your research in order to track their utilization outside of academe. As well, taking care to formulate your findings to maximize their uptake and considering new ways of disseminating these findings, may well bring you in closer contact with the end users of your work, providing new opportunities to work with individuals in implementing qualitative findings for maximum effect.

## Gen Y: The future of qualitative research

There are a number of committed, intelligent, articulate qualitative researchers in a wide range of disciplines, many of whom are Gen X and Gen Y, all of whom are working towards making a difference. When inviting contributors onto the writing team for projects such as this text and our previous publication *Grounded Theory: A practical guide*, we prioritize younger talent so as to tap into fresh ideas, while providing an opportunity for career development. Giving back through mentoring for career development is important to us because of our own experience of being expertly guided and supported over time. In saying this, we have also welcomed some traditionalist and baby boomer researchers to write about their areas of expertise and experience, thus valuing the wisdom of our elders also.

So what of Gen Y in today's mix of qualitative researchers? The approximate biological age range of this generation means that the oldest of this group are around 30 years of age. Therefore, Gen Y qualitative researchers are predominantly lecturers, associate lecturers, research fellows, research assistants, post-doctoral fellows or doctoral/masters degree candidates. Regardless of being at the beginning of their research careers, Gen Y qualitative researchers are very present in the literature regarding methodology and methods. A contributing factor to this proliferation of publications is the introduction of models of doctoral thesis by publication, particularly in education and health (Francis, Mills, Chapman and Birks, 2009). Mixed methods, the use of secondary data for qualitative studies (Birks and Mills, 2011) and emergent influences such as critical Indigenous research methodologies are becoming mainstream for a new generation of researchers for whom '[s]triking a balance between methodological rigor and the creativeness of the research design is imperative for innovative research' (Bainbridge, Whiteside and McCalman, 2013: 276). Methods of data collection and analysis including photovoice, digital storytelling and the analysis of social media are becoming more popular among Gen Y, and are effectively woven into classic research designs. An example of this is a participatory action research study using photovoice as a method of data generation conducted with young people living in socially and economically disadvantaged areas of Aberdeen, Scotland (Watson and Douglas, 2012). Photovoice provides for participants to take pictures that identify issues important to them in relation to the substantive area of enquiry, in this case the impact of neighbourhoods on adolescent mental health. Using these images as a basis for further discussion, researchers use methods of participatory action research to co-investigate issues, processes and actions in an iterative manner.

A recent discourse analysis of Gen Y university students (Sternberg, 2012) highlights issues that this group of qualitative researchers also face, mainly as a result of the proliferation of popular media images regarding their preferred ways of communicating and learning. Words used to describe Gen Y more generally include: social responsibility, volunteerism, flexible work arrangements, telecommuters, digital natives, needing constant feedback, living at home with parents, the emergence of adulthood (Glass, 2007; Favero and Heath, 2012; Sternberg, 2012). The concept of Gen Y as digital natives is particularly problematic in relation to how universities and workplaces construct their responses to younger adults. A critical review (Bennett et al., 2008) of the concept of digital natives found Gen Y's levels of skill in using the various technologies to be very diverse as opposed to the popular myth of general capability. A later research study supports this view with findings indicating inconsistencies between how different generational units within Gen Y sought information (Kilian, Hennigs and Langner, 2012). Sternberg (2012) builds on this argument of false homogenization, saying 'when constructing the generation y student, issues such as gender, sexuality, class, race and national identity tend to be, at best, subordinated, or at worst, neglected' (p. 537). In relation to other generations' assumptions about, expectations of, and interactions with, this new group of qualitative researchers these emerging debates and discussions are important to bear in mind.

# Conclusion

Qualitative researchers are in a stronger position than ever before in the quest to make a difference. As Flyvbjerg (2006) reminds us just because '… knowledge cannot be formally generalized does not mean that it cannot enter into the collective process of knowledge accumulation in a given field or in a society' (p. 227). For all qualitative researchers, being cognizant of generational difference, both within and between the ages will be important in ensuring respectful and yet lively debates and discussions about the future. Assessing the impact of qualitative research is one of the most important issues to be faced in the history of this tradition. While there are many philosophical and methodological arguments against notions of causality in qualitative research, the increasing pressure to report the impact of findings requires careful consideration of realist causality as a useful analytical heuristic. Developing rigorous, strategic, cumulative bodies of evidence derived from qualitative research studies will sustain these endeavours into the future.

## KEY POINTS

- Key debates in qualitative research differ globally
- The politics of evidence is largely argued by North American qualitative researchers
- Mixed methods is becoming more popular as a research design that includes qualitative methodologies
- There has been a transformation of higher education to become more corporatized
- Generational difference is one way of explaining the origins of different debates and issues in qualitative research
- Within each generation there are generational units who have concrete bonds that give voice to particular issues of concern
- Causality is an important consideration when thinking about 'what works' in qualitative research
- The utility of qualitative research findings as assessed by impact is becoming an important issue for Gen X
- Translating qualitative research findings into the language of interventions and implementation is becoming more important
- Assessing the impact of qualitative research equates to examining what was done, why it was done, what difference it made and how the research made it happen
- Popular images of Gen Y present a false homogeneity that could disadvantage particular generational units

## CRITICAL THINKING QUESTIONS

- How influential do you think the North American qualitative researchers are on the type of qualitative research undertaken in your country?
- Are there elements of the politics of evidence debate apparent in your workplace?

*(Continued)*

*(Continued)*

- What do you think of the suggestion that the impact of qualitative research is the next major challenge for qualitative researchers worldwide?
- Do you think that Gen Y is more diverse than popular culture would lead us to believe? How is this diversity played out in your workplace?

## Suggested further reading

### Journal article

Mannheim, K. (1952 [1923]) 'The problem of generations', in K. Mannheim (ed.), *Essays on the Sociology of Knowledge*, London: Routledge and Keegan Paul, pp. 163–195.

## References

Academy of American Poets (no date) *Audre Lorde*. Available at: http://www. poets.org/poet.php/prmPID/306.

Adams St Pierre, E. (2011) 'Post-qualitative research', in N. Denzin and Y. Lincoln (eds), *The Handbook of Qualitative Research*. 4th edn. Thousand Oaks: SAGE Publications, pp. 611–625.

Atkinson, P. and Delamont, S. (2006) 'In the roiling smoke: qualitative inquiry and contested fields', *International Journal of Qualitative Studies in Education*, 19: 747–755.

ATNU/Group of 8 (2012) 'Excellence in Innovation: Research impacting our nation's future – assessing the benefits'. Available at: http://www.atn.edu.au/newsroom/Docs/2012/ATN-Go8-Report-web.pdf.

Bainbridge, R., Whiteside, M. and McCalman, J. (2013) 'Being, knowing, and doing: a phronetic approach to constructing grounded theory with Aboriginal Australian Partners', *Qualitative Health Research*, 23: 275–288.

Bennett, S., Maton, K. and Kervin, L. (2008) 'The "digital natives" debate: a critical review of the evidence', *British Journal of Educational Technology*, 39: 775–786.

Birks, M. and Mills, J. (2011) *Grounded Theory: A Practical Guide*. London: SAGE Publications.

Bloor, M. (2011) 'The wider community', in D. Silverman (ed.), *Qualitative Research*. 3rd edn. London: SAGE Publications, pp. 399–415.

Cheek, J. (2011) 'The politics and practices of funding qualitative inquiry: messages about messages about messages', in N. Denzin and Y. Lincoln (eds), *Handbook of Qualitative Research*. 4th edn. Thousand Oaks: SAGE Publications, pp. 251–268.

Costanza, D.P., Badger, J.M., Fraser, R.L., Severt, J.B., and Gade, P.A. (2012) 'Generational differences in work-related attitudes: a meta-analysis', *Journal of Business and Psychology*, 27: 375–394.

Coupland, D. (1991) *Generation X: Tales for an Accelerated Culture*. New York: St Martin's Press

Creswell, J.W., Klassen, A.C., Plano Clark, V.L., and Smith, K.C. for the Office of Behavioural and Social Sciences Research. (2011) 'Best practice for mixed methods research in the health science', National Institutes of Health. Available at http://obssr.od.nih.gov/mixed_methods_research.

Damschroder, L.J., Aron, D.C., Keith, R.E., Kirsh, S.R., Alexander, J.A., and Lowery, J.C. (2009) 'Fostering implementation of health services research findings into practice: a consolidated framework for advancing implementation science', *Implementation Science*, 4: 50.

Denzin, N. (2009) 'The elephant in the living room: or extending the conversation about the politics of evidence', *Qualitative Research*, 9: 139–160.

Denzin, N. (2011) 'The politics of evidence', in N. Denzin and Y. Lincoln (eds), *The Handbook of Qualitative Research*. 4th edn. Thousand Oaks: SAGE Publications, pp. 645–657.

Denzin, N. and Lincoln, Y. (2011) *Handbook of Qualitative Research*. Thousand Oaks: SAGE Publications.

Donmoyer, R. (2012) 'Can qualitative researchers answer policymakers' what-works question?', *Qualitative Inquiry*, 18: 662–673.

Eisenhart, M. and Jurow, S. (2011) 'Teaching qualitative research', in N. Denzin and Y. Lincoln (eds), *Handbook of Qualitative Research*. 4th edn. Thousand Oaks: SAGE Publications, pp. 699–714.

Favero, L.W. and Heath, R.G. (2012) 'Generational perspectives in the workplace', *Journal of Business Communication*, 49: 332–356.

Flick, U. (2009) *An Introduction to Qualitative Research*, London: SAGE Publications.

Flyvbjerg, B. (2006) 'Five misunderstandings about case-study research', *Qualitative Inquiry*, 12: 219–245.

Francis, K., Mills, J., Chapman, Y. and Birks, M. et al. (2009) Doctoral dissertations by publication: building scholarly capacity whilst advancing new knowledge in the discipline of nursing', *International Journal of Doctoral Studies*, 4: 97–106.

Frieze, I.H., Olson, J.E. and Murrell, A.J. (2011) 'Working beyond 65: predictors of late retirement for women and men MBAs', *Journal of Women & Aging*, 23: 40–57.

Giddings, L.S. (2006) 'Mixed-methods research: positivism dressed in drag?', *Journal of Research in Nursing*, 11: 195–203.

Glass, A. (2007) 'Understanding generational difference for competitive success', *Industrial and Commercial Training*, 39: 98–103.

Gordinier, J. (2008) *X Saves the World: How Generation X Got the Shaft But Can Still Keep Everything From Sucking*. New York: Viking.

Hammersley, M. (2008) *Questioning Qualitative Inquiry: Critical Essays*. Los Angeles; London: SAGE.

Herrera, L. (2012) 'Youth and citizenship in the digital age: A view from Egypt', *Harvard Educational Review*, 82: 333–352.

Howe, N. and Strauss, W. (1992) *Generations: The History of America's Future, 1584 to 2069*. New York: William Morrow & Co.

Jorgensen, V. (1945) 'National Archives of the United States', in The National Archives US Government (ed.), ARC Identifier 520697/Local Identifier 520680-G-377094.

Kilian, T., Hennigs, N. and Langner, S. (2012) Do millennials read books or blogs? Introducing a media usage typology of the internet generation', *Journal of Consumer Marketing*, 29: 114–124.

Lather, P. (1993) 'Fertile obsession: validity after poststructuralism', *Sociological Quarterly*, 34: 673–694.

Lather, P. (2004) 'This is your father's paradigm: government intrusion and the case of qualitative research in education', *Qualitative Inquiry*, 10: 15–34.

Lincoln, Y.S. (2012) 'The political economy of publication: marketing, commodification, and qualitative scholarly work', *Qualitative Health Research*, 22: 1451–1459.

Lincoln, Y.S. and Guba, E.G. (1985) *Naturalistic Inquiry*. Beverly Hills, CA: SAGE.

Lyons, S.T., Schweitzer, L., Ng, E.S.W., and Kuron, L.K.J. (2012) 'Comparing apples to apples: a qualitative investigation of career mobility patterns across four generations', *Career Development International*, 17: 333–357.

Mannheim, K. (1952 [1923]) 'The problem of generations', in K. Mannheim (ed.), *Essays on the Sociology of Knowledge*. London: Routledge and Keegan Paul, pp. 163–195.

Maxwell, J. (2004) 'Causal explanation, qualitative research, and scientific inquiry in education', *Educational Researcher*, 33: 3–11.

Maxwell, J.A. (2012) 'The importance of qualitative research for causal explanation in education', *Qualitative Inquiry*, 18: 655–661.

Morse, J.M. (2011) 'Molding qualitative health research', *Qualitative Health Research*, 21: 1019–1021.

Morse, J.M. and Niehaus, L. (2009) *Mixed Method Design: Principles and Procedures*. Walnut Creek, CA: Left Coast Press.

National Health and Medical Research Council (2009) *Section 1: Values and Principles of Ethical Conduct – National Health and Medical Research Council*. Available at: http://www.nhmrc.gov.au/book/section-1-values-and-principles-ethical-conduct.

Pilcher, J. (1994) 'Mannheim's sociology of generations: an undervalued legacy', *British Journal of Sociology*, 45: 481–495.

*Rolling Stone* Magazine (2011) *500 Greatest Songs of All Time: The Who, 'My Generation'*. Available at: http://www.rollingstone.com/music/lists/the-500-greatest-songs-of-all-time-20110407/the-who-my-generation-20110516.

Saldaña, J. (2013) *The Coding Manual for Qualitative Researchers*. London: SAGE Publications.

Sandelowski, M. and Leeman, J. (2012) 'Writing usable qualitative health research findings', *Qualitative Health Research*, 22: 1404–1413.

Schwandt, T. (2006) 'Opposition redirected', *International Journal of Qualitative Studies in Education*, 19: 803–810.

Sternberg, J. (2012) '"It's the end of the university as we know it (and I feel fine)"': the Generation Y student in higher education discourse', *Higher Education Research & Development*, 31: 571–583.

Suau, A. (1989) *The Rise and Fall of the Berlin Wall – Photo Essays*. Available at: http://www.time.com/time/photogallery/0,29307,1631993,00.html.

Torrance, H. (2011) 'Qualitative research, science and government', in N. Denzin and Y. Lincoln (eds), *Handbook of Qualitative Research*. 4th edn. Thousand Oaks: SAGE Publications, pp. 569–580.

Twenge, J. (2010) 'A review of the empirical evidence on generational differences in work attitudes', *Journal of Business Psychology*, 25: 201–210.

Unknown. (1968) Photograph of Neil Armstong on the Moon. The National Archives US Government.

Watson, M. and Douglas, F. (2012) 'It's making us look disgusting … and it makes me feel like a mink … it makes me feel depressed!: using photovoice to help "see" and understand the perspectives of disadvantaged young people about the neighbourhood determinants of their mental well-being', *International Journal of Health Promotion and Education*, 50: 278–295.

Wilson, M. and Gerber, M. (2008) 'How generational theory can improve teaching: strategies for working with "millennials"', *Currents in Teaching and Learning*, 1: 29–44.

Yergin, D. and Stanislaw, J. (1998) *The Commanding Heights: The Battle Between Government and the Marketplace that is Remaking the Modern World*. New York: Simon & Schuster.

# Glossary

**Action research** An action-oriented methodology that aims to produce research-informed change to address live issues.

**Artefacts** Socially relevant materials such as photographs, artwork, relics or music that can be used as data in a qualitative research study.

**Bracketing** The use of reflexivity to maintain a position of objectivity as a researcher.

**Case study** An intensive study of an individual unit of interest, with a focus on the developmental factors of that unit.

**Causality** The linking of a concept or process with an outcome.

**Constant comparative analysis** An analytical process characteristic of grounded theory in which incoming data is compared with existing data in the process of coding and category development.

**Constructivism** A research paradigm that recognizes that reality is constructed by those who experience it and thus research is a process of reconstructing that reality.

**Critical ethnography** An approach to research underpinned by a critical ideological standpoint geared towards addressing social injustice and oppression through research.

**Critical realism** A research paradigm that recognizes an obdurate reality of fixed structures juxtaposed with the individual's ability to construct their own reality and influence change.

**Critical theory** A paradigm employed in the conduct of research that seeks to redress perceived societal injustices.

**Data** Raw material generated or collected through sources such as interview, observation, literature, documents and artifacts for use in qualitative research.

**Data analysis** The application of techniques in the treatment of generated and collected data for the purpose of achieving research outcomes.

**Data collection** A process of gathering data in which the researcher has limited influence on the data source, such as occurs when data is extracted from static materials such as documents and literature.

**Data generation** The process by which a researcher directly engages with a data source to produce materials for analysis, such as occurs during in-depth interviewing.

**Data sources** Persons, locations or materials from which material for analysis can be obtained through generation or collection.

**Discourse analysis** An umbrella term for qualitative methods that are used to study talk and text in social settings.

**Discourse tracing** A specific form of discourse analysis that involves tracing discursive practices across micro, meso, and macro levels of interaction and dialogue.

**Documents** Textual material that can be used as data and subjected to qualitative analysis.

**Epistemology** A branch philosophy concerned with the study of knowledge.

**Evaluation** The process of judging the quality and value of a research study using criteria designed for that purpose.

**Evidence** Research outcomes that lend support to the existence of a concept, phenomenon or theory.

**Evidence translation** The process by which research evidence is converted into knowledge that is applicable in practice.

**Fieldwork** A broad range of data gathering activities that include observation, informal conversation and accessing documents, in addition to formal interviews.

**Grounded theory** A research methodology that aims to produce a theory, grounded in the data, through the application of methods essential to the approach.

**Historical research** An umbrella term for the use of various sources of data to explore the ways in which the past shapes the future.

**Historiography** A written account representing the end product of historical research.

**Impact** The extent to which research findings have measurable utility in application.

**Interpretivism** A research paradigm concerned with human beings, which recognizes that actions are the products of judgements, reasoning and intentions.

**Lived experience** Reference to the concept of life as it is lived.

**Lifeworld** The term used to describe life as it is experienced rather than as it is conceptualized.

**Methodological congruence** Accordance between the researcher's personal philosophical position, the stated aims of the research and the methodological approach employed to achieve these aims.

**Methodology** A set of principles and ideas that inform the design of a research study.

**Methods** Practical procedures, strategies and processes used to generate and analyse data.

**Multiple case study** An approach to research in which more than one unit of study is subject to analysis.

**Narrative inquiry** The exploration of the stories humans tell to make sense of lived experience.

**Narrative research** A form of research employing narrative inquiry.

**Ontology** The study of the being, concerned with concepts of existence and reality.

**Paradigm** Frameworks that represent a shared way of thinking in respect of how the world is viewed and how knowledge is generated from that perspective.

**Participatory action research** An action research approach that involves participants as researchers in the process.

**Phenomenology** The careful and systematic reflective study of the lived experience.

**Philosophical position** The personal beliefs about reality that guide thinking about how legitimate knowledge can be acquired.

**Philosophy** A view of the world encompassing the questions and mechanisms for finding answers that inform that view.

**Positionality** The explication of the horizon in which the researcher stands.

**Positivism** The underpinning paradigm for scientific research that asserts the existence of a single reality that is there to be discovered.

**Postmodernism** A paradigm for the conduct of research that posits that the reality of a phenomenon is subjectively relative to those who experience it.

**Postpositivism** A paradigm that rejects the concept of a measurable reality that exists in isolation of the observer.

**Proposal defense** An oral or written submission that provides justification, clarification and/or responses to feedback in support of a research proposal.

**Procedural precision** The deliberate, planned and consistent application of methodological strategies in the conduct of research.

**Qualitative research** A research tradition that relies primarily on inductive approaches to the treatment of data, usually in the form of words, to explicate an understanding of a phenomena of interest from the perspective of those who experience it.

**Quality** Refers to research outcomes of value through the application of rigour throughout all stages of a study.

**Reflexivity** An active, systematic process used by the researcher in order to gain insight into their work that will guide future actions and interpretations.

**Research question** An interrogative statement of the research intent.

**Research proposal** A written outline of a proposed research study prepared to meet requirements for admission to study, ethical clearance or application for funding.

**Research plan** A framework that accounts for the philosophical, methodological aspects of, and methods to be used in, a research study.

**Researcher expertise** The skills, knowledge and abilities that a researcher brings to the conduct of their study.

**Rigour** Control of the processes employed in a study in order to accommodate or explain all factors that can impact on, and thereby potentially erode, the value of research outcomes.

**Story** A narrative that organizes events and/or experience to bring forward what is perceived as important and significant for the teller and the audience.

**Theory** An explanatory scheme comprising a set of concepts related to each other through logical patterns of connectivity.

**Unit of study** The person, group, social situation, or organization that is the subject of a research study.

**Utility** The usefulness and applicability of research findings.

# Index

content analysis, 97, 134
Conversation Analysis (CA), 73–74, **74**
Corbin, J.M., 108, 111, 114, 115, 225
Corey, S.M., 52
credibility, 192, 229
Creswell, J., 41, 43, 155, 191, 238
Critical Appraisal Skills Program (CASP), 230–233
*Critical Ethnography* (Madison), 92
critical performance ethnography, 99
critical realism, 20, 53
critical theory, 20, **20**
Crotty, M., 183, 186
Crowe, M., 71
cultural analysis, 97
Cutcliffe, J.R., 227

Darwin, C., 146
*Dasein*, 184
data analysis
    in action research, 56–57
    in case studies, 154–156
    in discourse analysis, 79–80
    in ethnography, 97–98
    in grounded theory, 113–115, **114**
    in historical research, 134–136
    in narrative research, 167–168
    overview, 42–44
    in phenomenology, 189–191
    software for, 43, 154, 227–228
data generation and collection
    in action research, 55–56
    in case studies, 150–154
    in discourse analysis, 75–79, **77**
    in ethnography, 41–42, 95–97
    in grounded theory, 113
    in historical research, 133–134
    in narrative research, 166–167
    overview, 37–42
    in phenomenology, 188–189
data saturation, 188
De Witt, L., 192
deconstruction, 134, 135
deduction, 23
Delamont, S., 242
Denzin, N.K., 6, 8, 92, 162, 238
dependability, 229
Descartes, R., 19
Dewey, J., 52
Dick, B., 240
Dilthey, W., 5, 19
discourse analysis
    data analysis in, 79–80
    data generation and collection in, 75–79, **77**
    ethnography and, 97
    historical research and, 134
    history of, 67–70, **69**
    overview, 67
    philosophical underpinnings, 70–71
    position of the researcher in, 71–73
    presentation and dissemination of findings in, 81–82
    purpose of, 73–75
    quality and rigour in, 80–81

Discourse Analysis (DA)
    data analysis in, 79
    data generation and collection in, 76, 78
    position of the researcher in, 73–74
    presentation and dissemination of findings in, 81–82
    purpose of, 75
*The Discovery of Grounded Theory* (Glaser and Strauss), 108, 110–111
documents and document analysis, 40–41, 43, 133–136
    *See also* memos
Donmoyer, R., 246
Dowling, M., 181
Duneier, M., 95
Dutta, U., 94–95, 96

eidetic reduction (bracketing), 183, 186, 188, 190
Eisenhardt, K., 147, 149
Eisenstadt, S.N., 132
Elias, N., 132
Elkind, P., 150
Ely, M., 168–169, 174
emancipatory action research, 54
embodiment, 185
empiricism, 18–19
epistemic validity, 99
epistemology, 18–19, 22–23, 148
*epoché* (bracketing), 183, 186, 188, 190
Erickson, F., 8
*Erlebnis* (lived experience), 182, 186
ethics
    ethnography and, 97, 100
    grounded theory and, 110–111
    narrative research and, 171–173
    overview, 21
    research proposals and, 215–216
ethnodrama, 99
ethnography
    data analysis in, 97–98
    data generation and collection in, 41–42, 95–97
    history of, 5–6, 90–91
    narrative research and, 163
    overview, 89
    philosophical underpinnings of, 91
    position of the researcher in, 92–95
    presentation and dissemination of findings in, 99–100
    purpose of, 92
    quality and, 98–99
ethnomethodologies, 90
Evans-Pritchard, E.E., 146
existential phenomenology, 184

face-to-face surveys, 56
Fals Borda, O., 52
Favero, L.W., 32–33, 34
feminism, 91, 161
feminist participatory theory, 32–33, 34
Feyerabend, P., 8
fieldnotes, 41
first-person action research, 54
Flyvbjerg, B., 147, 251

Locke, L., 206
logic, 23
Lorde, A., 239
Lugones, M., 164–165

Madison, D.S., 92
Magilvy, J.K., 230
Malinowski, B., 90, 146
Mann, M., 124–125, 132
Mannheim, K., 239–240
Marmon, S.L., 165, 174
Marx, K., 124
Marxism, 91
Maxwell, J.A., 58, 244
Maylor, H., 156
McClellan, S.E., **77**
McKenna, H.P., 227
McKernan, J.A., 53
McLean, B., 150
McTaggart, R., 55
Mead, G.H., 5–6, 110
member-checking, 192
memos, 26, 41, 111–112
Merleau-Ponty, M., 181, 184, 185
methodological congruence, 226
methodology
    critiques of, 35–36
    vs. methods, 32–34
    overview, 31–32
    paradigms and, 34, **35**
Miles, M.B., 148, 154
Minh-ha, T.T., 170
Mintz, S.W., 127
Mirivel, J.C., 71, 73, 76, 79, 81, 82
Mishler, E.G., 169
mixed methods, 33–34, 245
Molloy, E., 152–153
Moorthi, G., 93–94
Morgan, G., 148
Morse, J.M., 36, 245
Moustakas, C., 169, 183, 185, 191
Müller, M., 155–156
Munir, F., 33–34
Munn-Giddings, C., 53
Murray-Orr, A., 162

narrative analysis, 97, 134, 162–163
narrative psychology, 163
narrative research
    data analysis in, 167–168
    data generation and collection in, 166–167
    history of, 161–163
    overview, 161
    philosophical underpinnings of, 163–164
    position of the researcher in, 164–165
    presentation and dissemination of findings in,
        173–175
    purpose of, 165–166
    quality and rigour in, 168–173
narratology, 163
naturalism, 19
*Naturalistic Inquiry* (Lincoln and Guba), 244

Nestle, M., **77**
neutrality, 229
Newton, B.J., 26, 230

observation, 38, 41–42, 56
observer participant ethnography, 41
Olsen, M., 162
ontological authenticity, 99
ontology, 21–22, 148
open coding, 114
open-ended questions, 188
ÓRaigáin, R., 135–136

paradigm wars, 8
participant interviews, 37
participant observer ethnography, 41, 90
participatory action research, 58
participatory video, 56
*Pedagogy of the Oppressed* (Freire), 8, 52
Penrod, J., 203, 205–206
Peshkin, A., 26
phenomenological hermeneutics, 163
phenomenological nod, 186
phenomenology
    data analysis in, 189–191
    data generation and collection in,
        188–189
    ethnography and, 91
    history of, 182–183
    narrative research and, 163
    overview, 181–182
    philosophical underpinnings of, 183–187
    position of the researcher in, 187
    presentation and dissemination of findings in,
        193–194
    purpose of, 187–188
    quality and rigour in, 192–193
philosophy
    definition of, 17–18
    history of, 18–20
    research and, 23–24
photovoice, 56, 250
Plato, 21
Platt, J., 146
plausibility, 170
Ploeg, J., 192
Plummer, K., 202–203
Polakow, V., 169
politics of evidence, 238–239
Polkinghorne, D.E., 162, 169
position of the researcher
    in action research, 53–54
    in case studies, 149
    data generation and collection and, 37
    in discourse analysis, 71–73
    in ethnography, 92–95
    in grounded theory, 110–112
    in historical research, 128–130
    in narrative research, 164–165
    overview, 24–25
    in phenomenology, 187
    reflexivity and, 8, 25–27, 93–94, 112